LITERACY AND SCHOOLING

Monitoring Change in Education

Series Editor:
Cedric Cullingford
University of Huddersfield, UK

Change is a key characteristic of the worlds of business, education and industry and the rapidity of change underslines an urgent need to analyze, evaluate and, where appropriate, correct its direction. The series is aimed at contributing to this analysis. Its unique contribution consists of making sense of changes in education and in offering a timely and considered response to new challenges; the series, therefore, focuses on contemporary issues and does so with academic rigour.

Other titles in the series

Globalisation, Education and Culture Shock
Edited by
Cedric Cullingford and Stan Gunn
ISBN 0 7546 4201 1

Risk, Education and Culture
Edited by
Andrew Hope and Paul Oliver
ISBN 0 7546 4172 4

Race and Ethnicity in Education
Ranjit Arora
ISBN 0 7546 1441 7

Literacy and Schooling
Towards Renewal in Primary Education Policy

KATHY HALL
The Open University

ASHGATE

Published by
Ashgate Publishing Limited
Gower House
Croft Road
Aldershot
Hants GU11 3HR
England

Ashgate Publishing Company
Suite 420
101 Cherry Street
Burlington, VT 05401-4405
USA

Ashgate website: http://www.ashgate.com

British Library Cataloguing in Publication Data
Hall, Kathy, 1952-
    Literacy and schooling : towards renewal in primary
    education policy. - (Monitoring change in education)
    1. Literacy - Study and teaching (Elementary) - England
    2. Education, Elementary - England 3. Educational change -
    England 4. Education, Elementary - Government policy -
    England
    I. Title
    372.6'0942

Library of Congress Cataloging-in-Publication Data
Hall, Kathy, 1952-
    Literacy and schooling : towards renewal in primary education policy / by Kathy
Hall.
        p. cm. -- (Monitoring change in education)
    Includes bibliographical references and index.
    ISBN 0-7546-4179-1
    1. Education--Social aspects--Great Britain. 2. Education--Aims and objectives--
Great Britain. 3. Education and state--Great Britain. I. Title. II. Series.

LC191.8.G7H34 2004
379.1'12'0941--dc22

ISBN 0 7546 4179 1

2004012570

Printed and bound in Great Britain by
Athenaeum Press Ltd., Gateshead, Tyne & Wear

Contents

Acknowledgements   *vi*

Introduction   1

1   The Broader Context of Contemporary Education Policy   5

2   The Changing of the Guard: Teachers and Teacher Educators   25

3   Backing into or Facing into the Future? Literacy, Schooling   51
     and Society

4   Outstanding Literacy Teachers and their Teaching: Teachers not
     Packages!   70

5   From Monologic to Dialogic Classrooms   85

6   What Kind of Future? A Road to Better Things   103

Bibliography   *127*
Index   *142*

Acknowledgements

I would like to thank Joyce Tate for her patience and careful proof reading and for transforming the draft stages of the text. Thanks to Multilingual Matters for permission to use material which was previously published in *Language Culture and Curriculum* in Chapter 5. Thanks to Austin Harding for his research assistance on the project reported in Chapter 4 and for his contribution to Chapters 2 and 6.

For Tom

Introduction

The purpose of this book is to consider the recent and current thrust of government educational reform in England with particular reference to primary education and literacy. Taking account of such broad and complex themes as globalisation and technology, it develops a critique of government reactions and explores alternative re   ses to crucial issues of our time. Focusing on primary education generally, and on literacy in particular, the thesis is two-fold. First, that the discourse of current and recent reforms couches all initiatives in terms of human capital and ensures that only government voices are heard. This discourse has permeated the whole system of education from curriculum, pedagogy and professional development to accountability through policing and surveillance by unelected quangos. Second, that a discourse of renewal where other voices are also listened to is well overdue and that this can only be achieved through genuine alliances with other parties including pupils, teachers, parents, researchers, experts and community members more broadly. The bottom line of concern is whether justice and a participatory democracy are to remain subsidiary to economic efficiency as a defining aim of education. Optimistic but not naïve about the challenges of this thesis, the book focuses on key aspects of government policy that pertain to schooling, literacy and teacher professional development.

The reader is invited to consider what is happening in primary education generally, and in literacy education specifically, in a constructively critical way. The book is intended to be thought- and action-provoking. It is not a book that helps the reader to comply meekly with government initiatives, rather it is one that invites, indeed compels the reader to question some of those initiatives and to seek better ways forward. The book develops its critique of educational policy in a holistic way, that is in a way that recognises the inter-connectedness of policies. So, for example, the workings of the various agencies that are involved in monitoring and supporting primary educators such as the Office for Standards in Education (Ofsted) and the Teacher Training Agency (TTA) are analysed. Ways forward are offered for policy in relation to primary education and literacy education. The recommendations presented and discussed are based on empirical evidence drawn from several countries.

The first chapter provides a general overview of the origin and format of the educational reforms that were introduced not only in England but in other western democracies as well. The reason for beginning with this broader perspective is that issues affecting primary education and the literacy curriculum are influenced in various ways by the current changes in the global economy. The 'crisis', more imagined than real, that gave impetus to the changes is considered. What distinguished this particular period of crisis from other 'crises', leading to reforms in the past is noted. The manifestations and tactics of reform, with particular but not exclusive reference to England, are analysed. It becomes clear that the thrust and language of the reform agenda excluded opportunities for renewal and denied agency on the part of professionals while overstating the economic imperative in the lives of learners. Most importantly, the chapter begins to develop the argument that permeates the book which is that the reforms failed to engage with the complexity of the new realities facing society at the end of the twentieth century.

Two major levers through which pressure to conform is directed at primary teachers are discussed in Chapter 2. First, the Ofsted system of inspections and the associated publications of schools' performances are addressed. Second, the role of the TTA which 'oversees' not only the training and certification of new entrants to the teaching profession but also has important bearings upon teachers at all stages of their careers up to, and including, the role of the headteacher is reviewed. Drawing primarily, but not only, on developments in England, this chapter focuses on the effects upon schools and teachers of the new models of accountability. It is concerned with the impact of the policing and surveillance of teachers' practice by inspection systems like Ofsted, the use of league tables, the making public of results and the policies of naming, shaming and closure. Not only have teachers been expected to adapt rapidly to waves of changing legislation but they have also been manoeuvred into the position of executing tightly scripted teaching such that professional judgement is replaced by prescribed technicism. The national curriculum for teacher education, with its list of competencies, is yet another of a whole set of gateways through which would-be teachers are allowed to pass only if they are sufficiently conformist and accepting of their new technicist role. Managerialist ideology in the form of performance management legislation borrowed from the private sector, has created a number of gateways extending from initial entry into teaching and the award of Qualified Teacher Status (QTS), through the induction into the realms of the threshold, the Advanced Skills Teacher and headship. Movement through the career structure for teachers is more and more controlled by evaluation against explicit standards. Criticisms of the increasing 'control' of teachers by such managerialist machinery are examined here, as are the growing claims from some quarters that the reasonable claim of 'something for something' is, in reality, a more or less onslaught upon teachers as they increasingly experience work intensification, isolation and competition against colleagues and a growing sense that quality is less important than quantity. The very task of teaching seems to be being redefined. It is argued that the difficulties of teacher recruitment and retention and teacher discontent are logical outcomes of policies that minimise teachers' sense of professionalism and autonomy.

In Chapter 3 the focus of the previous chapters is narrowed to attend more specifically on reform through the lens of literacy. Drawing on empirical evidence, the chapter demonstrates the gap between the needs of our times and the policies we have in place to achieve them. The argument here is that everything about literacy today is more complex than it was in the past, yet national policies demand that we adhere to one type of literacy, that we assess against *the* standards, and that we specify *the* single best way of fostering literacy in our schools. The search for certainty and the narrowing of literacy, evident in current policies, coincide with increasing diversity and societal change. In the light of our more diverse society and new demands for multiple literacies the kinds of changes that are needed to maximise the life chances of all, and not just some, of the nation's children are debated. This chapter makes the case for a more inclusive and socially-aware literacy policy. A simple utilitarian view of literacy is simply inadequate for effective participation in modern societies which have left behind an agri-industrial past and have become post-industrial information-service economies. Just as the literacy product on offer is past its sell-by date, so also is the manner of its delivery via the direct instruction of the 'literacy hour'. By lacking 'authenticity' and by being insufficiently tied into the ways that literacy is needed and used in real life outside the school, the current policy on literacy fails to meet the demands of 'doing life' even if it meets the new demands of 'doing school'.

Chapter 4 develops a theme arising from Chapter 3. It explores the literature on outstanding literacy teaching in primary education drawing largely on a recent systematic review of evidence. The theme is not so much the relative effectiveness of various teaching methods, instructional programmes, teaching materials, or the 'natural' development of literacy in young children as it is about what characterises teacher expertise in the intentional promotion of literacy in the primary classroom. The evidence made available in this chapter is linked with the current policies on both teacher education and inservice professional development for teachers.

Chapter 5 narrows the focus still further. It considers some of the pedagogic changes that would be in line with a model of literacy outlined in the two preceding chapters. Based on a wide range of empirical studies from the United States (US) and the United Kingdom (UK), the chapter makes the case for the dialogic classroom. It considers the complexities involved in moving towards more active participation on the part of the learner in the literacy classroom.

The concluding chapter returns to primary education more generally. It offers a more speculative consideration of the implications of the issues raised in preceding chapters. It suggests issues that might contribute to a debate about renewal which can still incorporate economic considerations without ignoring personal and social dimensions. It is argued here that insufficient attention has been paid to the corollary of accepting such an important relationship. If education really is the key to economic prosperity then perhaps all of us, especially policy-makers, need to know much more about the relatively recent cutting edge developments in thinking and practices about how learning can be successfully stimulated in our schools. Certainly, the prescription and didacticism of some current approaches represented in some national initiatives will require some re-examination. If we are to have 21st century goals and aims for our educational system then we must also have 21st century pedagogies for achieving such goals. A dialogue between those who create educational policy and those who are expected to implement it, if there is the will and commitment on both sides, can simultaneously generate *personal* goals for education leading to fulfilment, mastery and self-improvement, *economic* goals leading to marketable knowledge, skills and competences as well as *social* goals leading to greater civic participation and engagement. A strategic imagination needs to be brought to bear upon important issues such that a reformulated set of educational goals can be creatively associated with a reconsidered and expanded set of educational practices and procedures. This chapter offers a framework which might help to formulate the shared agenda for an educational renewal initiative.

Chapter 1

The Broader Context of Contemporary Education Policy

Don't let us forget that the causes of human actions are usually immeasurably more complex and varied than our subsequent explanations of them. Dostoevsky 'The Idiot'

Introduction

This first chapter discusses the background to some of the educational reforms that have been introduced in England and other western democracies over the past few decades. The reason for beginning with this broader perspective is that issues affecting education generally are influenced in various ways by the current changes in the global economy. The way our education policy-makers responded to the changing economic, social and cultural scene in England is discussed. It is claimed that the thrust and language of the reform agenda excluded opportunities for 'renewal' and denied agency on the part of professionals whilst overstating the economic imperative in the lives of learners. More importantly, the chapter begins to develop the argument that permeates the book, which is that the reforms failed to engage with the complexity of the new realities facing society at the end of the twentieth century.

Before analysing some of the specific and now familiar changes that have been imposed on English education since the 1980s the chapter briefly explores some of the wider economic and social factors that were impacting and continue to impact on society. There are, firstly, two important forces of change that merit particular discussion: economic globalisation and the knowledge economy. Issues of faith in schooling and the blaming of schools for society's ills are further elements of the context of contemporary education that distinguish it from previous eras of major change. These inter-related factors partially explain the particular responses and reform tactics that governments adopted in the social sphere and particularly in education.

Economic Globalisation

Globalisation refers to social processes that transcend national boundaries. Economic globalisation describes a social change that is fuelled by economic activity that is beyond the control of individual nation states. So we have the notion of a 'world economy'. In his discussion of a world economy, Hobsbawm (1994) distinguishes between international and transnational dimensions. He describes the latter as 'a system of economic activities for which state territories and state frontiers are not the basic framework, but merely complicating factors' (1994, p.277). The emergence of transnational corporations with budgets larger than those of many nation states and with operations spread across the world is an important characteristic of economic globalisation. It is easy to appreciate the threat to the nation state when one considers that 500 companies control some 42% of the world's wealth and only 27 nation states have a turnover greater than that of Shell or Exxon combined (Korten, cited in Bottery, 2000). Multinational and transnational enterprises, not governments or national interests, control economic activity and nation states have to compete constantly to maintain and improve their relative advantage in the global market place. Sophisticated communication systems together with new market opportunities, particularly facilitated by free-trade agreements such as the North American Free Trade Association (NAFTA) and the European Union (EU), now allow multinational companies to shift production and services to more advantageous sites around the globe. Companies can move to those sites offering the best fit across skills, costs and stability and to those countries whose governments offer the most attractive inducements in terms of cheap, skilled labour and tax sweeteners. The terms of global competition are different now and labour markets and governments have had to respond to these new terms (Gee, 2000; Green *et al*, 1999). The consequences are that employers have to be more flexible and proactive in the face of continuous change and they have to expect to deal with different and changing occupational pathways. Manifestations of this changed scene are the greater responsibility employees now have to assume for the quality of their goods and services and the greater emphasis on communication and interpersonal skills as the balance shifts from manufacturing to the provision of services.

According to Davies and Guppy (1997) economic globalisation, with its stress on market competition and global capital, pushes towards a convergence in policies and practices – not just economic ones – among nations. Education systems, therefore, tend to become increasingly alike in these circumstances. It is important to understand how this convergence happens since it has a bearing on the mechanisms identified later in the book for countering some of the negative features of the education reforms in England.

Unsurprisingly, some industrialised nations are especially likely to show a convergence in social policy. Anglo-American countries, that is Britain, the US, Canada, Australia and New Zealand, show a good deal of similarity in education policy which Davies and Guppy (1997) explain with reference to their several common characteristics. First, they share a common language and have similar democratic governance structures, both of which foster the dissemination of ideas. More fundamentally perhaps, they share 'ideals of progress' based on individualism, effort and meritocracy which can be traced to the influence of Christianity in the US (see also Gray, 1998; and Gray, 2001). Third, due to their commonwealth connections, they have experienced similar immigration patterns making multiculturalism an issue for all five nations. Fourth, these countries operate open market economies and belong to one or more of the major trading blocs. In addition, as Davies and Guppy (1997) point out, all these nations play key roles in important international organisations such as the Organisation for Economic Cooperation and Development (OECD), the United Nations (UN), and the United Nations Educational, Scientific and Cultural Organisation (UNESCO). These nations, therefore, have a range of formal mechanisms for associating with one another. Fifth, these researchers and others (for example Goodson, 1991) claim that nations that once enjoyed economic superiority and dominance in the world are drawn to reform their education systems in order to win back economic advantage.

The example of the OECD is worth some elaboration here in relation to its influence in policy formation and in bringing about similarity in educational policy. Although it does not have a mandate over its members, being independent of the vested interests of individual states and governments, the OECD has been able to determine education agendas and set international performance indicators for educational systems (Taylor *et al*, 1997; Apple, 1992). It sees itself as providing a forum for governments to reflect on, discuss and shape their policies. It exerts influence through processes of 'mutual examination by governments, multi-lateral surveillance and peer pressure to conform or reform' (OECD, nd, cited in Taylor *et al*, 1997, p.68). The OECD is committed to fostering 'a market economy and a pluralistic democracy' as well as a 'post-industrial age' in which its members enjoy greater prosperity in an increasingly 'service-oriented world economy' (OECD, cited in Taylor *et al*, 1997, p.68, 1, 6). As Taylor *et al* (1997) demonstrate education, in OECD discourse, is justified as a mechanism for bringing about economic growth. For example, the 1988 inter-governmental conference, *Education and the Economy in a Changing Society*, explicitly linked the economic and social functions of education, placing unprecedented emphasis on 'the human factor'. The conference concluded that 'the skills and qualifications of workers are coming to be viewed as critical determinants of effective performance of enterprises and economies' (OECD, 1989, 18, cited in Taylor *et al*, 1997, p.69). Similarly, in 1993 it reasoned that the justification for education reform lay in economic considerations:

> Only a well-trained and highly adaptable labour force can provide the capacity to adjust to structural change and seize new employment opportunities created by technological progress. Achieving this will in many cases entail a re-examination, perhaps radical, of the economic treatment of human resources and education. (OECD, 1993, p.9)

What comes across from even a cursory reading of OECD documentation and some of the documentation of OECD countries is the conflation of economic and education priorities and the subordination of the latter to the former. This in turn has the effect of increasing the role of the market in education and reducing the role of the state. It is as if the state has been replaced by the market. Students are recast as 'consumers' or 'clients' and teachers and schools are recast as 'suppliers' or 'providers'. This point is taken up later in relation to specific policy initiatives in England. Although it cannot determine the nature of the take-up of its priorities by individual governments, there is little doubt that it and its related agencies have exerted considerable influence on the shape of educational policy in western countries.

While globalisation clearly brings obvious pressure for international convergence, the same process also exerts pressure in the opposite direction, towards empowering local groups to shape events at their local level – glocalization (see Green, 1999). The outcome is that control is at once centralised and de-centralised. In education this process reconfigures the power base: it 'squeezes power from middle levels of educational administration and redistributes it upward to more central states and downward to individual schools ...' (Davies and Guppy, 1997, p.438). This is a vital point since those who are 'squeezed' in this scenario are the professional educators, thereby presenting this group with an unprecedented challenge. This is considered in more detail later in the book with reference to how decentralisation, as a feature of globalisation, can be more fully explored and positively exploited by local groups, especially professional educators. For now the publication of several books that testify to the marginalisation of the voice of academics in educational policy-making, for example *Education Answers Back* (Simon & Chitty, 1993), *Education – Putting the Record Straight* (Alexander *et al*, 1993) and *Education, Policy and Ethics* (Bottery, 2000) is noteworthy.

Depending on who is doing the looking, however, different interpretations of the success of economic globalisation are made. For instance, David Henderson, former Head of the Economics and Statistics Department for the OECD, praises economies across the world for the effects of becoming freer and less regulated, citing the Republic of Ireland and New Zealand as good examples (see Mishra, 1999). Both countries enjoyed considerable increase in prosperity in the wake of adopting more open and less regulated policies in the economic sphere. On the other hand, with reference to the changes in New Zealand, John Gray, Professor of European Thought at the London School of Economics, says that '[a]mong the many novel effects of neo-liberal policy in New Zealand has been the creation of an underclass in a country that did not have one before ...'. He continues: '[o]ne of the world's most comprehensive social democracies became a neo-liberal state' (Gray, 1998, p.39). One outcome of globalisation has been described as 'a race to the bottom' (Brecher cited in Bottery, 2000, p.18) where the pay and conditions of work fall to the level of the most desperate. An advertisement placed by the Philippine government in the magazine *Fortune* captures another desperation: 'To attract companies like yours ... we have felled mountains, razed jungles, filled swamps, moved rivers, relocated towns ... all to make it easier for you and your business to do business here' (Bottery, 2000, p.18).

While levels of wealth and prosperity overall may rise, globalisation fosters a widening gap between rich and poor. Ramesh Mishra's analysis of globalisation, more generally, leads to the conclusion that it weakens the basis of social partnership by shifting the balance of power away from labour and the state and towards capital. A culture that prioritises private consumption over collective goods has been accompanied by criticism of, and a reduced willingness to pay for, social services. Reich's study, *The Work of Nations*, powerfully illustrates the scale of social fragmentation which follows from these trends in the US. Affluent Americans remove themselves from the public arena in that they establish their own private arrangements for health care, education, housing and transport. It is noteworthy, for example, that there are now more private security guards than police in America (Reich, 1991, p.269). The affluent are increasingly distanced from their considerably less well-off counterparts who no longer have a stake in society. As Green *et al* (1999) note, while America is not Europe, the forces that create such divides in society are global and therefore they require attention by all advanced economies.

Even more pessimistically, Noreena Hertz's study, *The Silent Takeover: Global Capitalism and the Death of Democracy* (2001), shows that politicians are now less responsive to democratic debate and more responsive to financial markets. She says: 'International forces are undermining government's ability to sustain the welfare state, and its ability to restrain economic forces so that society could be a more humane and equitable place' (p.60). This in turn has led to citizens' apathy when it comes to voting. Hertz adds: 'In a world where governments are proving less effective than corporations, trust in representative government is at an all-time low' (p.198). In a situation where governments seem to have less and less control, it is imperative that education should foster civic consciousness and social cohesion.

By the mid-1990s some countries, especially the UK and US, were beginning to recognise the negative effects of economic globalisation and of New Right policies on social justice and democracy. The so-called 'Third Way' was hailed as a way of achieving economic success *and* social cohesion (see Blair, 1998a and Halpern and Mikosz, 1998). In this model, education is seen as 'the main public investment that can foster both economic efficiency and civic cohesion' (Giddens, 2000, p.163). However, Tony Blair's manifesto of 'education, education, education', more specifically his contention that '[e]ducation is the best economic policy we have' (Blair, 1998b, p.9) testifies to the privileging of economics over civic cohesion. Witness also David Blunkett's (the then Secretary of State for Education) reference in Labour's first White Paper on education stating: 'We are talking about investing in human capital in the age of knowledge' (DfEE, 1997a, p.3) and the following year he stated in the Preface to *The Learning Age* (1998) that:

> Learning is the key to prosperity – for each of us as individuals, as well as the nation as a whole. Investment in human capital will be the foundation of success in the knowledge-based global economy of the twenty-first century. This is why the Government has put learning at the heart of its ambition.

The Knowledge Economy

Globalisation is about far more than economics. Giddens (1994, p.4) says it is 'action at a distance' and he suggests that what has facilitated this is the 'means of global communication and mass transportation'. Territory or place no longer dictates social life. It could be argued that the internationalisation of the new economy, that is much of what was described above, is not really new. Rather what is new is the technological infrastructure which facilitates economic transactions at an unprecedented speed. This brings us to the second force of change in education policies – the knowledge economy.

In a White Paper entitled, *Our Competitive Future: Building the Knowledge Driven Economy*, Britain's Department of Trade and Industry (1998) (http://www.dti.gov.uk/comp/competitive/main.htm) defined a knowledge driven economy as follows:

> A knowledge driven economy is one in which the generation and the exploitation of knowledge has come to play the predominant part in the creation of wealth. It is not simply about pushing back the frontiers of knowledge; it is also about the more effective use and exploitation of all types of knowledge in all manner of economic activity. (para 1.2)

The White Paper endorses the definition of the knowledge driven economy put forward by the World Bank, stating that:

> [f]or countries in the vanguard of the world economy, the balance between knowledge and resources has shifted so far towards the former that knowledge has become perhaps the most important factor determining the standard of living ... Today's most technologically advanced economies are truly knowledge-based. (para 1.2)

The foreword to the White Paper (1998), written by Tony Blair, refers to the role of education in creating a 'culture of enterprise' in the UK. It is clear that knowledge is not simply greater understanding or more information, it is about its application and exploitation, especially and significantly, for wealth creation. The White Paper justifies this emphasis by referring to the importance attributed to knowledge by the OECD and the World Bank, the latter emphasising the ways in which education and technology are now central to economic growth. In 1999 Tony Blair asserted that:

> The role of government today is to equip people and business for the new economy in which we are going to live and work. To encourage innovation and entrepreneurship; to improve education; stimulate competition; broaden access to new technology ... Above all, we are embarked on a fundamental reform of our education system. (Blair, 1999)

Michael Barber, Head of the Education Standards Unit in the DfEE in 1998, claimed that 'in the future learning society the imagination will be king'. His book, *The Learning Game* (Barber, 1996) elaborated on this claim. This in turn echoed the National Commission on Education's *Learning to Succeed: A Radical Look at Education Today and a Strategy for the Future* (1993). Here Lord Walton observed: 'We, along with many other countries round the world, are in the throes of a "knowledge revolution" which has already created a society in which the basic economic resource ... is no longer capital or natural resources but knowledge'. As a result of the communications revolution, globalisation encapsulates more than goods, capital and labour but also services, knowledge and ideas. And the transfer of knowledge is a key factor in economic development (Green *et al*, 1999).

One of the best descriptions of received, mainstream understanding of the knowledge economy was offered by Michael Peters in a series of lectures he delivered at the University of Auckland, (http://www2.auckland.ac.nz /ipa/Publect%201.htm) and published in 2001. He prefaced his characterisation by saying that the received view is both untested and uncritically adopted. He distinguishes the 'knowledge economy' from the 'traditional economy' with reference to five features which he calls, 'the economics of abundance', 'the annihilation of distance', 'the de-territorisation of the state', 'the importance of local knowledge' and 'investment in human capital'. Here is his description in full:

Characteristics of the Knowledge Economy

- Economics of abundance: The economics is not of scarcity, but rather of abundance for unlike most resources that become depleted when used, information and knowledge can be shared, and actually grow through application.
- The annihilation of distance: The effect of location is diminished through new information and communication technologies; virtual marketplaces and organizations offer round-the-clock operation and global reach.
- The de-territorisation of the state: Laws, barriers and taxes are difficult to apply on solely a national basis as knowledge and information 'leak' to where demand is highest and the barriers are lowest.
- The importance of local knowledge: Pricing and value depend heavily on context as the same information or knowledge can have vastly different value to different people at different times.
- Investment in human capital: Human capital (competencies) is the key component of value in a knowledge-based economy and knowledge-based companies seek knowledge locked into systems or processes rather than in workers because it is a higher inherent value.

The knowledge economy is most associated with the acceleration of change itself. The speed of change has quickened and unprecedented change is now more common. Over thirty years ago Alan Toffler's *Future Shock* described the way forces are being released which we are only learning to control. He says:

We no longer 'feel' life as men did in the past. And this is the ultimate difference, the distinction that separates the truly contemporary man from all others. For this acceleration lies behind the impermanence – the transience – that penetrates and tinctures our consciousness, radically affecting the way we relate to other people, to things, to the entire universe of ideas, art and values. (Toffler, 1970, p.18)

Recognising that there are benign and less benign versions of the knowledge economy, Peters (2001) goes on to critique the knowledge economy as conventionally perceived and is especially critical of the 'economic definition of knowledge and education' underpinning education policy documents. The major problem, as he sees it, is summed up by Chisholm (cited in Peters, p.16): 'New information and communication technologies offer ultimately non-controllable access to diverse and plural worlds – yet they do not assure the acquisition of the ethical and critical faculties needed for personal orientation and balance in negotiation of those worlds'. He says that while knowledge societies have, in theory, the potential to transform society for the better, in practice, he argues, they tend to reproduce systematic social inequalities and to exacerbate existing economic and social polarisation.

As discussed in more detail below, the response of governments in England and elsewhere to globalisation and the knowledge economy has been to redefine education as a market and to recast pupils and teachers as customers and suppliers respectively. Schooling has been harnessed to the task of creating a flexible, skilled workforce able and willing to respond to changes in this very new kind of market. Economics and schooling are interlocked. Social cohesion would seem to be low on the list of priorities. In 1987 Margaret Thatcher proclaimed at a Conservative Party Conference that 'If education is backward today, national performance will be backward tomorrow' (TES, 1987). In 2001 Estelle Morris, the then Secretary of State for Education, asked the head of the Financial Services Authority (the City's Regulator) to lead an enquiry into how the government could inject business and entrepreneurship into the school system. The dominant philosophy underlying schooling in this scenario is a utilitarian assumption about human capital. That is, children are viewed primarily as competitive individuals whose overarching values lie in their eventual potential to generate wealth. Educating children then is a matter of developing the 'human infrastructure' to 'complement new investments in the physical infrastructure' (Lawton, 1992, p.151). As Corson (2000) observes, in the past economic priorities were limited in their impact as long as capitalism was kept a little separate from government. This close coupling of economics with education is indeed a recent development. The integration of education and employment into one ministry of government, the Department of Education and Employment, is another indicator of this close coupling.

At the time of writing this chapter (September 2003) Tony Blair has opened what is called a 'City Academy' in Bexley, London. This state-of-the-art specialist secondary school, part-funded by private enterprise, incorporates a life-size model of the London Stock Market where students can experience and play out some of the core practices of the capitalist system. Several studies point to the dangers of promoting business values in schools. With particular reference to the English and Australian contexts, John Smyth, for example, alerts us to the danger of so embracing the enterprise culture in schools, including its more negative aspects like greed and individualism, that critiques of it are silenced or discouraged (Smyth, 1999). Moreover, the responsibility for producing economically enterprising, innovative and flexible people is placed squarely on schools and individuals themselves – those institutions one might hope would be bastions for the promotion of a civil and democratic society. Shifting this responsibility to schools at least partially absolves governments from grappling at a collective level with the consequences of the new transglobal order where there is massive global restructuring leading to deindustrialisation and where a country's ability to compete in the global market is a constant issue. But this economic background tends to be ignored as governments simplify the issues and pass them to schools to solve (Smyth, 1999).

There is one further and related theme that exerts another kind of pressure on governments to reform their education systems and that is the apparent inability of schooling to deliver in relation to society's expectations.

Faith in Schooling Questioned

A perusal of the history of schooling and of the history of school literacy, more particularly, leaves one in no doubt about their significance for the health, wealth and welfare of society. People look to schooling as the most important vehicle for improving society. It is believed to be the means by which one can gain upward social mobility, it is believed to be a mechanism for providing equal and fair access to the world's material and cultural goods, and it is believed to be the means by which people acquire and share values. It seems society has faith in schooling. It is believed to be the certifying agency that identifies and legitimates categories of achievement and competence, it defines what counts as legitimate and worthwhile knowledge, it publicly assesses and classifies people and gives or denies access to valued positions in society (Broadfoot, 1996; Collins, 1979; Popkewitz, 1988). Literacy, frequently presented as the most significant focus of schooling, is assumed to lead to rational and analytic thought (Olson, 1977), to lead to democracy and even social justice and to lead to economic prosperity and political stability (Goody, 1977). The literate person is assumed to be achievement-oriented, liberal and humane and to be law-abiding and not likely to become a drain on society.

This faith in schooling, and more specifically in literacy, for society's health goes hand in hand with the blaming of schools for society's ills. The blaming of schools is by now a familiar mantra in the speeches of politicians and in the scribblings of those who have become, arguably, the new experts – journalists and other media people. Such ills range from inability to meet the needs of business to unemployment, and from irresponsibility and teenage pregnancy to dysfunctional families and crime.

The field of (il)literacy powerfully exemplifies such connections. Recently, a US-based organisation calling itself the National Right to Read Foundation outlined the societal costs of illiteracy. In juxtaposing statistics on literacy levels and crime, it reached the conclusion that poor literacy levels cause crime. 85% of delinquent children and 75% of adult prison inmates are illiterate, it pointed out (http://www.nrrf.org/index.html). It continued – 90 million adults in the US are at best functionally literate and the cost to taxpayers of adult illiteracy is US\$24 billion a year in welfare payments, crime, job incompetence, lost taxes and remedial education. In addition, it stated US companies lose nearly US\$40 billion annually because of illiteracy. Drawing on these statistics an influential body, the National Reading Panel (NRP, 2000), convened by the US Congress to determine the best way of teaching early reading, concluded that there are significant societal gains from early reading success.

Here we have an assumption that there is a simple and causal relationship between learning to read early and lawful behaviour in adulthood. Perhaps the US government's commissioned report, *A Nation at Risk* (National Commission on Excellence in Education, 1983) is the most well known US example of the attribution of society's ills to the education system, not least because it was among the first reports giving impetus to a host of new reforms in US education. Here national leaders attributed economic recessions to young workers who, it claimed, had not been equipped by their schools for the new global economy. This thinking continues to be reflected in US policy. In 2001 the new Business Coalition for Excellence in Education in the US (http://www.nab.com/pdf/bcee_victory_dec102001_pdf) claimed that:

> ... the time is now to take action to bolster the mathematics and science competency of our young people ... or risk losing our position as the world's technological leader in the knowledge-driven 21st century global market.

In England, however, such claims had been made in the mid-1970s. In his famous speech at Ruskin College, Oxford in 1976, Labour Prime Minister, James Callaghan, criticised schools for their lack of engagement with the world of business. He linked economic decline to a decline in educational standards which, he argued, were the result of the use of 'progressive' teaching methods. Callaghan called for a 'Great Debate' on educational policies. His speech pushed education into the public and political arena and high level politicians since then have been intervening in the system on a variety of fronts. In England that speech marked the shift from more or less passive political involvement in education to such active political intervention that the professionals, heretofore front and centre in policy initiatives, have been sidelined and even excluded. From then, education was seen as too important to be left to the educators.

Following the Labour government's public acceptance in the late 1970s that schools were not measuring up to the demands of business, consecutive Conservative governments took up this discourse of blame but were more aggressive than their predecessors in how they attributed it to schools. To prepare people better for the world of work, reforms would have to include stronger curricular emphasis on the attitudes, skills and knowledge that is assumed to be important in business. Hence the subsequent greater emphasis on science and technology and on literacy and numeracy.

What is especially noteworthy in the discourse of blaming schools, however, is the pessimistic tone of the criticisms, leading sometimes to an attack on state education itself. This contrasts sharply with the optimism that characterised other periods of educational reform, for example, the period after World War Two which saw enormous expansion of school systems and the 1960s which saw the adoption of progressive methods. In addition, the current attack is not merely confined to more conservative quarters but permeates the thinking of those who claim to champion equity and social justice. In 1999, for example, President Clinton's Secretary of Education, Richard Riley (1999), commenting on the national assessment data, stated that:

> new data (tell) us that our nation's reading scores are up for the first time in all three grade levels – 4th, 8th and 12th – But 38% of our 4th graders are struggling to learn this very first basic ... We have a stubborn achievement gap between the well-off and the poor. This is a hard, cold reality; too many of our schools are failing some of our children and some of them shouldn't be called schools at all. (http://www.ed.gov/Speeches/02-1999/990216.html)

His explanation for poor children's unfair share in the overall progress in reading is not down to their poverty but down to schooling itself. The simple assumption is that teaching is a predictable activity entirely dependent upon the teacher and the school. Absent from this crude thinking is a notion of teaching as 'conflictual ... dilemma-ridden ... constrained by factors beyond an individual teacher's control' (Woods, 1989, p.84).

The point here is that education reform is currently happening against a background of government and media criticism of schools and teachers. There is an assumption that schools have failed their pupils, that they have failed to develop human capital for the benefit of both individuals and society, despite increasing expenditure on education. Education systems have become inefficient. The tax payer, it is assumed, is short-changed. Moreover, there is an assumption, at least on the part of governments, that schools, left to themselves, are not willing or able to change appropriately, that they are resistant to change and that, therefore, change has to be imposed upon them. It is thought schools cannot be trusted to reform themselves. The notion that the education system is organised to be self-serving, summed up in the phrase 'producer capital' – that is to benefit primarily those who work in it – is an assumption that some argue has achieved the status of common sense (Lawton, 1992; Levin, 1997). Some school reform advocates argue that significant school improvement can only be obtained through the introduction of a market in schools and through the removal of those factors that inhibit the operations of a market, that is the strangulating effects of bureaucracy and of professional self-interest (Chubb and Moe, 1990).

It is this set of assumptions, more than any other factor that, arguably, accounts for the radical nature of the reforms that were adopted in Britain and that accounts, in turn, for the lack of emphasis on renewal and acknowledgement of what was good in existing policy and practice. Interestingly, such assumptions appear to be unfounded, or at least not shared by all interested parties. Livingstone (1995) for example provides evidence from the UK, the US and Canada indicating that the general public has greater confidence in schools than have governments or business. There is also evidence that parents believe that their local schools are actually doing a good job (Barlow and Robertson, 1994). Referring to the US, Maddaus (1990, p.289) concluded that 'many parents have a more holistic view of "good schools" than appears to be held by policy-makers. This view encompasses moral, social, emotional and cognitive dimensions of education'.

Responses and Fixes: Education Re-formed

The belief that schools should address the challenges of globalisation and other trends, real or imagined, has been a motivation for radical change in education policy. Central to the changes introduced during the 18 years of Conservative government in England and Wales is the imposition of a market model where schools are positioned as suppliers that must compete in the market place of other schools for its customers, that is pupils. Whilst New Labour, elected to power in 1997, does not accept that the market is the answer to all social problems, there is little substantial change in the thrust of its initiatives. It is noteworthy, for instance, that when the Conservative government introduced the 1988 Education Reform Act, which gave unprecedented powers to the Secretary of State for Education, Labour politicians were vehemently opposed to such a shift in the power base. Yet, since coming to power New Labour has increased the power of the Secretary of State (through the 1998 Education Act) rather than repeal the existing acts. Furthermore, New Labour has gone along with virtually all the reforms that were put in place to establish an educational market (Gillborn and Youdell, 2000; Power and Whitty, 1999; Whitty, 2002).

It is now appropriate to sketch out and discuss some of the major educational reforms that British governments introduced in England and Wales and, where appropriate, to identify common strands in other countries to show the tendency towards convergence in the broad orientation of education policy.

Curriculum Definition and Control

The Education Reform Act of 1988 altered the basic power structure of the education system, increasing as it did the powers of the Secretary of State for Education. It restored to central government powers over the curriculum that had been surrendered between the wars. It also set up mechanisms whereby these powers were enforced. One of the major elements of the Act was the creation of the National Curriculum that teachers in all state schools were obliged to implement. It is arguable that the National Curriculum was the most significant centralising force (Paterson, 2003) since, by its introduction, the curriculum role of the local education authorities was downgraded. The National Curriculum standardised what was to be taught, it provided the local authority, the school governors, the headteachers and the teachers with 'their marching orders' (Maclure, 1988, p.9). Schools were now obliged by law to implement a centrally-prescribed curriculum and to adhere to the assessment regulations laid down by law.

The National Curriculum, which is intended to take up some 80% of the timetable, is designed to ensure that all pupils of compulsory school age follow the same course with English, mathematics and science forming the core, and history, geography, technology, art, music and physical education (and a modern foreign language in the case of secondary schools) forming the foundation subjects. The national assessment programme is a crucial accompaniment to the National Curriculum for it is through the assessment programme that standards are to be raised. Subjects are divided up into a number of components called attainment targets that are articulated at a series of progressive levels. The attainment targets are described at each of the levels by a series of criteria or statements of attainment that form the basic structure of a criterion-referenced assessment system. There are two main assessment methods: external tests or assessment tasks known as standard assessment tasks and tests (SATs), and teachers' own informal assessments of pupils' attainment called Teacher Assessment (TA). Although the National Curriculum was revised in 1995 to make it more manageable and to free up some extra time for schools to pursue areas of study they deem important, the overwhelming emphasis remains on 'the basics' and the core subjects. Indeed the Chair of the review of the curriculum recommends that the most of the time released through the slimming down of the curriculum should be devoted to 'the basics' (Dearing, 1994, p.7).

Most people were not against the idea of a national curriculum for schools. Several arguments were put forward in its favour. These included that all children are entitled to a worthwhile curriculum; that educational chances should be equalised so local differences in provision should be reduced; that schools should share common standards in order to ensure reasonable levels of teacher expectation; that a national curriculum should facilitate easy mobility of pupils across schools; and that a national curriculum should enhance the accountability of schools (Lawton, 1989). However, as Lawton and others have pointed out, the version of a national curriculum we got lacked a philosophical basis. It was almost entirely concerned with what pupils should know and paid little or no attention to what they should become. With reference to the subjects-bound nature of the National Curriculum, Lawton rightly says 'Subjects may be useful as means to curriculum ends, but they are not ends in themselves' (1989, p.33).

Policy-makers and curriculum designers in this case assumed or behaved as if there were a general consensus about the aims of schooling. A convenient assumption adopted was that since all agreed about its aims, it was only common sense to define the curriculum in terms of subjects. One would expect there to be a world of difference between a curriculum that would be needed to promote, say, pupils' willingness and readiness to fit into a social world already organised according to certain occupational and class lines and a curriculum designed to promote, say, pupils' awareness and critique of that particular social world. Schooling may be designed to create autonomous individuals, to create good citizens, to safeguard democracy, to promote social justice *and* to equip pupils for jobs in later life, that is it may be designed to fulfil multiple purposes. The point is, as Postman (1970) so well reminds us, that educational policies and practices are designed to produce one sort of human being rather than another kind. Or, in other words, an educational system operates on the basis of some model of what a human being ought to be like which in turn means that all educational policies and practices are deeply political. On the philosophical level the National Curriculum in England and Wales is especially silent.

On the question of subjects, it is worth pointing out how England and Wales differ in this regard from Scotland and Northern Ireland. Some researchers (Hamilton and Weiner, 2000) have argued that the dominance of subjects and the concentration on knowledge in the curriculum in England and Wales can be read as a sign of neo-liberalism and market-orientation where the overarching emphasis is on equipping pupils to meet their eventual responsibilities as workers. Their responsibilities as citizens are very much secondary. In other parts of the United Kingdom they point out, in contrast, questions of citizenship and personal and social relationships have more prominence and are stronger features. Such differences in education policy, even within the United Kingdom point, at a general level, to how the details of policy, and in this case the curriculum details, vary from country to country, according to the existing culture, history and those individuals who manage to exert influence at the time (Green, 1999). However, it must be acknowledged that citizenship education has been emphasised in New Labour policy, especially in the government's second term of office. Comprising three components, social and moral responsibility, community involvement and political literacy (DfEE, 2001) citizenship education is compulsory for both primary and secondary pupils.

What is undoubtedly the case though is that the curriculum in England and Wales, with its strong emphasis on mathematics, science and technology, owes much to the perceived need of governments to make the education system meet industry's needs. Subjects perceived to be associated with economic advancement (for example mathematics and science) are accorded higher status than subjects perceived to involve more personal interest (for example music and physical education) despite the fact that pursuits like music arguably tend to occupy young people's leisure time outside of school. So strong is the emphasis on mathematics and science in some official reports that these subjects are sometimes viewed as synonymous with education. The well-known Ofsted review entitled *Worlds Apart? A Review of International Surveys of Educational Achievement Involving England* (Reynolds and Farrell, 1996), for example, is about comparative achievement in mathematics and science, but the title could be read to imply that it is about comparative educational achievement in general (see Foster and Hammersley, 1998 for a full discussion). Reynolds and Farrell justify their focus on both these subjects on the grounds that 'mathematics and science are universally recognised as the key skills needed in a modern industrial society, and particularly in the new "information age" economies' (p.1). The review assumes that the main goal of education should be to enhance economic competitiveness and it is taken as axiomatic that the greater economic success of the Pacific Rim countries is down to their superior performance in these subjects as measured by international tests.

Performance Tables and Target Setting

While teaching methods or mode of delivery are not specified in the National Curriculum, practice at the level of the school is audited through inspections carried out by Ofsted.   While making the education system accountable and providing information for parents underlie this approach, its effects, as more fully discussed later, are experienced by its recipients as policing performance and as intrusive surveillance.   Teachers are no longer trusted to do their jobs correctly, efficiently and effectively.   Furthermore, they are not trusted to do their work ethically, though it is worth pointing out that auditors are trusted to ensure correct, efficient, effective and ethical performance (Scott *et al*, 2001).

In addition, the publication nationally of the results of the SATs and GCSE in the form of performance (league) tables is used as a means of assessing the quality of provision and the standards obtained by individual schools and LEAs.   League tables are designed to inform parents, the consumers of the education service, of how well schools are operating and so furnish them with information on which to make choices about schools in their area.   Gillian Shephard, the last Conservative Secretary of State for Education, likened performance tables to 'a bright light into every classroom in the land' (TES, 1997).   Choice and standards continue to be the obsession of the New Labour government as signalled in its mantra 'standards not structures' promulgated by a White Paper on education in Summer 1997 (Brighouse, 2001).   As other researchers have observed, not only have performance tables been retained under New Labour, but new elements have been added (Gillborn and Youdell, 2000; Power and Whitty, 1999), indicating that the quasi-market, originated by the Conservatives, is being refined rather than rejected.   In 1997, Estelle Morris, then Secretary of State for Education, stated:

> This year secondary tables will include for the first time measures of how schools have improved.   They will show the proportion of pupils who, on reaching school leaving age, achieved at least five higher-grade GCSEs in the last four years.   This school improvement index will be presented in easy-to-understand bar charts so parents can see how well a school is improving – or whether its results have been falling back. (TES, 1997)

So, it is clear that continued progress is expected year after year no matter how good a school does in any given year.

New Labour's initiative of target-setting at national, local and school level is designed as a means to raising expectations.   All State schools now have to set targets for improving the performance of 11 year olds' assessments in the primary phase and of secondary pupils' GCSE results.   Teachers' pay is linked to student and school performance, representing just how much New Labour policy has adhered to market perspectives.

As will be demonstrated more fully later, central control in matters of curriculum in the 1980s was extended to include pedagogic control in the 1990s through the national literacy and numeracy strategies.

Parental Choice

A major aim of the Conservative governments in the 1980s was the extension of parental choice and the vehicle they adopted for this was the market.   New Labour also enshrines parental choice as a key part of its educational policy although the market rhetoric has subsided a little. Underlying the aim of parental choice was the perception, as noted above, and especially among Conservative politicians, that teachers and LEAs were running the education service in their own interests rather than in the interests of children and parents. Conservative policy was that schools should be more aware of parents' needs, that they should offer what parents wanted, that those schools so responsive would thrive and that those schools that were not responsive to parents' needs would simply cease to be. The best schools, it was assumed, would become beacons of excellence while the worst would close as parents took their children elsewhere. It should be added that, as well as a desire to empower parents, Conservative politicians wished to remove any forces of resistance to their centrally-orchestrated reforms and local education authorities were seen as one potential source of resistance. This group had to be weakened or entirely removed from the scene (for example the Inner London Education Authority) in order to maximise the impact of the new reforms.

The mechanisms adopted by the Conservatives to achieve parental choice were numerous, ranging from the expansion of the powers, duties and responsibilities of governing bodies under a series of Education Acts through to rights to parents to vote for their school, that is to 'opt out' of local authority control, to be funded directly by government, and thus become grant maintained. Such a school could develop its own distinctive character and become selective if it wished. The 1993 Education Act extended local management so that all schools could opt out if they wished (Whitty, 1996).

Different types of schools were created to provide more diversity and therefore more choice to parents, grant maintained schools (GMSs) and city technology colleges (CTCs) being prime examples. These particular institutions were established to operate independently of the local authority and were allocated disproportionately high levels of funding. Under the Conservatives, these schools were offered greater freedom to select and admit pupils according to ability. Interestingly, although the New Labour government is against selection at the point of entry in principle, it has refused to weaken such powers where they have already been granted. A ballot of local parents is expected before selection on entry can be removed (Gillborn and Youdell, 2000).

More recently, New Labour extended diversification through its 'specialist' schools (DfEE, 2001). These schools are the result of public private partnerships – a private contractor owns the school but leases it to the local authority. Such schools are allowed to select up to 10% of their intake according to their aptitude for the specialism on offer. In June 1998 David Blunkett announced 51 more schools had been given specialist status bringing the total number of specialist schools to 330 broken down as 227 technology colleges, 58 language colleges, 26 sports colleges, and 19 arts colleges (Power and Whitty, 1999). The government intended that 25% of secondary schools would have 'specialist' status by 2003. By 2001 about one-fifth of secondary schools had already become specialist (Smithers, 2001, cited in Paterson, 2003) but the official intention is that their number will increase significantly (Labour Party, 2001; Blair, 2001).

'Open enrolment' was another strategy designed to offer more parental choice. It was introduced to allow parents to send their children to schools outside of their catchment area and schools were obliged to admit such pupils up to a pre-defined number (Maclure, 1988). This approach seeks to mimic the characteristics of the market and is based on the assumption that schools will improve if they have to compete for students.

New Zealand introduced a similar strategy to England's 'open enrolment' to increase parental choice but other countries adopted different mechanisms for promoting choice. American states have experimented with a range of approaches. Charter Schools, for example, were designed to offer more diversity in provision. These schools are not unlike the specialist schools being promoted currently by the New Labour government in England in that they are set up around a particular focus or purpose. Charter schools have a different funding formula from regular public schools and are often exempt from various government regulations applying to public schools (Levin, 2001). Provision of greater choice to parents regarding the education of their children featured in many countries. However, as Levin and others have shown, the way different countries seek to give parents more choice varies considerably and, he argues, it is these differences that to some extent allow politicians across the spectrum to support parental choice:

> Choice plans ... differ greatly not only from one country to another, but within countries or states. Many jurisdictions have begun with an ideological commitment to choice, but choice plans in practice vary widely. Indeed, it is hard to find two that are very much the same ... Some plans include private schools, while others do not. Some plans allow choice at any point in a child's schooling, while others focus it at certain transition ages. Some plans require schools to achieve equity targets while other do not ... The combination of these details can result in huge differences in the practical implications of choice. These differences are one reason that one can find people on opposite ends of the political spectrum arguing in favour of choice plans. (Levin, 1997, p.260)

One of the far-reaching changes made through the Education Reform Act (1988) was the introduction of 'local management of schools' (LMS) whereby the vast majority of schools' budgets (75%) was removed from the control of the LEAs and devolved to schools themselves. These devolved budgets were based largely on the number of registered pupils at the school – the more pupils a school had, the greater its budget (Maclure, 1988). In addition, schools were obliged to make public their aims, procedures, selection criteria, examination and test results and truancy levels so parents would be better informed and therefore better positioned to make choices between schools. As already noted above, regular school inspections were also part of this process since the full reports of individual school inspections are make public on the web and in public libraries, and parents themselves are sent a summary report of their own school. It is noteworthy that local management of schools, together with parental representation on school governing bodies and councils, were among the strongest trends in education reform across national boundaries. By 1989 the OECD reported that many countries were experimenting with these forms of decentralisation (Levin, 2001).

The policies designed to enhance parental choice in England would appear to have had mixed impact and 'success'. Schools are now much more likely to market themselves quite assertively to parents and to use a range of means to this end (Gewirtz *et al*, 1995; Woods *et al*, 1996) but the extent to which schools have made substantive changes in teaching and learning is quite another matter. To date there seems to be no evidence to show that these policies improve the quality of teaching and learning. Evidence suggests that efficiency in terms of balancing budgets was more easily achieved and demonstrated than was effectiveness in terms of educational outcomes (Huckman and Fletcher, 1996).

A study by Power *et al* (1996) indicates that policy on GM schools shows little sign of achieving its objectives. These authors conclude that in fact its outcomes may run counter to its stated intentions of empowering parents and enhancing their involvement. Although the policy invites schools to specialise through selecting pupils with particular aptitudes in areas like languages, music or sport, the reality is that few GM schools are pursuing these options. According to Power *et al* the typical form of specialisation relates to academic selectivity rather than curricular diversity. Moreover, even those parents who are mandated to govern schools do not seem to be very interventionist. Parents would appear to participate little in relation to matters of curriculum and teaching activities. Power *et al*'s evidence is in line with that from governing bodies from other schools – that is women, working class and black governors are not very directive in school decision making (Brehony, 1992). With reference to parents on governing bodies more generally, Rosemary Deem described them as 'neither particularly efficient nor democratic' (1996, p.66) and some governing bodies had members who were not representative of the communities the schools served.

In relation to the specific function of financial management and financial decision-making, it seems that budgetary control remains firmly the domain of the headteacher, despite the fact that it officially is the responsibility of the school governors (Thomas and Martin, 1996). Overall it seems that the research on the impact of policies to do with school choice and parental empowerment is at best mixed in terms of the fit between policy and practice and is at worst negative in its consequences for the education of pupils. Whitty (2002) has argued that they may merely help advantaged schools and already privileged families to enhance their advantages. The point is that parental choice is assumed to be an unproblematic good. Politicians continue to defend it as the highest democratic virtue. But is it really available to *all* parents? Can *all* parents access and, more particularly, use the information that is on offer about schools or is this only the privilege of the middle classes? The evidence so far suggests that it benefits the middle classes disproportionately.

Education and Responsibilities Redefined

Taken together the reforms introduced in England and Wales represent a most dramatic shift in terms, firstly, of the conception of education itself, secondly in the way education policy is made, and thirdly, in regard to who is responsible for the operation of the education system.

The conception of education as a life-enhancing, public good and welfare right has given way to a notion of education as an economics-enhancing commodity to be traded in the market place. The problems of the economy have been repositioned as the problems of education and educators. While one should not deny the importance of education in fulfilling an economic imperative, the excessive prioritising of economic ends and the consequent marginalisation of broader humanitarian ends of social justice, social integration and democracy should be of major concern. However, setting aside these important reservations for a moment, the central tenet in Conservative and New Labour governments that education is merely about the development of human capital to make the country more competitive internationally can be shown to be misguided, even economically.

It is noteworthy that among the four historic weaknesses in the UK's economy, only the last one bears on education – the skills base. The three factors considered by the Treasury (cited in Coffield, 1999) as more important causes of the UK's relative economic decline are the direct responsibility of business and not education. These three factors are the absence of a culture of innovation and enterprise, the failure of capital markets to provide sufficient investment, and the need for more competition in business to tackle vested interests. So even in its own terms it seems the human capital project will fail. One might well ask, as Coffield does, why the human capital theory is so popular? Among the reasons he offers are that it deflects attention from the need for economic and social reform and that it offers the illusion that every complex problem has a simple solution. Educational policy then opted for unambiguous formulations of problems and solutions that pointed to clear ways forward.

The notion of managing public services like education by seeking a consensus, no matter how difficult, across partners in central and local government through practical experience, rational argument and theoretical insight is no longer a reality – if ever it was. Prior to the 1980s educational policy in England was decided largely through the deliberations of teachers, politicians, local education authorities, employers and other bodies interested in education. However, parents and students were not key partners in this decision-making. Undoubtedly teachers enjoyed a great deal of professional autonomy. Decisions about what should be taught and assessed, even how it should be taught (discussed more specifically later) have been removed from the control of professionals, signalling a dramatic break with the professional autonomy once accorded to educators in England and endorsed in official policy.

While the purposes and content of education are now defined through central governments' policies, not through a dialogue with professional educators, the operation and implementation of this new model of education have been passed to schools. Paradoxically, the challenges have been passed partly to the very people who are responsible for the loss of confidence in the education system in the first place. That this responsibility placed on teachers for the effective operation of the education system is not matched by an equal measure of professional control or autonomy is an understatement. Neither is it matched by teachers' remunerative status nor by their conditions of work. Indeed the current recruitment and retention problems testify to a) the mismatch between professional responsibility on the one hand and professional autonomy on the other, and b) between professional responsibility and pay and conditions. In relation to a) while educators and schools are expected to devise strategies for the realisation of externally defined educational aims, which are primarily economic in nature, they are denied the opportunity to influence and inform those aims themselves. Their job is merely a technical one – to find the best means of achieving the ends, not to determine the ends.

Bourdieu (1998, quoted in Scott *et al*, 2001) offers an interesting analysis of the current trend in capitalist economies towards a split between those who work 'with money' and those who work 'with people' which is especially pertinent in the English education case. It is also a suitable point on which to conclude this chapter. It is arguable that there is a similar split between the decision-makers or reformers of social policy and those who implement those decisions. Bourdieu talks about the 'Right and Left hands of the State'. The former refers to the institutions that have shaped and driven the reforms and these include cabinets, finance ministers and treasuries, banks and businesses. The 'left hand of the State' refers to those concerned with public interest and welfare, including education, social services, health and so on. He says the 'left hand' includes 'family counsellors, youth workers, rank and file magistrates, and increasingly primary and secondary school teachers' (Bourdieu, 1998, cited in Scott *et al* 2001). Those in the caring or people-oriented professions are 'sent into the front line to perform so-called social work to compensate for the inadequacies of the market' (p.3). He suggests that the 'right hand' does not know and does not want to know what the 'left hand' is doing and it is also reluctant to pay for the 'left hand's' activities. Decline in the status of those professions that perform the work of the 'left hand' witnessed a decline in their relative salaries. This decline is paralleled by an increase in the status and salaries of the 'right hand' professions, that is all those who work with money.

The next chapter focuses more closely on the way teaching and teacher development have been reconceptualised and redefined in a new policy context which promotes schooling primarily for economic ends.

Chapter 2

The Changing of the Guard:
Teachers and Teacher Educators

Introduction

One of the principal ways in which the State attempts to exercise strong control over both the content and the quality of public services like the prisons, the health service and the education system is through the use of a vigorous and regular monitoring and inspection of those services coupled with the eventual making public of the outcomes of such scrutiny. The drive is to use monitoring as a means of obtaining measures of performance against normative criteria and also to create a mechanism through which the State as purchaser of services is able to influence and, some would say, define the scope, nature and delivery of such services by the contractors. Schools, in particular, have been subjected to inspection on a hitherto unknown scale; the use of performance measures has been extended to Higher Education where teaching quality is assessed through the Quality Assurance Agency (QAA) and research quality by the Research Assessment Exercise (RAE). The providers of teacher education are also subject to regular inspection under the aegis of Ofsted and, all in all, teachers do, indeed, appear to live and work in what might truly be described as an evaluation or audit culture.

With a national curriculum, a national system of assessment and national strategies for literacy and numeracy in place, the control of teachers at all stages in their careers assumes huge importance. Only through persuading teachers into this new vision for education could the whole new machinery operate effectively and efficiently. The two major levers through which pressure to conform is directed at teachers are the Ofsted system of inspections together with the associated publications about the performances, and also the Teacher Training Agency which 'oversees' not only the training and certification of new entrants to the teaching profession but also has important controlling influences upon teachers at all stages of their careers, up to and including the role of head teacher.

The 1992 Education (Schools) Act inaugurated new national arrangements for the inspection of schools by Ofsted, an ostensibly independent body but one which nonetheless appears to operate within the value boundaries of marketisation and managerialism. The initial establishment of Ofsted and the subsequent extensions of its remit to include the inspection of teacher training arrangements represent a firm and consistent drive by central government to secure and maintain strong control over the education system. This chapter describes the nature and functioning of the Ofsted and TTA processes. It shows how teachers are kept 'on task' in relation to the National Curriculum and the literacy and numeracy strategies and shows how the publishing of league tables and inspection reports, and sometimes the associated provision and deprivation of funding, act as powerful mechanisms for establishing and maintaining the government views on education. It will also critically examine some of the weaknesses and difficulties associated with such tight prescription and supervision and will explore some tentative suggestions for improvement.

Ofsted Inspections of Schools

Pierson (1998) discusses how one clear expression of central government's enthusiasm for new forms of accountability and management is its wholesale reform of the process of schools' inspection. Her Majesty's Inspectorate of Schools (HMI), suspected as being part of the liberal educational conspiracy that had presided for too long over supposedly declining educational standards, was sidelined and its responsibility for inspecting schools was transferred to the Office for Standards in Education. Ofsted's remit was to 'identify strengths and weaknesses so that schools may improve the quality of education they provide and raise the educational standards achieved by their pupils' (Ofsted, 1995a, p.9). Inspections are to be carried out by independent inspection teams, each including a lay member, and such teams are awarded inspection contracts on a competitive basis. Inspections are to be conducted according to a standardised Framework of Inspection (not based on any acknowledged or explicit theoretical analysis of the workings of a school) and are to be repeated, initially, at four-yearly intervals. An Ofsted Handbook contains the 'framework' that gives advice on inspection requirements as well as the guidance on the collection of evidence and also on the inspection process itself (Ofsted and TTA, 1996). The language of the framework is a technical one based upon the concepts of audit and managerialism. There tends to be a concentration on those aspects of the work of a school and its teachers that are measurable and the model of teaching employed appears to be a transmissional one in which the teacher passes information to pupils. Teachers are charged with managing the learning of their pupils so that they acquire the skills thought to be useful in a competitive market.

Reports emerging from inspections are made available to parents and give rise in schools to 'Action Plans' through which head teachers and governors indicate how the recommendations of the inspectors are to be implemented. The watchwords of this new regime, under the combative leadership of Chris Woodhead during the formative early years, were independence (from the teaching profession), standardisation (of evaluation procedures), bench-marking (of national standards) and public disclosure (of assessment outcomes) (Pierson, 1998).

Though in some important ways the setting up of Ofsted represented an improvement on the earlier arrangements involving HMI and Local Education Authority (LEA) Inspection Services (they are much more systematic, for example) the situation is regarded by many authorities and researchers as being unsatisfactory and unacceptable in a number of important respects.

The competition amongst contractors for inspection contracts and the associated financial arrangements are seen by some commentators as running the risk of producing unstable and frequently changing memberships for inspection teams. It is argued that this makes for an overall inconsistency of judgement and, together with the earliest Ofsted inspectors' inability to offer advice, represents poor value for money. The costs of Ofsted are high (around £140 million per year) and such expense is resented, especially in schools where shortages of books and equipment are a fact of daily life.

As well as concerns about cost there are more critical voices questioning the soundness of Ofsted's methods (Fitz-Gibbon, 1997; Gray, 2000). Gray, for example, comments on the proliferation of the many unreliable and unfair judgements about the achievements and progress of pupils without sufficient attention being given to social factors or the use of thorough value added analyses. Weaknesses in quality control, unreliable data, small sample sizes, random variations in the amount of observations, inconsistencies within and between inspection teams and the undue emphasis of inspectors' own orthodoxies on their judgements have all been cited as examples of Ofsted's questionable methods (Taylor, 1998; Thrupp, 1998).

In response to the growing unreliability of the Ofsted process a small, independent group of academics set up the Office for Standards in Inspection (Ofstin) to encourage the analysis and accountability of Ofsted's work. The Ofstin group accepts the need for schools to be inspected and held to be accountable but are strongly critical of the Ofsted approach which they find to be poor value for money and only moderately effective in improving schools. Ofstin calls for the appointment of a fully funded inspectorate staffed by well qualified members and whose quality, efficiency and effectiveness are open to public scrutiny. The work of such a body should, in Ofstin's view, integrate with and support, validate and accredit the processes of internal school review and development (Ofstin, 1996; 1997).

Another particularly critical line of attack on Ofsted is that which brings the inspectorate to account for constructing pupils' failure as almost the sole responsibility of schools and teachers. Using what Thrupp (1998) describes as the 'politics of shame' they use school effectiveness research to bolster their accusations whilst playing down those aspects of that research which acknowledge the contribution of broader social and political factors to educational failure. A sociologically blinkered Ofsted has been criticised for its 'erasure of social class'. Angus (1993) tells how they have regarded factors such as social class and family background as 'noise', as outside factors that need to be controlled then stripped away so that research can concentrate on the important domain of school factors. This, despite the fact that some research indicates that such factors account for between only 8% and 15% of educational achievement (see William and Raudensbusch, 1989 for a discussion). Whilst never seeing these methodological defects as intentional, Angus describes the school effectiveness project as 'sitting quite comfortably with the conservative educational project' (p.342).

In asking the question, 'School Effectiveness for Whom?' Slee *et al* (1998) argue powerfully on the dangers of too readily accepting the current orthodoxy of the school improvement and school effectiveness movements:

> The danger of signing up to the school improvement charter is that there is a separation of the school from the education policy and social context. What transpires is a policy of naming and shaming whereby schools are blamed for being solely responsible for educational failure and drastic measures are introduced to improve failing schools. That these measures frequently involve systematic population cleansings such as was the case with the Ridings school and large injections of funding previously not delivered to the school is not dwelt upon by those chronicling the histories of schools that are 'turned around'.

When politicians like Stephen Byers (1997) can blandly insist that poverty must not be seen as an excuse for failure and the New Labour government emphasises 'standards not structures', it is time to assert even more strongly that whilst one cannot explain away all failure in terms of home background, it is a fact that disadvantage and poverty are associated with low academic performance. Children from disadvantaged families do suffer physically, emotionally, psychologically and educationally. Disadvantage is a cause of, rather than an excuse for, failure (see next chapter).

As Ofsted gradually took a campaigning role to raise educational standards upon itself, it put pressure upon research, both external research and its own internally conducted studies, to fit in with this new campaigning style and approach. Smith (2000) contends that this led to a sidelining of some research findings and an over-emphasis and prominence being placed on other studies. There is a general reluctance to publish any contradictory and thus unwelcome findings; a 'rubbishing' of the value of much research is now commonplace.

The campaigning approach has been especially associated with the leadership of Chris Woodhead who had a strong interest in promoting information and findings that furthered the Ofsted cause or message. Woodhead acted as the principal spokesman for the campaign to raise standards; he personally spoke to the press and appeared on television in a manner and to an extent unprecedented for a civil servant. This sometimes led to Ofsted's downplaying of certain findings like those of Adey *et al* (1999) whose evidence favoured teachers choosing from a wide variety of teaching approaches and strategies. It also involved a 'rubbishing' of other research, including a strong personal attack upon one of the research authors when the team of Gillborn and Gipps (1996) explored the achievements of ethnic minority children. In a *Politiea* pamphlet the Chief Inspector (Woodhead, 1995) almost held Professor Gipps personally responsible for the educational failure throughout the system. Delays in publication, numerous re-draftings and failure to publish as well as a calculated use of press releases were just some of the ways in which certain research findings were sidelined. Work by Sammons and her colleagues (1994) also fell foul of Ofsted for underlining a very heavy association between ratings of school performance and the social settings of the schools.

Ofsted saw the taking of social factors into account as a way of lowering expectations and shifting attention away from teaching.

A similarly biased approach was also evident in research conducted by Ofsted (1995b) itself. Even though the research into class size and the quality of education found that for Key Stage 1 pupils and for older, lower ability children class size did matter, the press release issued by Ofsted was headed 'Ofsted finds no clear link between class size and lesson quality' (cited in Smith, 2000). Although the research findings were tentative, exploratory and not clear cut, the Ofsted interpretation was to give such results an unwarranted authority claiming that 'except in the early years, reductions in the class size of one, two or three are not likely to have an educational benefit which justifies the increase in public expenditure' (Ofsted, press release cited in Smith, 2000). Increasingly over the 1990s, it would appear that policy-making based upon research was 'cut off at the knees' (Ball, 1990). Maguire and Ball (1994) argued that although research and evaluation were still being funded by central agencies, the work was subject to delay in reporting, or was not being reported at all, or was being misreported in the public press.

Another important focus within the debate surrounding Ofsted and the surveillance of teachers has been concerned with the impact of inspection upon teachers' professionalism. Gewirtz (1997) describes how in her study of secondary schools she perceived strong moves to align school activities with the technicist requirements associated with Ofsted inspections. Such internal adjustments to external demands made manifest through Ofsted inspections resulted in emotional, social and pedagogical changes. Staff talked of working at a 'frantic pace' and of feeling 'squeezed dry'. They felt an increasing loss of control over their work and felt that their schools had become less sociable places in which to work despite an increase in the number of occasions on which teachers met together in groups. They told of deteriorating and competitive relationships between subject departments (balkanisation) and of relationships between staff and students as approximating to those of the production line. They reported a decline in the vitality and creativity of their teaching and its replacement with more utilitarian, examination-oriented approaches to teaching and learning.

Researching in primary schools Troman (1997) vividly describes the emotional phases which teachers and schools go through in preparation for the inspection process. An anticipation of surveillance is associated with the telling of 'horror stories' about inspectors who 'leave no stone unturned' and 'don't miss a trick'. This initiates intense self-surveillance during which teachers move their teaching well away from anything which they perceive as being unpopular with Ofsted. An accompanying attempt at impression management occurs in which schools strive to show outsiders, including Ofsted inspectors, that they run schools which are rational, efficient and effective and that through their carefully planned, implemented and evaluated work they provide education which is good value for money. A variety of accommodations like rebellious talk, bitching and humour helps to ease some of the stress associated with the sense of surveillance but it often still succeeds in generating a fragmentation as happy and collaborative informal working together is structured into formal, hierarchical and threatening groups with an increased sense of 'Indians' working for 'chiefs'.

Jeffrey and Woods (1996; 2002) describe the technicist approach of Ofsted inspections as impacting upon the more holistic and humanistic values of the teachers. This produced a high degree of trauma for the teachers and resulted in them feeling uncertain, confused, anxious, anomic and lacking in confidence even in schools that had been rated as satisfactory by Ofsted. Inspections make no allowances for emotional responses: they define teaching quality in terms of technical competences (Troman, 1997) and operate in a mechanical, clinical fashion. Teachers feel that they are under strong critical surveillance and that far from being part of the solution to educational problems, they are rather part of the problem (Carr and Harnett, 1996). The research of Peter Woods and Bob Jeffrey (1998; Jeffrey and Woods, 1996) sees Ofsted inspections as functioning as an assault on teachers' sense of professionalism and also upon their sense of self. They are put through a kind of rite of passage which, against their will, moves them from their values as professionals to the status of technician. To avoid any repetition of the trauma of inspection they can either leave teaching or become instrumental and technicist in their approach.

In the light of its purpose of helping schools to identify strengths and weaknesses, as mentioned earlier in this chapter, it is noteworthy that a detailed examination of the language of Ofsted inspection reports concluded that:

> ... the disciplinary culture of inspection reporting ... results in a weak and questionable product, a thin base on which to build and develop school improvement and effectiveness. The real outcome is too often a demoralising and demotivating chastisement of the effort and commitment provided by the majority of staff in our nation's schools. (Field *et al*, 1998, p.138)

The conflict in values between the teachers and the inspectors seems to be centred around four important areas – knowledge, pedagogy, assessment and culture. Whilst teachers adopt a holistic approach and recognise and value complexity and difference the inspectors want uniformity and compartmentalisation of knowledge. The individual and small group approach to teaching and learning favoured by many primary school teachers contrasts with that suggested in, say, the National Literacy Strategy, and looked for in Ofsted inspections. There appears to be an implication that more rational, unemotional approaches to pedagogy are needed and that there has been too much 'caring' and not enough 'direct teaching'. Ofsted Subject Reports for 1999-2000, for example, praises the 'direct teaching of reading skills' and describes how the National Literacy Strategy has concentrated effectively on raising the general standard of literacy by enhancing class teaching of English.

Whilst the teachers want to look to inspection for advice and guidance, the inspectors seem concerned with secretive checking, policing, archiving and recording. They bring the world of audits and quality control right into the world of teaching and teachers become calculable, describable and comparable. They are subjected to what Foucault (1977) describes as an 'examination', a surveillance that makes it possible to quantify, to classify and to punish. Teachers want advice but get scrutiny and judgement. The supportive, friendly, collaborative culture of the school is replaced with a 'contrived collegiality' as structures are formalised to suit the scrutiny of roles and responsibilities by Ofsted. Teachers develop 'persecutory guilt' and feel a strong sense of failure and blame. Whilst teachers are described as employing coping strategies like demonising inspectors, secretly reaffirming their own teacher values and beliefs, agreeing to 'give the inspectors what they want to see', most of them ultimately feel powerless against the inspectors; they are colonised, taken over and strive to change their teaching to bring it in line with the technicist approach of Ofsted. Jeffrey and Woods (1998) use a very powerful 'undressing' metaphor to describe how things are in many schools after an inspection is over:

> ... schools are left in no doubt that Ofsted's priorities and pedagogy are paramount and that Ofsted has the power to undress you, gaze at you and in the spotlight of their supporters redress one with care or with brutality as they see fit. They have effectively colonised the primary teachers' domain, their classroom and their identity.

Ofsted, Ofstin and Self-Evaluation

Yet more criticism of the Ofsted approach is that which questions the effectiveness of the inspection system and speculates that the slogan 'improvement through inspection' is rather more rhetoric than reality. Several authorities suggest that Ofsted has made only limited contributions to school improvement (Fitz-Gibbon, 1998; Lonsdale and Parsons, 1998). In considering especially the situation of the poorest schools where inspection visits are the most frequent it has been suggested that although most of such schools are usually removed from 'special measures' they do not generally make disproportionately large improvements in their examination performances (Gray, 2000). Brimblecome, Ormston and Shaw (1996) found that only about one third of secondary teachers said that they intended to change some aspect of their teaching as a result of a school inspection. Feedback to teachers about their performance was only introduced in 1998 and many argue that, even when it is part of the inspection process, the conditions and circumstances of a school inspection are hardly the best opportunity for the discussion of teaching and serious consideration of and reflection upon inspectors' suggestions.

Despite its many critics the Ofsted process has been given a general recognition for some of the strengths associated with and attributable to the inspection process. In their submission to the House of Commons Select Committee Fidler, Ouston, Earley and Ferguson (House of Commons Select Committee, 1999) acknowledge, amongst other things, the bringing of much information about schools into the public domain. They also recognise the ways in which Ofsted inspections have been spurs for concerted school development and improvement measures, with schools going as far as using for themselves the detail of the Ofsted Handbook. Their evidence does, however, also cite the increased stress and demoralisation often associated with inspection and they are especially critical of the reporting of schools' outcomes against national norms and how there needs to be a more sophisticated approach to the recognition of children's abilities on entry and their social background.

Although much has been written about possible alternatives to Ofsted (Ofstin, 1997; MacBeath, 1999; Ferguson *et al*, 1999, 2000; Learmonth, 2001) it would appear that such radical changes are still a long way off. Indeed, few have argued for the total replacement of the Ofsted system although many argue for a substantial acknowledgement of the crucial nature of internal self-evaluation assisted and supported by external review. Most commentators acknowledge the continued need for both internal and external perspectives but urge a move away from the current highly pressurised model where external evaluation dominates, to a position where there is a better balance between pressure and support with internal self-evaluation given a higher profile.

The process of scrutiny needs to continue to be rigorous and thorough but also needs to be sensitive to the schools' capacity for change. An ongoing collaboration between the school and an inspection team is required in order to implement, monitor and support change. MacBeath (1999) outlines the Evaluating Quality in School Education, a European Commission study involving 101 schools in 18 countries. The purpose of this study was to pilot self-evaluation in different countries so as to draw policy conclusions about national frameworks and school-based practice. Of the 101 participants 98 wanted to continue beyond the end of the project, 94 asserted that it had improved their schools and the policy-makers from 18 countries agreed that the project had made a significant impact on thinking about school evaluation. The project results show that carefully conducted self-evaluation in schools succeeds in revealing much valuable data, improves teaching, enhances management and is reliable, valid and cost-effective.

From 1993, the year in which Ofsted first started to carry out school visits, external inspection has been seen as the main driving force in terms of the evaluation of school and pupil performance. Ten years on, however, it has become apparent that the processes and frameworks used as a basis for inspection need to be modified so as to take greater account of a growing drive for internal self-evaluation, arising from the desire of schools and teachers to assess for themselves how well they are doing. By 1996, for example, a new inspection framework was introduced which gave greater emphasis to a school's own evaluation of its strengths and weaknesses (Earley *et al*, 1996). In the past year there has been a small shift in the right direction with the introduction of a school's right to identify some areas for Ofsted scrutiny as well as a greater emphasis on the school's own evaluation. As this book goes to press Ofsted's consultation paper 'The Future of Inspection' (Ofsted, 2004) is published. It proposes that the burden on schools is to be reduced. It is suggested that each inspection 'should be a short, sharp review' (p.3) with a very short period of notice given before a school is inspected. Demands for documentation from schools may be reduced and the proposal is that individual teachers will not receive repeated lesson observations and that school self-evaluation will become more important. Of note is the suggestion that 'the increased emphasis on school self-evaluation should be seen as reflecting increased confidence in the professionalism of school management' (p.4). Of particular note is the welcome suggestion that '[i]t is time to trust schools more, and to draw on the professionalism of teachers' (p.8).

Publications from Ofsted such as *School Evaluation Matters* (1998) have focused directly upon self-evaluation and have offered advice to schools about the processes involved in carrying out evaluation. It is clear that Ofsted now views external inspection and self-evaluation as complementary activities. Thus the Handbook for Inspecting series (1999a; 1999b; 2003) states that 'Ofsted is committed to promoting self-evaluation as a key aspect of the work of schools'. The nature of the relationship between Ofsted inspections and school self-evaluation is described as follows:

> It is advantageous to base school self-evaluation on the same criteria as those used in all schools by inspectors. A common language has developed about the work of schools, expressed through the criteria. Teachers and governors know that the criteria reflect things that matter. (Ofsted, 1999b, p.138)

Whilst it is true that a majority of schools view the inspection criteria as being a suitable basis for self-evaluation, research reveals that some difficulties still remain, arising from the fact that self-evaluation and school inspection are not the same thing. It is evident that there are still some tensions between the (external) requirement for inspection and (internal) school-based desires for self-evaluation and improvement.   This is why a number of schools and Local Education Authorities have made use of frameworks other than that supplied by Ofsted, including quality assurance standards, such as 'Total Quality Management', British Standards indicator BS 5750, 'Investors in People' and school-driven frameworks such as that suggested by MacBeath (1999) in his influential work 'Schools Must Speak for Themselves'. Typically, schools or LEAs make use of a combination of elements of the Ofsted framework (including relevant checklists from the Ofsted Handbooks) and customised, LEA-produced evaluation tools or elements from other frameworks such as those mentioned above.

Rudd and Davies from the National Foundation for Educational Research (NFER, 2000) discuss the need for some modification of Ofsted's processes and frameworks so as to take greater account of the growing drive for internal, self-evaluation by schools. They refer to the 1996 version of the Ofsted Inspection Framework and also cite Ofsted's Evaluation Matters (1998) which focuses directly upon self-evaluation and collaboration. In their work, however, the researchers detect strong tensions between the external requirements for inspection and the internal school drives for self-evaluation and improvement as teachers draw upon and use a range of other criteria and checklists as well as those employed by Ofsted. In trying to get underneath the rhetoric to see whether there was a genuine culture of self-evaluation in schools and LEAs, the researchers wanted to find signs of a flourishing of such cultures which might eventually supersede external inspection as the dominant way of driving a school forward. Using a scrutiny of one primary and one secondary school in each of nine LEAs the team compared and contrasted the perspectives of the LEAs and the schools. Their findings for LEAs were generally positive, with LEA representatives enjoying the challenge of self-evaluation and welcoming a lessening of hostility between LEAs and their schools. Both parties were in agreement that inspection is something which is done to you but that self-evaluation is something of which you are a part.

Tensions were still evident though and LEAs were unconvinced that some schools were sufficiently self-critical and were unclear as to whether schools were yet capable of self-evaluation or whether they still required steerage from the LEA. Schools also were generally positive about their involvement and wanted what one of their number described as 'a thinking, changing school and a thinking, changing teacher who will develop a thinking, changing child'. Most schools believed in setting their own improvement agendas but enjoyed the help of a 'critical friend' in the form of an LEA member, a paid consultant or a colleague from another school. Many schools also used packages and toolkits either in-house or bought-in since they did not feel the need for each school to re-invent the wheel. Like their LEA colleagues, school representatives also saw difficulties and uncertainties in their situations. Few saw themselves as being allowed to be totally free of LEA help, which was sometimes seen as interference, and even within the school some teachers felt that they had not achieved a genuine 'bottom up' approach since most power remained in the hand of senior staff.

The general conclusion reached by the researchers was that although the self-inspecting school is a long way off yet, self-evaluation is at least beginning to flourish and show promise. The main issue that remains unresolved concerns the point of self-evaluation – is it a method of internal self-improvement for schools or is it a better and more successful way of preparing for and succeeding in satisfying an Ofsted inspection team? Could internal self-evaluation ever be an alternative and replacement for Ofsted?

A case for self-evaluation is powerfully made by MacBeath (1999) who maintains that to be truly effective self-evaluation needs to be built into, rather than bolted onto, the work of the school. It needs to be an integral part of a school's routines and processes so that it might facilitate enhanced professionalism, better management, improved teaching and learning as well as reducing the need for the present system of costly external inspection. School self-evaluation needs to be based upon carefully collected and thoroughly analysed data about such factors as pupil attainments, attendance and behaviour as well as data from pupils themselves. It must also draw upon data collected from parents and the totality of information needs to be used to drive up standards from the inside of the school. In addition, most schools are likely to benefit from external support, review and challenge by an external body like a reformed inspectorate, the LEA, a local university or some kind of critical friend. This external evaluation can provide a new external perspective, additional evaluation expertise and a readiness to share issues and challenges and to provide supportive and critical feedback. There must be, of course, mutual trust between a school and its review agency and there will need to be a structure and mechanism for this co-operative venture to work.

Much internal evaluation is based exclusively on Ofsted documentation which runs the risk of becoming an orthodoxy on how a school should be run. Schools which slavishly follow only Ofsted criteria are likely to fail to develop their own critical and innovative thinking and practices. Such narrow adherence to the Ofsted protocols runs the risk of becoming a cynical 'how to please Ofsted' activity. In a genuinely co-operative approach the external body would work in real partnership with schools to develop and agree criteria for evaluation; the indicators, measures and targets would be jointly negotiated and agreed. Instead of the 'hit and run' model of Ofsted there would be a genuine working hand-in-hand to ensure that improved teaching and learning improved the quality of education. Presently it would appear that a minority of schools are confident enough to view an Ofsted inspection as an opportunity for genuine development where they present, to quote Ofsted's consultation paper 'a warts and all' picture (Ofsted, 2004, p.10). The majority, it appears, 'bury their bodies' and adopt an accountability stance as they conceal their weaknesses and strive for a 'perfect' inspection. Much bridge-building will need to be done before schools will be prepared to present for inspection a 'warts and all' picture as proposed by Ofsted in early 2004 (Ofsted, 2004, p.10).

Recent refinements to the policy and procedures within Ofsted indicate that some welcome change is likely although, realistically, whether this is sufficient to change the relationships between schools and inspectors remains a moot point. Whilstever Ofsted remains perceived by teachers as a coercive piece of State apparatus which robs them of their professionalism and replaces it with a prescribed technicism it will be resented by all, subverted by the brave or resourceful and unwillingly complied with and obeyed by the many. Small wonder that the recruitment and retention of a teaching force proves to be such a difficult task for government.

Origin and Workings of the Teacher Training Agency

The increased central control over the school curriculum and the associated assessment that occurred during the 1980s was extended in a similar way to incorporate teacher education in the 1990s. Using a medical metaphor of the 'repeat prescription' Hartley (1998) describes how first the 'ailments' of the school system and then those of teacher education were 'treated' by the prescribing in both cases of a detailed curriculum, a framework of assessment and the use of a system of strict inspection to guarantee compliance. The structures imposed in both cases and the legitimation arguments surrounding their implementation were broadly similar. From as far back as Labour Prime Minister James Callaghan's (1976) lecture at Ruskin College, Oxford there had been a strong and consistent criticism of the perceived excesses of child-centred education, the 'crack in the pedagogical code'.

Although the prescriptions of the National Curriculum and Ofsted's surveillance of schools appeared to be suppressing progressive pedagogy the Government also had plans to mount a strong assault on what it perceived to be the source of such aberrations, namely the teacher training institutions. Whilst the Government had shown an interest in imposing more control over teacher education (or teacher training as it is now called), as far back as the 1970s when Area Training Organisations (ATOs) were abolished, it was only in the 1990s that the full force of government attention was directed at the area of teacher education.

Following suggestions made by the Cross Commission in 1888 the universities had begun to establish their own departments of education for the training of teachers in order to make up for the failings of the learning-on-the-job pupil-teacher apprenticeship system. As well as founding their own education departments the universities also had oversight of the mainly denominational colleges that were also training teachers. This system of oversight was eventually formalised in 1947 with the creation of the Area Training Organisations which supervised all aspects of teacher training courses and recommended students to the Minister for Education for the award of Qualified Teacher Status (QTS). By 1960 these ATO colleges and departments were considered to be sufficiently effective and reliable to have their training courses extended from two to three years' duration with a fourth year added in 1964 for those students wishing to stay on for their BEd degrees. For about 150 years these ATOs had developed and supported courses of teacher preparation which rejected school-based pupil-teacher apprenticeship schemes and moved towards the generation of courses which stimulated professionalism through the bringing together of practical training and theoretical study based in both school and college.

As part of the centralisation of control over teacher education the ATOs were abolished in 1975 and in 1983 the Council for the Accreditation of Teacher Education (CATE) was set up to advise the Secretary of State for Education on the approving of courses for initial teacher training. Only a few members of CATE were actually drawn from those directly involved with teacher training. Teacher education was, in effect, 'thoroughly disenfranchised' and treated with a 'lack of trust, indeed, suspicion by the Secretary of State' (Gilroy, 1998).

The voices of teacher educators were neither heard nor heeded and a one-sided critical attack was mounted from right wing think tanks like the Centre for Policy Studies as well as from influential individuals like the academic Anthony O'Hear (1988) who attacked the colleges for their 'spurious and questionable studies (with no) solid grounding in the real world'. Their graduates were seen as having insufficient practical skill and too much of what Sir Keith Joseph described as 'jargon ridden theorising' that served as 'a lamentable substitute for serious thought and training'. It was felt that by increasing the amount of time that students spent in schools, by giving a bigger part of their training to school teachers, by enforcing the practical implications of the CATE criteria like encouraging college staff to renew their own practical school experience and by recruiting new lecturers who had recent and relevant practical experience of teaching in schools, teacher education would be brought under closer central supervision and control. It was planned that this would also promote a move from theory to practice and a corresponding power shift from college lecturers to school teachers in the preparation of new recruits. Such moves were strongly welcomed in parts of the media where, for example, as described by Whitty (2002) an editorial in *The Spectator* portrayed teacher educators as Marxists who peddle an irrelevant, damaging and outdated ideology of anti-elitism to students who, in order to qualify as teachers must undergo 'a period of Marxist indoctrination' (*The Spectator*, 27 February, 1993).

Despite such changes, however, it was still subsequently thought that courses were still not practical enough, that the criteria had only been partially successful and that a National Curriculum for teacher training should be developed. This was the view of Anthea Millett, the first chief executive of the TTA. Just like school teachers in the 1980s the college staff were now deemed not to be trustworthy of self-regulation and were subjected to increased central government control and prescription. This culminated in the establishment of the unelected TTA in 1994, the setting up of a national framework for the assessment of teacher education by Ofsted/TTA in 1996 and the establishment of a national curriculum for initial teacher education, now called Initial Teacher Training (ITT).

Little is known in any detail about the workings of the TTA. Its membership was generated not by election but by direct ministerial appointment. It is not known what procedures and criteria were used to structure such appointments and there appears to be a similar lack of transparency about the composition of its many Committees and Boards. There is very little access to its agendas, minutes and proceedings and, with such centralisation of power, nobody on the outside of the policy-making process knows who is doing what, with whom, in what manner and for what purposes.

The new managerialism, which had been imposed earlier in schools, has been extended into the world of teacher training where a centrally prescribed curriculum and assessment framework have been imposed almost without any serious negotiation and consultation. These centrally imposed activities have to be implemented and delivered locally within the colleges and universities, where compliance is more or less guaranteed by the use of Ofsted inspections and the potential for having recruitment targets set, funding withdrawn and the closing down of courses by the TTA. Gilroy (1998) describes how the New Labour government inherited and continued with the top-down, centrally imposed control mechanisms for schools, and now also continued with 'a similar negative and ugly inheritance ... with regard to teacher training'.

A whole raft of policy initiatives on teacher education appears to have been framed specifically to change the nature of teacher professionalism and to increase a focus upon craft skills at the expense of reflection and professional understanding. By emphasising competencies the dominant discourse of liberal humanism is undermined and replaced with a discourse of technical rationality; technicians are preferred to reflective practitioners whose skills are theoretically underpinned. Whilst central government holds on tightly to strategic control it relies increasingly on intermediary agencies like Ofsted and the TTA, headed up by government appointees, to implement and facilitate its vision.

Many criticisms have been made about the imposition of control over schools and teacher education institutions by central governments. The University Committee on Teacher Education (UCET) saw the replacement of CATE by the TTA as 'a serious threat to quality [which] would lead to an increase in political control'. The retiring chairman of CATE, Professor Taylor, argued that the TTA would do nothing to improve the quality of initial training, that it would not provide better in-service education, and that it would not solve the problems of teacher recruitment. Making teacher education subject to a different funding body to the rest of higher education also raises the possibility of universities withdrawing from teacher training (and some have done so). Shifting the emphasis from university-based work to school-based training and expecting teachers to make a bigger input into the teaching of students places a huge strain on schools and runs the risk of diverting their attention and energy away from their major role, the education of school pupils.

The TTA has as its policy the centralised control of all aspects of teachers' professional development. It set itself up, with government backing, as the sole arbiter of what is to count as meaningful in-service education for teachers, what is considered suitable classroom-focused research and has outlined plans for teacher professional development from initial training onwards with teachers themselves having little, if any, say in these new arrangements. The vision of the TTA is based upon a series of proposed National Professional Qualifications (NPQs). Student teachers proceed through a government-approved training course and achieve Qualified Teacher Status. They then serve an induction year, structured by their Career Entry Profile (CEP), which they bring with them from their training course and which indicates their strengths as well as the areas where improvement is required during the induction year in a school. If they are successful they are recognised as teachers. After several years of teaching they become eligible to apply for passage through a Performance Threshold and may continue to proceed through further stages of professional development up to and including headship, with each critical step governed by the application of Standards emanating from the TTA. In short, there is a clear career pathway mapped out for teachers by the TTA with only somewhat questionable consultation procedures involved in the development of such a path.

Critical Issues: Consultation and Underlying Model

The nature and quality of the consultation processes associated with the development of Standards and career gateways are revealing (Mahony and Hextall, 1997; Hextall and Mahony, 2000; Mahony and Hextall, 2000). Pat Mahony and Ian Hextall argue that the consultation process by which the TTA lays such store is a good indicator of the health of democracy and that consultation should involve genuine invitations for appropriate agencies and individuals to give advice and for that advice to receive, in turn, genuine, thorough and responsive consideration. Unfortunately, the research reveals considerable deviation from this pattern; important imperfections are revealed in the scrutiny of the consultation process involved with the QTS Standards. Such Standards are obviously important since they constitute the mandatory first gateway into the profession and provide a baseline on which the Induction Standards, the Performance Threshold Standards and the Standards for Advanced Skills Teachers are built.

The research called into question the ways in which the agenda for consultation seemed to be constrained by pre-ordained, non-negotiable parameters. It was not always clear how consultation responses were interpreted or how weight and importance were given to some representative bodies in comparison to individual responses. Schools did not appear to play a significant role in the consultation process and some important and relevant bodies like the Campaign for Racial Equality and the Equal Opportunities Commission were not included in the formal invitation lists. Furthermore, there was a lack of clarity and openness about the ways that working groups were set up and friendships, networking and recommendations seemed to have influenced what has been called the recruitment of 'people like us'.

It appears that such a lack of transparency and accountability prompted a defensiveness more closely associated with something like national defence than with the standards of our teachers. As the audit of public institutions by Weir and Beetham (1999, p.487) revealed 'Government consultation of interests and the general public is unsystematic and opaque … Overall, the absence of firm rules for consultation gives rise to concern'. The work of the TTA does not warrant the defensiveness, secrecy even, which surrounds some of its work. Neither does it warrant the 'manufacturing of consent' to the QTS Standards revealed in the research. The use of consciously 'toned down' language in reports, the systematic deletion of terms like 'criticism' and their replacement with words like 'comments' were all part of a process of glossing in the consultation and the increasingly positive account of responses which is given in the written documents as they proceed from First Draft to Final Draft to Summary Draft. Positive feedback was played up and negative feedback was played down; the half-empty jug was always described as being half-full.

Hextall and Mahony (2000) conclude that this is not the way to produce a policy text or to ensure its endorsement and the full involvement of the teachers who will be required to deliver such a policy. Rhetoric and managed consent can never replace real ownership and genuine confidence in a policy – factors which are critical for its implementation. As it is, those policies which are imposed prompt teachers and teacher educators to ignore the policies if they can, appropriate them and alter them to suit if they dare, or accept with sullen resignation that to which they have no commitment or real engagement.

In examining the actual Standards produced in this questionable process Reynolds (1999) describes how the TTA used the Standards produced by the Management Charter Initiative (MCI) as a source of reference. Both sets of Standards have the same shared aim of making transparent the basis upon which the accreditation of practice is made; professional requirements would be unambiguous and a benchmark of acceptable practice would be established. Unlike the MCI however, the Standards for teaching were not based upon a systematic and rigorous analysis of the main roles, skills, abilities, attitudes, knowledge and understanding required for teaching. The use of the word 'Standards' may have a rhetorical function to exhort a bettering of performance but it does not explain what is fully involved in teaching. The word seems to have more of a symbolic than an explanatory function; the Standards spell out details of subject knowledge, craft skills and familiarisation with documents but they have nothing to say about the personal qualities appropriate to the teacher's role, the social contexts which constrain it nor the purposes and values which it seeks to serve.

The Standards cast the teacher as a technician who must match classroom practice to the view of effective teaching embedded in those Standards. They seem to imply that values and attitudes are not centrally important for ITT. Teaching must be 'effective' but little is said about its appropriateness; it must be skilled but little is said about the ways such skills will be operated in the diverse racial, class and gender situations in which new teachers will be expected to work. Additionally, there is very little mention of the need for teachers to be educated in matters relating to social justice. Matters relating to social justice seem to feature little in the policy and practice of the TTA and the assertive restructuring of teaching has neglected social justice issues. Whilst teachers, parents, pupils and all involved in the life of a school will inevitably be faced with issues of race, social class, gender, sexuality and other socially and politically defined identities, the TTA has practically nothing to say about how to deal with such issues. Teaching is discussed in a decontextualised manner where it always appears to be seemingly simple and non-problematical. The TTA appears to deny or to ignore the fact that schools exist within, and are influenced by, inequitable social relationships; it seldom makes explicit reference in its documentation and practice to where pupils come from, the nature of their life experiences and their prospective destinations. Education is conceived by the TTA in a mechanical way and is seen as a 'set of techniques to be employed by technicians on malleable pupils' (Angus, 1993, p.337).

In a recent paper Peter Cope and John I'Anson (2003) describe a significant dimension of teaching which they call 'social contingency' – an aspect, they argue, which is currently marginalised in official discourse. Nowhere is this more applicable than in the case of the TTA Standards. Social contingency, they suggest, is characterised by unpredictability, relationality and ethical demands and its neglect, they say, can be explained with reference to the assumptions of teacher sovereignty that are philosophically and ethically unsustainable. One indicator of the lack of an appreciation of social contingency in the TTA Standards is the development of assessment profiles which treat generalised competence as precise assessment criteria. A second problem, they argue, is that such 'high-inference descriptions' give power to those who use them. This power, they add, 'can be amplified and misused if the outcomes are presented as resulting from objective measurement rather than complex and error-prone judgement' (p.229). In presenting the act of teaching as a value-free activity and unproblematic, the work of professionals is devalued accordingly. At the same time, it protects policy-makers and managers from the complexity of the educational arena.

Similarly, Mahony and Hextall (2000 and Hextall and Mahony, 1999a) discuss how the 'modernisation' of teachers has its roots deep in the private sector and is based on an assumption that systems of personnel management can be simply moved from one context to another. Management and modernisation are seen as being a technicist 'free floating technology' capable of being universally applied in a range of public service arenas like health, education and the prisons. It sets out, by implication, to redefine teachers on an individualistic model in which their individualism comes to be seen as more important than a communitarian commitment to collaboration and non-competitive shared actions and values. By adopting a discriminatory approach based upon Standards, and an increase in salary for some, 'earned' by progress through hurdles, thresholds and gateways, central policy-makers seem to believe that the lone teacher jealously guarding his or her money-earning professional accomplishments and skills and competing for progress and promotion against colleagues will generate effective, efficient and economical teaching – the virtuous 3 Es.

Lawn (1996, p.119) describes this version of the teacher that is being redesigned as 'individualistic not collective in orientation, differentiated but not homogenous, competent not responsible'. Such a 'more for less' approach will inevitably lead to work intensification, de-skilling, lower salaries for some teachers and the isolation of individuals. For the Government it will, it hopes, lead to a reduction in public sector expenditure and a lowering of tax levels. It will also probably promote an image of the Government as a wise, rational and responsible holder of the public purse strings and guardian of our well being. By tightening things from the centre the Government can employ a 'hands off' approach to steerage by facilitating decentralisation and delegation. Hoggett (1996, p.9) discusses this centralisation/decentralisation nexus, which is also referred to as the tight-loose coupling approach, in which 'there is a pronounced shift towards the creation of operationally decentralised units with a simultaneous attempt to increase central control over strategy and policy'.

Room for manoeuvre is highly constrained; the parameters are highly centralised and largely non-negotiable but they have to be put into practice in sites and localities that are diverse in their nature and needs. The TTA seems to want to impose consensus where none exists, to put an end to debate and to close critical and contestational spaces for teachers.

The view of leadership embedded in TTA documents about headship is interesting in this respect. Right from its beginning the TTA directed initiatives towards head teachers and this concern has remained centre-stage from that time with the training, re-skilling, re-orientation, managerialisation and certification of heads occupying a key place in TTA strategy. The TTA views effective teaching as requiring good management that will set the tone and purpose of the institution and will make plans, implement them and appraise and monitor their effectiveness. A predominantly hierarchical model of leadership seems in favour with the TTA which places other participants in the school community in a largely responsive position to the head teacher's vision. As Angus (1994, p.86) says 'other teachers, parents and students are generally viewed as essentially passive recipients of the leader's vision ... the main skill required of most participants is for them merely to adopt the leader's vision and slot into the leader's definition of the school culture'. Making hierarchical places like schools even more hierarchical seems to be predicated on a particular version of leadership which de-legitimates space accessible for other competing visions and values.

There are quite serious risks of course for central policy-makers to attempt to stifle a teaching culture that has previously thrived on co-operation and collaboration. Whilst all public sector workers will hope for increased remuneration for their work, many of them have very strong commitments to the values and beliefs of public service. The potential divisiveness and jealousies amongst colleagues promoted by the extra pay for some, but not all, might threaten the collegiality of schools if 'good' teaching becomes a jealously guarded and personal commodity to be sold on the 'internal market of the school' (Mahony and Hextall, 2000, p.75). Co-operation and team-work might be replaced by distrust, low morale and counter productive competition. Technicist measurable targets from policy-makers may clash with the values and beliefs of many public service workers.

Mahony and Hextall (2000 and Hextall and Mahony, 1999a) are critical of the way that the Standards for QTS emanating from the TTA are not accompanied by an explicit account of how teaching is conceptualised within the Standards and the way that, without explanation, justification or rationale, they have foisted upon teachers and teacher educators a view of teachers as technicians rather than critical practitioners. The use of tight regulation and surveillance transforms teachers from being decision-makers into technicians or semi-professionals who are expected to know and follow curricular, pedagogic and assessment frameworks so that they can be trusted to safely 'deliver' content through procedures established from above. Circumscribing the degree of choice and decision-making of teachers might even discourage prospective teachers from entering an occupation characterised by decreasing levels of autonomy. Standards may have the appearance of being merely mechanisms for measurement but they are, in effect, constructing new definitions of teaching. They are definitions, however, which inadequately frame the social and political contexts within which teaching occurs and the values and purposes which it seeks to serve. The 'dreary utilitarianism' of the Standards may, for example, prompt a familiarity with anti-discrimination legislation but have very little to say about tackling racism in the classroom and teaching in a non-discriminatory manner. There is no space within which disagreement and debate can flourish and a veil of seemingly neutral technicism is drawn over any potential dissent and dialogue; teachers' voices are marginalised and the values, purposes and content of education are rendered as not being up for discussion.

Since compliance to central diktat had been largely achieved through Ofsted inspections of schools, the same apparatus is imported into the world of teacher education where inspectors, working on behalf of the TTA, produced data upon which target recruitment figures, funding and threats of closure guarantee compliance. Since inspection evidence and judgements based upon visitations to teacher training institutions can have such profound consequences like the closure of courses, staff redundancies and redeployment, it is imperative that Ofsted methods and reliability are subjected to thorough scrutiny.

Since 1995 the allocation of funding and training places quotas by the TTA have been based upon evidence of 'quality' in teacher training institutions as measured by Ofsted inspections. Such institutions may have their accreditation withdrawn where they receive an Ofsted grade of poor quality or are deemed not to have complied with statutory obligations. It is, therefore, of critical importance that there is full confidence in the method used by Ofsted and in the judgements it makes. Ofsted, for its part, has not made clear how it seeks to ensure its reliability, for example in such matters as inter-observer agreement, the representativeness of the behaviour they observe and the methods they use to minimise and control observer bias. There are no clear exemplification criteria used to support their judgements and little, if any, constructive dialogue between assessors and the assessed. As Campbell and Husbands (2000) observe 'to simply impose criteria by Circular is unacceptable'. They go on to argue that to impose criteria and to make judgements without dialogue, explanation or contestation other than in law are all signs of a system which has little interest in improvement but is seeking compliance through control and surveillance.

The TTA and Ofsted together developed their *Framework for Inspections* of teacher training institutions in 1996 and revised it in 1998. Around this time, as already noted above, Ofstin was founded as a voluntary, unfunded group which espoused the aim of 'securing the highest standards of inspection and support and the most effective methods of improvement and accountability'. They obtained funds to support their sponsorship of research, the results of which were both supportive and critical of Ofsted and were provided to the House Of Commons Select Committee on Education and Training which was examining the work of Ofsted (House of Commons Select Committee on Education and Employment, 1999). The research found a broad acceptance of the idea of inspections and praised the way that much more evidence about educational institutions was finding its way into the public domain. It acknowledged also that inspection had stimulated a good deal of internal self-evaluation in both schools and colleges. It was very critical, however, of the general ineffectiveness of Ofsted as far as improvement was concerned and was also critical of its methods and its failure to offer much dialogue and advice. Amongst other things, Ofstin recommended to the parliamentary committee the appointment of a full-time professional inspectorate and an end to the contracting arrangements. It also proposed the encouragement of much more self-evaluation in institutions and a more complementary relationship with Ofsted.

The parliamentary committee considered a wide range of evidence. UCET (1998), for example, described the 'Byzantine complexity' of the Ofsted scoring system and regretted the frequency of inspections such that institutions had not finished with implications arising from one inspection before they were faced with yet another. In the end, however, the House of Commons Select Committee was broadly in favour and supportive of Ofsted and the status quo. Indeed, David Blunkett (1999) responded to the Select Committee with a ringing endorsement of Woodhead and Ofsted:

> Under the leadership of Chris Woodhead Ofsted is making significant contributions to the government's drive to raise standards in schools, LEAs and teacher training colleges. Inspection helps us to identify when things go wrong and, more recently, good practice which can now be spread. I am glad that the Select Committee has recognised this and sees no case for radically changing the system.

The General Teaching Council: A Way Forward?

With teacher professionalism firmly in the pincer-like grip of Ofsted and the TTA, one can only conjecture whether the recently instituted General Teaching Council for England (GTCE) might represent an opportunity for teachers to reclaim their professional identity and, in the process, revive their demoralised spirits.

Aspirations for a council for teachers akin to those like the Law Society and the British Medical Association (BMA) have a long history. A lack of parliamentary support, however, together with internal squabbles amongst teacher unions have failed to dent the reluctance of successive governments to surrender their control over teachers to the teachers themselves. Even during the educational reforms of the Thatcher and Major years, when there was an intensification of the campaign for such a council, all of the lobbying and arguments were rebuffed by the ever suspicious Tory politicians' mistrust of 'producer' interests. Despite the campaigners' readiness to allay government anxieties by proposing an advisory rather than an executive role for a teachers' council, they met with consistent failure. Their campaign did, however, manage to secure a commitment for a General Teaching Council in the Labour Party Manifesto and when New Labour came into power in 1997 consultations about the nature, composition and powers of the Council were initiated.

The General Teaching Council for England was legislated for in 1998 and began to operate in 2000. It was heralded with much brio by politicians like Byers (1997) who saw it as offering teachers 'a measure of self-regulation' and the 'ability to offer an expert view on professional development and career progression'. David Blunkett was equally effusive in claiming that 'the GTC will have a crucial role to play in promoting high standards and raising the standards and morale of the profession' (Blunkett, 1997). Another nameless but less convinced Member of Parliament is quoted by Kirk (2000) as describing the GTCE as the 'rather toothless poodle of the Secretary of State'. Nigel de Grouchy (1997), a leader of the National Association of Schoolmasters/Union of Women Teachers (NAS/UWT) union, is also quoted as saying that the GTCE was 'a very pale shadow of what a real teaching council should be'. Whilst it is far too early to rule out the possibility of the GTCE becoming the authentic and authoritative voice of the teaching profession in England and the custodian of standards, a number of convincing authorities have cast strong doubts, given its current powers, about its likely future as such an important body.

Comparisons between the Scottish GTC and its English counterpart make clear the limits of the recent creation. Existing since 1965, the GTCS has established itself as a key member of the policy community and speaks authoritatively on educational issues. Its powers are more executive than the essentially advisory powers of the Council for England. Only time will tell whether the government's preference for a more minimalist English Council is an expression of a belief in 'hasten slowly' approaches or whether they continue to lack any real confidence in teachers in England.

Of course, it could be argued that teachers in England got what they deserved; campaigners for the GTCE went out of their way to assure government that their proposals for the GTCE would involve minimal interruption and interference with the work of Ofsted and the TTA. They seemed willing to accept a rather limited advisory role and, although they succeeded in securing a teacher majority on the Council, they settled for 'the best GTC possible rather than the best possible GTC' (Kirk, 2000).

The GTCE will consist of 63 members of which there will be 25 teachers elected by the profession (11 primary teachers, 11 secondary teachers, one primary head teacher, one secondary head teacher and one special school teacher). In addition, there will be 16 appointees from representative bodies, 13 appointees by the Secretary of State and 9 appointees from teaching unions: NAS/UWT, National Union of Teachers (NUT), National Association of Head Teachers (NAHT), Association of Teachers and Lecturers (ATL), Secondary Heads Association (SHA) and Professional Association of Teachers (PAT). One extra member will be appointed by the Disability Rights Commission.

In almost 40 years and with considerably more powers than the English council, the GTC (Scotland) has still failed to earn the full confidence of Scottish teachers who appear not yet to identify or commit fully or warmly to its mission. Perhaps it is not surprising that teachers in England are showing such little enthusiasm for their own GTC. A lack of confidence about the currently functioning GTCE is evident in the writing of academics like Hextall and Mahony (1999b) who point out that the GTCE came into being in a context of the well established TTA which was already vested by the government with strong powers in relation to teacher education and professional development. The largely advisory powers of the GTCE contrast strongly with the clear decision-making and control capabilities of the TTA. An intentionally 'hazy' interface between the GTCE, whose majority members are elected or nominated by the teaching profession, and the un-elected TTA quango with its Board appointed by the Secretary of State has seemingly been left by the government.

The research into the consultation processes surrounding the emergence of the GTCE indicates that a majority of the respondents wanted the removal of the TTA as an unrepresentative, unaccountable and undemocratic body. Many responses argued for the activities and functions of the TTA to be transferred to a more professionally accountable body, the GTCE. Mahony and Hextall (2000) argue that the GTCE ought to occupy a more central role in the deliberative processes concerned with teacher education and professional development. As it is, the council is simply one of a number of consultative groups which gives advice. The TTA, it can be argued, possesses neither the status nor experience to define and endorse standards for the teaching profession. Its poor track record on consultation and the Ministerially-appointed Board are no substitute for a properly established system of professional debate and decision-making with its associated acceptance of accountability, transparency and ratification.

Government's behaviour is ambivalent; it talks of enhancing professional status and standards of teaching but invests all the power in an un-elected quango, the TTA. Important issues relating to matters like teacher supply and recruitment, pay and conditions of service are the business of the DfEE, TTA or the School

Teachers' Review Body with the GTCE only giving advice when asked. Time will tell about the extent to which the GTCE is a 'token gesture, a chimera which pretends to take a body of teachers seriously as professionals whilst effectively re-engineering them as cohorts of workers under the auspices of new managerialism' (Hextall and Mahony, 1999b, p.10).

In preferring a government-appointed quango over a more democratically established GTCE, the government appears to be attempting to mollify the teacher profession without giving it very much real power. Conformity and compliance, it still seems, remain the distinguishing features of the educational landscape with teachers still located at a distance from decision-making. The government still consults on a narrow base and fails to heed the voices of those excluded or marginalised from positions of power. Certain interests seem to be privileged over others. This may not be intentionally malicious but it is certainly poor democracy from a government that talks in such warm words about it. Decision-making in education needs to become much more responsive to and representative of the various constituencies involved. Spaces need to be created in which these voices can speak and be listened to. When discussing the discourse of derision which envelops teachers Maguire and Ball (1994) describe how:

> Some voices, some modes of articulation and forms of association are rendered silent. Certain possibilities are offered and others are closed down, some ways of thinking are supported and empowered others are inhibited … Actors are positioned and constructed differently within different discourses, different values and ends and purposes are operant within different discourses. The task then for the progressive educator is to re-appropriate key discourses, to deconstruct dominant meanings and reassert more democratic, participatory and socially just meanings. (p.7)

It may not be an easy task to listen to such a variety of voices and viewpoints but it must be attempted by government. At the moment, unfortunately, there is little evidence that such spaces exist. Certainly it appears that for the time being at least the GTCE will not be a space wherein teachers will re-assert their professionalism. Teachers are obviously not trusted by government; their professional activity has been submerged under a sea of audits and prescriptions. Inspection and prescription control their daily activities and, in the name of accountability and transparency, their work is choreographed by instruments of control, regulation, monitoring and enforcement with the net effect of undermining their professional independence and integrity (O'Neill, 2002). Far from increasing trust in educational institutions and their personnel, the audit culture has prompted teachers to be more concerned with satisfying centrally prescribed requirements than meeting the varying needs of their students and the communities which they serve.

Under avalanches of legislation, regulations, instructions and demands for more detailed record-keeping, closer adherence to procedures and protocols and improved achievements in meeting targets, teachers end up serving their government masters rather than their pupils' educational needs. The real work of teachers is damaged as they are, for example, obliged to spend more time assessing students' achievements with less time remaining for the actual purpose of teaching. Over-concern with measurable outcomes may well result in teaching to the test. It may also result in teaching which is primarily concerned with avoiding public criticism and punishment rather than teaching which is tailored to the strengths and needs of individuals. Time spent covering their backs gives teachers less time and energy for interacting with their students. If individual personal agency by teachers has such scant opportunities for its expression, it will perhaps require social agency by the teaching profession, ideally not fractured and separated by allegiances to various unions and professional associations, to reclaim a sense of ownership over its general direction.

Whitty (2002) sees the creation of the GTCE as a possible opportunity to rebuild a sense of common professional identity but warns against some backward-looking power struggle wherein the GTCE simply tries to seize for itself all the decision-making currently in the grasp of the government. Teachers need to redefine their professionalism, possibly through the GTCE, but in a newer context in which a broadly based alliance of support, which will include hitherto ignored voices like those of parents and pupils, is mobilised. This will not be an easy task since in recent years governments and the media have created a climate of mistrust between society and its educators. Teachers need to address the critics of schools and teachers who argue that they have misused their professional mandate. They must seek to defend education and to include in such a defence those voices which have hitherto been ignored or silenced. The teaching profession needs to become more open to the needs and concerns of other groups in our democratic society. Writers like Ginsburg (1997) and Apple (1996) in the USA argue for a 'democratic professionalism' for teachers. Democratic professionalism would seek to demystify their professional work and build alliances between teachers and excluded constituencies of students, parents and members of the community on whose behalf decisions have traditionally been made either by professions or by the State. New forms of association and a new professional identity are needed in the 21st century.

Useful insights from an Australian context are provided by Sachs (1997; 2001) who tells how for the Australian Teachers' Union (ATU) the core of democratic professionalism is an emphasis on collaborative, co-operative action between teachers and other stakeholders. Teachers must be accountable and responsible for that work which is under their control but they must also seek to demystify their professional work and not restrict reasonable access to that work. Their democratic professionalism must facilitate the participation in decision-making by students, parents and others and seek to develop a broader understanding of education and how it works in the community. Instead of being defined by governments and their agencies, teachers within a more democratic perspective need to define themselves as they negotiate their identities through collaborations between stakeholders within a community of practice. Democratic professionalism has clear emancipatory aims; it favours an open flow of ideas and practices such that all people can be as fully informed as possible. It has faith in individuals as well as in the collective capacity of people to create strategies for resolving problems. Ideas, problems and policies are evaluated through critical reflection and analysis. There is a shared concern about the welfare of others and the dignity and rights of individuals and minorities. Democracy, equity and social justice are cherished as a set of values by which people work and live. Schools need to become social institutions which promote and extend the democratic way of life; they must be concerned to reduce or eliminate exploitation, inequality and oppression. Such schools will seek to share their vision not only amongst their staff but with the broader constituency of parents and students. They see themselves as part of a rich and complex community where there is mutuality, respect and communication.

The individualism promoted in the Government's dominant managerial discourse stands in stark contrast to the collaboration and collegiality that are the cornerstones of a democratic discourse and the development of democratic professionalism. Such an open, sharing culture will provide opportunities for all stakeholders to communicate with each other about issues of policy and practice covering curriculum, pedagogy and assessment. To engender such a professionalism which would facilitate such a community will be a challenging business but will eventually improve the way teachers work and how they and others see that work. The new professionalism for teachers will be borne out of their attempts to equip themselves with allies as well as tools to contest the agendas that are at work transforming them into technicists; teachers must learn to challenge the taken-for-granted ends towards which their teaching is being directed. To be successful requires that the teaching community begins a process of reclamation or rebuilding of their professionalism. They must build a network of associations and forge a newly restated set of aims and purposes together with a shared set of strategies for attaining its goals. This will not be an easy task for teachers. Part of the 'reform' discourse has been the denigration of teachers as a self-serving group whose practices were in need of being 'opened up' by the market so as to wring out of them an improved service. Serious doubt was cast upon their altruism and this campaign of derision, ably aided and abetted by the news media, created an overworked and exhausted workforce which had neither the time, energy or interest to cast a critical eye at the forces that had produced its condition. Scrutiny of the wider picture from whence their changed circumstances emerged was beyond most teachers who were understandably too busy getting on with the job, implementing government initiatives and living with the rising public scrutiny and criticism. Bottery (1998) quotes one, too typical teacher who said:

> It's profoundly dispiriting to come home after an exhausting and frustrating day to know that you've got another two or three hours' work in front of you after you've finished your tea, to switch on the television to find that you're watching some minister telling you how you can't be trusted, how you're the cause of the country's educational and social problems, and to find your educational ideals are disparaged and belittled. (p.36)

Many teachers, it would appear, have become what Hoyle (1974) has called 'restricted professionals' who lack a wider vision of their role and who have taken on board a technical-rational-implementational approach to their work and have become understandably preoccupied with implementing initiatives, responding to reforms and doing a 'better job' in the classroom instead of engaging in critical debate about the purposes of education. Their silence, for example, was deafening about the imposition of the literacy and numeracy strategies: given practically no say in the decisions about the content and pedagogy of these initiatives, their silence was clear evidence of a weakened and supine teaching force.

Time for Teachers to Re-Define their Professionalism

It is time for teachers to re-assemble and re-define their professionalism which extends beyond simply being 'good' in the classroom. They need to take up a view that teaching transcends the classroom and requires that they take a more active interest and participation in the issues that are currently steering education. To do this will necessitate them forging and rebuilding mutually helpful alliances and relationships with universities, interest groups, community leaders, school students and, perhaps most importantly, with parents.

Talk about the importance of home and school relationships has a long history dating back, in the UK for example, to the Plowden Report in 1967. For the most part, however, it has remained at the level of talk, with schools acknowledging the importance of the home but remaining reluctant to stimulate and support true parental involvement which goes beyond the supporting of the school's mission and the fulfilment of its own agenda. If teachers are to seek a more democratic professionalism they will need to make genuine and consistent efforts to forge truly collaborative links with parents and the communities served by the school. Such a move will help schools move away from 'deficit' explanations for the failures of many children to progress within the school system which tends to locate the source of failure within the pupil, the family or the community. More open relationships with parents will reveal failure to achieve as reflecting discrepancies and mismatches between the culture of the school and the culture of the home and community (Au, 1993). Children who enter school having already been partially apprenticed or enculturated into the social practices of schooling invariably perform better at those practices than children for whom there has been no such preparation. If teachers are increasingly able to recognise learning as a socio-cultural practice they will better understand the mismatches between the learning practice of the home and those of the school. Parental involvement will help teachers to understand more fully the cultures of the home and community whilst at the same time teachers will be able to explain more clearly their ways of working in school. A greater understanding of the diversity of children's backgrounds will help schools to adapt curriculum content and methods to suit the needs of those children. Democratic professionalism makes possible a much more equal sharing of agendas between teachers and parents. An improved, open dialogue will ensue with more collaboration and partnership. Too often it appears that cultural differences and mismatches between teachers and their local communities result in poor communication with parents, poor interaction with children in the classroom and unsatisfactory learning. Too often home and community culture is ignored, rendered invisible or considered irrelevant.

Improved alliances with parents will help teachers to better understand their pupils' home and community culture and help them to be more ready and able to reform their curriculum and pedagogy to accommodate and respond to such cultures. It would appear that there are too few schools in which there are genuine, reciprocal partnerships between the school, the home and the community. In too many schools home and school partnerships consist of little more than the marshalling of parents into an acceptance of the perspective and agenda of teachers and schools. There is a need for a significant shift in schools' understanding of the type of relationship which is desirable and possible with their communities. The one-way transmission of information and knowledge from the school to the home must be replaced by more genuine reciprocity and a shared search for ways and means of reaching a mutual consensus, a shared focus of attention and a shared understanding of the ways in which all parties involved define, value and facilitate learning. In learning from parents, teachers will be better able to adjust schooling to better meet the needs of families. At the same time parents can be helped to observe more closely and understand schooling and how it can empower their children to take their place in society.

If a more democratic professionalism can engender the building of genuine partnerships between teachers and parents, it can lead to more equitable learning outcomes for all children, irrespective of their social and cultural background. The task will not be easy but the prize makes the efforts worthwhile. Parents are rightly suspicious of a view of teaching as an ancient and arcane craft with rituals beyond their understanding. Parents would welcome a view of professionalism that is a visible reality, not a handy defence of the status quo, a weapon to beat off parental opposition or a shield with which to fend off the rightful and legitimate wishes, needs and suggestions of parents. They understandably resent the use of notions of 'teacher professional judgement' used to disguise complacency and conservatism. Teachers should be open and sensitive to such feelings and use every opportunity to forge alliances with parents who could help them to persuade government to end repressive surveillance and begin to encourage self-evaluation in which parents and pupils play an active role. Teachers should not cling to their weakened powers and defend valueless territory. In alliances with other stakeholders they might be able to show that schools can be effective and efficient whilst still being vital, democratic, interactive and self-motivating learning communities.

This 'making things happen' by teachers instead of things just happening to them is unlikely to occur without the sympathy and trust of the public. To open up to parents, and to be open to their concerns in return, represents an important way forward. Teachers need to appreciate the fact that their jobs as educators are likely to meet with more success if they form mutually supportive alliances with parents. They will also enhance rather than diminish their standing as professionals if they can take the initiative in building relationships with parents based upon notions of coequal concern, shared decision-making and working towards common goals.

Chapter 3

Backing into or Facing into the Future? Literacy, Schooling and Society

Introduction

This chapter narrows the focus of the previous two chapters to attend more specifically to reform through the lens of literacy. As already mentioned in Chapter 1, literacy has been relentlessly emphasised in policy initiatives and media representations of schooling, while poverty or equity have effectively been ignored or silenced, hence the focus on literacy in this book. However, literacy education has the potential within the curriculum to generate the kind of critical citizen that can 'position take' to engage critically with global or glocalised economies. This chapter demonstrates the gap between the needs of our times and the policies we have in place to achieve them. The argument is that everything about literacy today is more complex than it was in the past, yet national policies demand that we adhere to one type of literacy, that we assess against *the* standards, and that we specify *the* single best way of fostering literacy in our schools. The search for certainty and the narrowing of literacy, evident in current policies, coincide with increasing diversity and societal change. In the light of our more diverse society and new demands for multiple literacies the kinds of changes that are needed to maximise the life chances of all, and not just some, of the nation's children will be discussed. Just as the argument is made for multiple literacies, so the argument is made for multiple voices in policy decision-making and for a more inclusive and socially-aware policy. A simple utilitarian view of literacy is inadequate for effective participation in modern societies which have left behind an agri-industrial past and have become post-industrial information-service economies. Just as the literacy product on offer is past its sell-by date so also is the manner of its delivery via the direct instruction of the 'literacy hour'. By lacking 'authenticity' and by being insufficiently tied into the ways that literacy is needed and used in real life outside the school, the current policy on literacy fails to meet the demands of 'doing life' even if it meets the new demands of 'doing school'. The chapter is structured by posing three broad questions:

1. What kind of world must school literacy address?
2. How are governments and education policy-makers responding to this changing and complex world?
3. What might constitute an alternative and more satisfactory vision for literacy education?

What Kind of World Must School Literacy Address?

At the level of society there are two significant areas of change with implications for literacy: one economic, the other cultural and demographic. At the level of literacy itself, there are changing definitions brought about by the new technologies and the ubiquity of popular culture; there are new perspectives on how literacy is acquired; and there is the growing gap between the literacy 'haves' and the literacy 'have nots'. These are the inter-related issues that make up the complexity of the field of school literacy that is being described here.

The World of Work

First the economic context needs to be noted. As already noted in the first chapter, multinational and transnational enterprises, not really governments, control economic activity and nation states have to compete constantly to hold onto and improve their relative advantage in the global market place. Sophisticated communication systems, together with new market opportunities, now allow multinational companies to shift production and services to more advantageous site: around the globe. The upshot for workers, in a freer and more open world market, is that they have to be more flexible and proactive in the face of global competition. They have to expect to deal with different and changing occupational pathways.

What is especially noteworthy here, from the perspective of literacy, is not so much the internationalisation of the economy with its consequences for employers' and employees' shifting and changing occupations, as the knowledge-based infrastructure that facilitates all this. The basic economic resource is no longer capital or natural resources but knowledge and ideas or human capital. What is key for wealth creation is the more effective transfer, use and exploitation of all kinds of knowledge. Indeed one could argue that firms sell knowledge, not products or even services, since it is the knowledge required to design, produce and market the product or the service that is so important in what has been called the New Work Order (Gee *et al*, 1996; Gee, 2000a).

Moreover, this knowledge is distributed as James Gee explains (2000b). It is not so much in heads as in networks of relationships, it is not so much what individuals can do on their own that counts as what they can do with others. Workers in this scenario, he says, are expected to work collaboratively, flexibly and in non-routinised ways. Their sense of identity and security comes less from some occupation, fixed set of skills, permanent job or employment, rather it comes from their employability. And employability is a matter of one's skills, experiences and reputation accumulated through a variety of contexts including the workplace, the school or college, the family, the community, etc. To remain employable workers have to keep upgrading their skills and redefining their identities in the light of rapid change and those who fail to do this run the risk of becoming economically marginalised in society. Economically then, life is not stable – it is changing faster than at any previous period in history.

Poverty, Demographic Change and Equity

While a major outcome of globalisation in western democracies is increased wealth and affluence, this is far from evenly distributed (see Chapter 1). Cross-national analyses of earnings and income show that the long term trend towards equality was reversed in the 1980s and 1990s. Inequality of income widened markedly in the UK in that period (Instance, 1997). In fact the gap between the rich and poor widened over the 1990s and into 2001. This claim is based on the government's own official statistical measure of inequality in Britain (see the Office for National Statistics website). On 2001 some four million children lived in poverty in the UK, compared with 1.4 million in 1979 (Joseph Rowntree Foundation, 2001). However, at the time of completing this chapter (December 2003) the statistics show that poverty in Britain has fallen to the levels of the 1980s (Palmer *et al*, 2003). The authors of the report concluded that, while there is still a long way to go to combat poverty, the reduction in poverty levels to below those of the 1990s is an important achievement. We should note that it is the relative difference in income/wealth between people in society that is so significant for life chances, as Wilkinson (2000, p.62) reminds us. He says '... as income inequality increases, the quality of the social environment seems to deteriorate: trust decreases, involvement in local community life decreases and hostility and violence increase. In other words, as hierarchical dominance becomes stronger, egalitarian social relationships weaken'. What creates disadvantage in education is the fact that upper socio-economic groups have superior access to resources, wealth and power, including the power to decide what knowledge is of most worth. This enables these groups to avail of the opportunities presented in education in a relatively more successful manner than other groups (Lynch, 1999). However, the rhetoric of 'standards' rejects such structural issues. As the first Labour Education Secretary for almost two decades, David Blunkett proclaimed more than once that 'Standards not structures are now the prime concern' (cited in Gillborn and Youdell, 2000, p.19). The assumption is that opportunities have been equalised – all have an equal opportunity to succeed.

Historically, as a nation we have not been good at bringing poor children to the same levels of literacy achievement as their better-off peers, resulting in a literacy achievement gap. Similar trends are evident in the USA (Au and Raphael, 2000). In recent years researchers in this country have been using a sophisticated statistical approach, multi-level modelling, to explain achievement. Based on some 5,300 children in over 100 schools in one large LEA, Marchant and Hall (2003) are interested in how school and pupil factors influence achievement. Taking eligibility for free school meals (FSMs) as an indicator of social disadvantage, our research shows that poverty is closely implicated with underachievement. An eleven year old girl not on FSMs, for instance, has a chance of success in English of 0.8, that is an 80% chance of getting level 4 or above in the SATs. But if we change one variable so now we are talking about an eleven year old girl on FSM, her chances of success are much reduced – the probability drops to 0.5 – a 30% difference. This pattern of findings is also evident in the research of others (Croll, 2002; Haverman and Wolfe, 1995; Mortimore and Whitty, 1997; and Strand, 1999). Poverty is still all too often a powerful predictor of literacy performance.

British society is becoming more ethnically diverse. Data collected by the Office for National Statistics (ONS) between 1992-1994 and 1997-1999 showed that the number of people from minority ethnic groups grew by 15% compared to 1% for white people. More than half of the growth in the working age population over the next decade will occur among ethnic minority groups. In a recent quarterly *Population Trends* report the ONS estimated that the number of people from minority ethnic groups in Britain had hit four million – 7% of the population. Minority ethnic groups as a whole account for 12% of pre-school children. Projections for the future indicate that the population of school-going children will be larger and more ethnically diverse. Clearly, Britain is changing demographically and culturally. While ethnic minorities are not homogeneous groups, the incidence of poverty is higher in them than the mainstream population. When compared to white children, children from ethnic minority families are three times as likely to live in poverty. Unsurprisingly, inequality of literacy achievement, and education achievement generally among these groups, is higher than in the rest of the population (Gillborn and Gipps, 1996). The fact is that children who are most often under-achieving or failing are most often poor; because children from ethnic minority groups are more often poor, they are over-represented in the lower achieving pool.

In short, present demographic trends indicate the urgency of addressing the literacy achievement gap. If nothing else, this short discussion flags how literacy and politics are inseparable. One cannot debate ways of closing the literacy gap without reference to political and social issues.

New Perspectives on Language and Literacy Learning

Anthropological, socio-cultural and discourse analytic studies have shown that literacy is not a unitary phenomenon. Rather, language is something that is contested, dynamic and provisional, and new perspectives on it expose its contested nature. One socio-linguist, Brian Street (1999) highlights this through a good example. He cites the case of the latest version of the Oxford Dictionary of English. It bases its entries, not on the traditional position of lexicographers which was to seek a single definitive meaning of a word or term, but on actual usage. Usage allows in, so to speak, the split infinitive and clauses ending with prepositions. Of course the language police have been quick to criticise this stance, lamenting what they see as pandering to fashion and failing to uphold 'correct' and 'high' standards.

In the light of our developing understanding about how language works and particularly how humans develop their linguistic competence, it makes more sense to talk about literacies as plural, changing and, above all, socially situated. Learning to read and write cannot be separated from the context in which these activities happen, which includes why they happen, and how they are valued by significant others in the culture. For example, one's experience of reading is first of other people reading; it is in experiencing other people's reading, and in experiencing one's own attempts in certain structured settings (like school) that one learns what counts as reading. As sociolinguists put it, becoming literate involves learning a specific discourse, that is, it involves learning particular ways of thinking, acting and valuing (Michaels and O'Connor, cited in Hiebert and Raphael, 1996). Reading, like any social activity, involves a set of cultural practices that are embedded within webs of relationships. This is a stance that sees learning to be a better reader and writer as social as well as cognitive, as involving motivational and emotional dimensions as well as intellectual and academic ones.

In this socio-cultural view of literacy (Hall, 2003a) the classroom itself has a context and a culture in its own right – that is that it has its own system of socially-made beliefs, values and ways of doing things and that these in turn guide people's thoughts, feelings and behaviours (Au, 1997a). The classroom or school or home or community is a community of practice with, in the case of literacy, its own ways of being literate and demonstrating literacy. Various groups or communities may have patterns, habits and ways of dealing with the world that differ in all sorts of ways and so their literacy patterns will vary accordingly. Importantly, a single individual is likely to be a member of several different communities of literacy practice. Each different literacy practice is the result of some particular community going about its special business (Lemke, 1998). As Rassool (1999) shows so well, learning to read the Koran involves rote memorisation and people are not usually expected to decode the written passages or interpret what they say – the latter being the job of the 'learned scholars'. The religious purpose of prayer does not necessitate comprehension. Literacy is used in a specific way here and the context promotes particular skills. On the other hand graffiti artists operating in the underground are expected to devise their own trademark logos. School literacy is no less specialised and some research on literacy (Hall, 2002) attempts to show how learners succeed with it according to how they understand, take on board, or resist the identities, the behaviours and the codes associated with it. School literacy is of course a very important form of cultural capital since without it one is unlikely to have access to the knowledges and understandings that are highly valued in the culture. The point to emphasise here is that participation in the social practice provides the context for the use of the particular skills that are valued – this participation tacitly teaches you how to behave in linguistically-appropriate ways. Socio-cultural studies of literacy have shown how literacy gets shaped and transformed inside different socio-cultural practices and these practices vary in relation to what counts as acceptable identities, ways of knowing, and behaviours (Gee, 1999). In other words, non-language elements like ways of behaving, interacting, thinking and believing are all part-and-parcel of what it means to be and to become literate.

New, socio-cultural perspectives on our understanding of literacy see children not as mastering school literacy practice (or any school practice for that matter) without being motivated to enter into and identify with that practice, and without believing that they will be able to function within it and use it in the here and now of their lives. Young children are not simply learning to read or write but they are getting enculturated into a range of literacy practices, where each one is linked to specific forms of language, specific activities and specific identities (Gee, 1999). However, many fail in school and fail because they are 'latecomers' to the school literacy game (Gee, 1999). They may not have been exposed to the middle-class discourse patterns in their families and communities and they may receive inadequate bridging between their out-of-school literacy practices and those valued by the school to compensate for this. This point is revisited later in the chapter in the context of the challenges of meeting the literacy needs of all learners. For now, the complexities of becoming literate make it unlikely that a search for one infallible method or programme will suit all learners or, for that matter, particular groups of learners. As some wise person once observed, 'to every human problem there is a solution that is simple, neat and wrong'. In the case of literacy we must accept that there are no simple solutions or rather that there are no simple solutions that are right.

The New Technologies and Media Culture

At a technological level hardly a day goes by without the opportunity to marvel at technological innovations and the social and cultural consequences they produce. As Au and Raphael (2000) remind us, in the past 50 years we have moved from computers that filled buildings to equal or more powerful ones that fit on our laps or can be held in our hands. Over the past 20 years or so technology has allowed us to communicate across time and space and to link a wide range of textual information into our communications: photo images, video clips, sound effects, music. A multi-modal take on literacy places viewing and visual representation alongside the more traditional areas of reading and writing, listening and speaking – a trend captured in the term 'the communicative arts' (Au and Raphael, 2000; Flood and Lapp, 1995). While traditional print literacy remains essential, for without it so much learning is inaccessible, the potential of the new technologies is advancing our definition of literacy. Children nowadays are not just learning via print but through a combination of media including hypertext, video, graphics and sound.

   Moreover, there is an increasing recognition on the part of researchers that media representations help construct our images and understanding of the world, making it imperative that children are taught how to be critically aware of the various media. Such skills should not be deemed 'advanced' and assumed to follow only after print literacy has been mastered. They need to be part and parcel of what literacy learning means right from the beginning of schooling. The challenge for educators, therefore, is not only to enhance print literacy, the kind historically used and taught in schools, but also to enhance the literacies likely to become more important in the future.

   We must consider the literacy debate in the context of contemporary challenges. The challenge for literacy educators and policy-makers is to provide people with the tools to participate in an increasingly complex world. Like any field of human endeavour, such as medicine, building construction or space exploration, the field of literacy is changing and making new demands in terms of the skills required. Over the past three decades there have been dramatic shifts in the way researchers talk about the processes of language and literacy. So the question is: are we facing into the future? Or, are we backing into the future? In his book about modernity and post-modernity, the philosopher, Stephen Toulmin (1990, p.203, cited in Green and Dixon, 1996) talked about 'two attitudes to the future' – one of imagination and one of nostalgia. Of the first he says: 'we may welcome a prospect that offers new possibilities, but demands novel ideas and more adaptive institutions; and we may see this transition as a reason for hope, seeking only to be clearer about the novel possibilities and demands involved ...'. Of the second, he says, 'we may turn our backs on the promises of the new period, in trepidation, hoping that the modes of life and thought typical of the age of stability and nationhood may survive at least for our own lifetimes'.

Importantly, he notes that these two attitudes do not imply different expectations about the future, merely attitudes to dealing with it, the one of imagination 'facing into' the future and asking about possibilities open to us, the other 'backing into' the future without plans or ideas but hoping to preserve the status quo. Applied to literacy, which disposition do we imagine to be necessary? Which attitude are we taking as a nation? How does literacy policy reflect this changing and complex scene? This brings me to the second question posed at the beginning of this chapter.

How are Education Policy-Makers Responding?

A Literacy Crisis?

While this question is being addressed here mostly in relation to England, there are parallels in several western democracies although the precise details vary. Policy analysts have shown the considerable convergence across western democracies over the past two decades or so in relation to the thrust of literacy education policy. For instance, see Luke *et al* (1999) regarding the Australian policy context and Gee (1999) in relation to the US.

Over the 1980s and 1990s politicians 'discovered' a crisis in education and the media colluded with them in not just reporting this claimed crisis, but in reporting it in a way that undermined the authority and professionalism of teachers and their educators in universities and colleges of teacher education. So politicians, in the interests of fixing what they decided was broken, and journalists, in the interests of newsworthiness, together represented educational issues in a way that downgraded teachers, state schools and teacher educators. The claimed crisis was falling standards of print literacy. There are several incidents one could take to illustrate how this crisis was engineered going right back to Prime Minister Callaghan's famous Ruskin Speech in 1976 in which he linked economic decline to what he saw as a decline in educational standards. That speech heralded what became known as the 'great debate' in education and, as noted in Chapter 1, from then on, not wholly unreasonably, education was considered too important to be left to the educators. The case of just one official research study illustrates the point that the so-called crisis in literacy was manufactured.

In 1995 Ofsted began a study of the teaching of reading in 45 primary schools in three inner London boroughs. The three LEAs (Islington, Southwark and Tower Hamlets) reluctantly agreed to participate in the study. On the same day that the

LEA and Ofsted planning group was meeting to discuss the study design the then Prime Minister, John Major, was addressing the Grant Maintained Schools' Association in Birmingham (Smith, 2000). In his speech he alluded to the reading study and stated that 'from now on, inspections will increasingly focus on those schools or authorities where standards are poor; those responsible need not be surprised if "an inspector calls"'. Writing about the controversy surrounding this study, George Smith notes that the Ofsted press release on the same day (12th September, 1995) stated 'Ofsted launches urban literacy project'. Here, in contrast, we have the collaborative nature of the project highlighted. Two months before the report of the study was published, *The Times* devoted its lead news item on the front page to the study with the headline 'Poor White Boys in Cycle of Failure' and Chris Woodhead, the then Chief Inspector of Schools, commented selectively on the results on an inside page referring to how girls outperformed boys in Year 2 but neglected to mention that at Year 6 there were no gender differences found. Smith describes how the report went through several drafts, how 'a sharper and more critical' (p.347) commentary section was added prior to publication, and he tells how the LEAs were given less than an hour to read through the final report and respond, after which they collectively withdrew from the exercise. Chris Woodhead justified the difference between the first and final version with the comment 'the conclusions are now presented as clearly and dramatically as they deserve to be' (Smith, 2000, p.350).

The report of the study was eventually published in May 1996 (Ofsted, 1996). It concluded that 40% of pupils had reading ages of two or more years below their chronological ages. However it downplayed the fact that less than half (49.3%) of the Year 2 and just over half (54.5%) of the Year 6 pupils had English as a first language. Of those whose families spoke another language 77% of Year 2 and 70% of Year 6 had been categorised as non-fluent. In one school 98% of pupils had English as a second language. Some 57% of the sample consisted of children who received free school meals and in three of the schools the figure was as high as 80%. The research was based upon a one-day visit to schools to observe 358 lessons. This was used as a basis, not only for some 13 separate points, but also for the further 31 pages of discussion about the teaching of reading, noted above, in which the roles of LEAs, the schools, the head teachers as well as the classroom approaches and initial training of the teachers were all discussed. A recent re-reading of that report leaves me in no doubt about the gloomy picture being painted of reading standards and the repeated statements about the importance of phonics in the teaching of reading more than hint at the changes that were to come. Commenting on what he called the 'appallingly low levels of literacy' as if it represented the reading attainment of primary pupils nationally, Chris Woodhead claimed that the cause of this state of affairs was poor teaching. He blamed poor achievement on the lack of emphasis on tried and tested or traditional teaching methods, by which he meant specifically phonics and whole class teaching. It is worth mentioning that Mr. Woodhead was, and remains, addicted to the phrase 'trendy teaching methods', a phrase he uses to castigate progressive approaches to teaching and learning. Over the years he has frequently characterised teachers, and more particularly their educators, as subversives bent on lowering standards, indoctrinating children and destroying our literary heritage. In this case, he once again took the opportunity to publicly criticise teachers and to threaten them, their LEAs and teacher education departments in colleges and universities with increased surveillance in the form of inspection visits and yet more league tables. He represented teachers as intransigent and essentially lacking in professionalism. His tone overall in commenting on the research was both negative and adversarial.

Mortimore and Goldstein's (1996) analysis of the report points to the intermingling of research evidence and inspection description as if they are both of the same standing. Mortimore and Goldstein conclude that it is not possible, in reading the report, to ascertain how much of the discussion emerges from the investigation and how much is an expression of the general approach towards the teaching of reading adopted by Ofsted. They criticise the study on the grounds of inadequacy of the sample, flawed methodology and misleading interpretation of the results.

While one must acknowledge that poor reading standards are often, indeed, the result of poor teaching, the fact that other factors in the case of the Ofsted study might be much more important was not even considered by the Chief Inspector or by journalists. One assumes that, as far as the Chief Inspector was concerned, to include such factors in the debate about reading would only give sociological alibis to incompetent teachers and headteachers.

Journalists went even further than Mr. Woodhead as the quote above from *The Times* shows. In a culture where nearly every institution is subject to high levels of accountability, the media, as well argued by Onora O'Neill (2002) in last year's Reith Lectures, is one exception and have unaccountable power to agenda-set. One journalist admits that when he began working as The Observer's Education correspondent in 1996, he was told by an old hand that there were only three stories in the field that made the front page and these are: 'Standards are falling', 'Teacher sleeps with Pupil' and 'Pupil Hits Teacher'. Some newspapers, and not just the tabloid press, have engaged in hype, spin, misinformation and disinformation about literacy standards. Here are some examples of the way the newspapers coin misleading headlines to represent the so called crisis:

> At the bottom of the class: Something on a grand scale is required if Britain is to avoid the humiliation of continuing decline. A profound change in attitudes is needed if Britain is to cease to be the most ill-educated nation in the developed world. (Peter Jenkins, *The Independent*, 8 February 1990)

> Only tougher testing can halt this classroom rot (Ferdinand Mount, *The Daily Telegraph*, 31 August 1990)

> It is astonishing that the world's fourth largest economy still cannot do what most third world countries which teach phonics properly manage to do – teach every single child to read. (Melanie Phillips, *Daily Mail*, 14 January 2002)

However, back to the Ofsted report of reading standards. It is no coincidence that inner-city schools, with their implicit racial identity, were chosen for that study. Such schools play a symbolic role in promoting the conventional wisdom that schools in general, and that inner-city, culturally-diverse schools in particular, are failing in their responsibility to produce the kind of person needed to compete in the knowledge economy (Berliner and Biddle, 1995). Statistical correlations between assessed literacy standards and unemployment, the prison population, school dropouts etc. are recurring themes, thus supposedly demonstrating the social ills caused by the literacy problem. This fallacy then legitimates 'back to basics' policies and high stakes testing of narrowly constructed notions of literacy.

What was particularly interesting, if not surprising, about the fall-out from the 1996 Ofsted report on reading was the way it seemed to produce a consensus among the main political parties about a) the existence of a literacy crisis and b) what should be done about it. The report was used to justify the Conservative Government's back-to-basics drive, a national curriculum for student teachers, inspections and league tables of teacher training providers. A press campaign ensued for an emphasis on phonics and whole class teaching. In the run up to the election in 1997 New Labour bought into the Conservative policies about standards and literacy. It is worth reminding ourselves that by this time – the mid 1990s – the battle for the curriculum itself had already been fought and won by Conservative politicians eager to dictate from the centre regarding what pupils should know, understand and be able to do in various areas of the curriculum and at various key stages of their school careers. As we noted in Chapter 1, teachers were already obliged by law to implement the National Curriculum. To further ensure that teachers would comply with what had been centrally decided and to provide information to parents about how well the system was doing, an assessment framework had been devised and implemented to test pupils. The results of these tests were being published in the form of league tables of results for individual schools. And as explained in Chapter 2, teacher education colleges and university departments were heavily scrutinised and graded for their compliance with Ofsted policy. So what control remained in the hands of teachers?

The last bastion of teacher control was the how of teaching and learning – pedagogy. And it was to pedagogy and to a *de facto* national curriculum for university departments of teacher education that political attention now turned. The latter was dealt with in the previous chapter and it is now opportune to consider the former. However, it is necessary to refute the existence of the literacy crisis, at least the particular literacy crisis framed by the popular press, politicians and politically-driven policy-makers.

It is simply untrue to suggest that standards of literacy are lower now than they were in previous generations. Exactly the opposite is the case. As recently as 150 years ago rudimentary literacy was defined and measured as the ability to write one's name. The 20th century saw the definition of literacy expand to integrate listening, speaking, reading and writing and to the attainment of functional literacy on the part of the vast majority of citizens. The literacy demands of the times have increased and so have standards. Greg Brooks' (1998, p.1) investigation of literacy standards spanning most of the second half of the 20th century shows convincingly that 'literacy standards have changed very little in that time'. The only caveat is that standards among eight year olds fell slightly in the late 1980s but recovered again in the early 1990s. One explanation for the dip offered by Brooks was the introduction of the National Curriculum which resulted in less time being accorded to reading. Incidentally, Brooks' study received very little press coverage, probably because it did not fit either the definition of newsworthiness or the agenda of so many journalists that teachers were incompetent and had distanced themselves from the so-called tried and tested, traditional methods.

Another and more recent study worth noting here is a comparative one by researchers at the University of Bristol and Canterbury Christ Church University College involving tests of French primary children on the English assessments and tests of English primary pupils using the French tests. The researchers conducted a detailed analysis of pupil errors (Broadfoot *et al*, 2000). This study revealed that, unlike their French counterparts whom the researchers described as 'typically "technicians" applying skills they had been taught, often in a decontextualised way', English pupils were described as 'explorers' who were 'coping well with tasks where the route was not clearly laid out' (p.203). English pupils were better at problem-solving, taking risks, having a go than their French peers. They adopted a more creative approach to all the tasks and tests set for them. In commenting on their findings the research team advised that it is important to recognise the strengths of the English tradition while also observing that the skills the English pupils were particularly good at are the most difficult to measure by conventional means and hence not often recognised. These are also the skills that are most relevant to the global economy and to lifelong learning.

However, back to the national policy response. It should be no surprise that since it had been decided that there was a crisis, a literacy crisis, drastic action would be required.

Control over Pedagogy: The National Literacy Strategy

New Labour continued rather than resisted centralisation and state control of most aspects of education despite its pre-election promise to value local flexibility and the professional discretion of teachers and to guard against stifling teachers' creativity (Labour Party, 1994; Labour Party, 1995; for a full discussion, see Davies and Edwards, 1999). It was (and remains) preoccupied with standards and their measurement. This preoccupation is at once reflected by and created by the media: a report in the *Times Educational Supplement* on the buzz words of 1998 (Howson, 1999) claimed that the word 'standards' was mentioned 2,272 times, almost twice as often as reading – the next highest – and it was mentioned in almost 25% of all the articles in the *Times Educational Supplement*. In relation to measurement, evidence shows that there is no other country in the world that subjects its pupils to more external testing or spends more money on it than England (Whetton, 1999).

With more specific reference to literacy, a year before New Labour was elected the Shadow Secretary of State for Education, David Blunkett, launched the preliminary report of the National Literacy Strategy at a conference held at the Business Design Centre in London. The Final Report of the Task Force (DfEE, 1997b) set out details of a strategy for raising standards of literacy – that being its *raison d'être*. The target suggested was that every child should be able to read well by the age of eleven, unless they had a specified educational need. The key national target was that by 2002, 80% of 11 year olds should reach the standard expected for their age in English in the National Curriculum tests for Key Stage Two (7-11 year olds). (This target was not achieved.) According to Chris Woodhead it was the inspection evidence gathered in those inner-London primary schools that provided the impetus for the introduction of the National Literacy Strategy.

There are now termly teaching objectives in literacy for each year of the primary age range. A structure for time and class management of a daily Literacy Hour is specified (DfEE, 1998a and 1998b). It is expected that for at least 60% of the time pupils should be working with the teacher. Three broad elements of literacy are the focus of the Strategy, i) word-level work (phonics, spelling and vocabulary); ii) sentence-level work (grammar and punctuation); and iii) text-level work (comprehension and composition).

Closer attention to some of the prescriptions and directives for the early years of school reveals the control exercised over teachers' pedagogical imaginations. For example, the language describing what teachers have to do during the 15 minutes of word-level work which is to take place in a whole-class setting bears on content, sequence and objectives:

> There must be a systematic, regular and frequent teaching of phonological awareness, phonics and spelling throughout Key Stage 1. Teachers should follow the progression set out in the word-level objectives carefully. It sets out both an order of teaching and the expectations for what pupils should achieve by the end of each term. (DfEE, 1998a, p.11)

There are 14 precise objectives associated with word-level work to be achieved by children in their first year of school; a further 14 in term one of their second year; and a total of 87 up to the end of the year in which they reach seven years of age – all to be addressed in the specified sequence. Further sets of objectives are prescribed for these children in sentence-level and text-level work.

As a policy text the National Literacy Strategy has few spaces for teachers to exercise their own judgement. The same approach is assumed to suit all contexts and all types of learners. If one only has one teaching approach in one's pedagogic tool kit, then one is not equipped to deal with the diversity of learners in today's classroom. As argued elsewhere in relation to the centrally-defined competencies for teachers, if one only has a hammer, pretty soon everything begins to look like a nail (Hall, 1999). The thrust of the NLS is to package instruction and to standardise teaching approaches, regardless of the needs of local cultural or linguistic contexts. Although not legally compulsory, David Blunkett described the NLS as non-negotiable. In practice, it is clear that the professional educator does not have a choice about its implementation. The decision to separate the design of the curriculum from its execution, thereby taking teachers out of the decision-making process, has to be resisted by anyone attempting to define teaching as a profession.

This diminution in teachers' power over curriculum and pedagogy has to be considered in the context of an assessment framework that, as Economic and Social Research Council (ESRC) funded research has shown, has increasingly marginalised the role and the status of teacher assessment in favour of externally-set assessments (Hall and Harding, 1999; 2002). Primary pupils are assessed via externally-set tests in reading and writing (and in other areas of the curriculum) at ages seven and eleven in the primary school and a school's results are published in league tables. Teachers' own evidence-based assessments of pupils originally had parity with these results and were also published alongside the test results. In the best cases, that is where this work was well-supported, research showed that teacher assessment had the capacity to provide the evidence behind the numbers and the grades. However, over the last several years the financial and professional support for enhancing the validity and reliability of teacher assessment has been reduced to a minimum and newspapers no longer bother to publish these results. Attention is directly solely to the SATs. So significant are the end of key stage assessment results that schools prioritise them at the expense of other educational values like inclusion (Benjamin *et al*, in press; Hall *et al*, 2004). Against such a background the teacher is positioned as deferential, compliant and mechanically obedient – the recipients, as Stephen Ball (1994) describes them, rather than the agents of reform. Is it really so surprising that there is an unprecedented problem of recruiting and retaining teachers in the profession?

The most recent pronouncements of the Secretary of State for Education, Charles Clarke, about reducing the emphasis on the external assessment of seven year olds must be acknowledged as a step in the right direction, at least with reference to assessment.

To return to the literacy crisis. In summary, both the diagnosis and the remedy can be queried. One cannot be complacent about literacy standards. There is a crisis, or rather a potential crisis, but it is not the one framed in the popular press or the one the National Literacy Strategy is designed to counter. The potential crisis lies in the narrow, singular conception of literacy that so dominates current educational policy. If not addressed, this could lead to a situation where pupils can pass reading tests as early as age seven but cannot evaluate what they read and write or be successful in the new knowledge-based economy or think critically about the social and political issues in their communities and society (Gee, 1999).

An Alternative Vision of Literacy Education

In the final part of this chapter a modest step is taken in sketching out an alternative and more satisfactory vision for literacy education. It is suggested that there are three things that need to happen in order to face into, rather than back into, the future.

1.   Shift from a Uni-dimensional to a Multi-dimensional View of Literacy

Multi-Media Texts

To make the shift from a uni-dimensional to a multi-dimensional perspective requires firstly a recognition of the evolving nature of literacy. Literacy is a relatively recent development in terms of human development – a mere 6,000 years old. It has evolved from pictographic to logographic to alphabetic in representation to suit different purposes. The refinement of alphabetic writing is recognised by many historians as a landmark point in development (Barton, 1994). To prepare our pupils for new types of literacy we must be receptive to new definitions of the term itself. We have to refigure our notions of literacy in an electronic world. In his essay entitled 'From Pencils to Pixels', about the stages of literacy technologies, Dennis Baron (1999) explains that computers are the latest and most sophisticated in a long series of communication tools that have included the invention of writing itself, the pencil and the telephone. The electronic medium is not merely a change in the form of transmission of written text, it is changing the ways in which we create, structure and process texts – it is changing our notion of text. It is very likely that in due course literacy historians will deem the shift to multi-media communication yet another landmark in the history of literacy.

What does it mean then to function competently in the communicative arts in an electronic age? It means the ability to express and share meaning through the integration of non-verbal elements like pictures, icons, movies, animations and written prose into electronic texts. In electronic texts, images and sounds compete equally with alphabetic symbols forcing us to consider their respective contribution and value towards expressing meaning. This adds up to what Jay Lemke has termed 'representational literacy' or the ability to communicate ideas flexibly, using multi-media forms. As researchers like Lemke (1998), Gunther Kress (2000) and Cope and Kalantzis (2000) and many others have argued, we need to help children discover and refine strategies for reading and evaluating electronic, non-linear texts, which often mix and meld the visual and verbal. Schools obviously need to embrace more than print literacy.

The almost exclusive focus on the printed word in the National Literacy Strategy means that there is insufficient education in the visual arts and on electronic media. While written language skills are even more important in today's world than they were in the past, written language is only one symbol system which humans use to express and share meaning. Bearing in mind that nowadays the media, especially television, are, for most people, the most dominant sources of information about the people and events in the universe, an exclusive emphasis on print in school is inadequate and out of kilter with real life outside of school. When the motor car first made its appearance in America, those in the railroad business had to decide whether they were in the railroad business or the transport business. Those who saw themselves as just in the railroad business went to the wall while those who defined themselves as in the transport business prospered. As literacy educators, policy-makers, and researchers, we have to ask ourselves whether we are in the print business or in the literacy business (Flood and Lapp,

1995). Certainly literacy policy-makers need to redefine the nature of their business if the next generation is going to prosper in the new electronic world.

Literacy is about Citizens and Society: Critical Literacy

To shift beyond print literacy to embrace electronic media more enthusiastically is not enough. There are other ways in which our definition of literacy needs to be broadened. We have to ask what kind of literate person we need and wish to create through our school system. This literate person is not just someone who is technically skilled in the use of print and the use of the keyboard and computer applications to produce multi-media texts. Most people would probably agree that the kind of literate persons that society needs are citizens who:

- are able to analyse texts (in the broadest sense of that word) for their implicit, taken-for-granted assumptions about the way the world is and ought to be;
- challenge the identities that texts offer when they run counter to principles of fairness and equity; and
- use their literacy to make a difference to their world.

Literacy learners need to learn how texts have power, how power is exercised in texts, how literacy works to privilege some knowledges, beliefs, attitudes and values and to marginalise others. Critical literacy involves asking learners to question the taken-for-granted assumptions about the world. It is based on the assumption that language reflects the way the world is and the world is to some extent the way it is because of the way our language is (Morgan *et al*, 1996, p.9). A critical perspective on literacy seeks to make explicit the various positionings and identities that are on offer in texts but that are mostly left implicit. Learning literacy then is about understanding how attitudes and beliefs about the world are manipulated by language. Understanding how one writes to position oneself and others and how one is positioned by a text to view the world is a prerequisite to developing other possibilities or opposing interpretations. It is worth noting here, however, that the purpose of a critical literacy orientation is not merely to help learners appreciate that texts can be manipulative or stereotype people. Whilst this is part of the process critical literacy, as so well demonstrated by writers like Barbara Comber (2001a, 2001b) is essentially about understanding how texts work to achieve certain effects. A critical literacy classroom involves teachers and pupils working together to see how texts construct their worlds, their cultures and their communities. In addition, it involves reworking or using those texts to reconstruct different worlds, worlds that are more equitable and fair. This is to recognise that learning to read and write is as much about learning identities and values as it is about learning skills and codes.

If we are to help children do more than pass tests, if we want them to evaluate the textual world they inhabit, then a critical perspective has to be part of school literacy from the earliest stages. The Australians Allan Luke and Peter Freebody (1999) present a useful model against which one could judge any literacy policy or set of practices in this regard. In the case of reading, for example, they suggest that learners can be described as having four types of competence:

1. Code breakers (How do I crack this code?)
2. Meaning makers (How do the ideas represented in the text string together? What possible meanings can be constructed from this text?)
3. Text users (What do I do with this text, here and now?)
4. Text critics (What is this text trying to do to me? In whose interests? Which positions, voices, and interests are at play? Which are silent and absent?)

Each one, these sociologists of language suggest, is best thought of as a 'family of practices' to emphasise their dynamic, fluid and changing nature as well as to stress the fact that they are undertaken by people in social contexts. It is in the fourth family of practices that the scope for critical literacy particularly lies. What is important is that children do not begin with code-breaking and move in a linear way through the four, only becoming a text critic once decoding, comprehension and application have been established. Literacy learning is not about moving from the reductive and the simplistic to the sophisticated and the more complex. All four aspects, they suggest, are relevant and essential from the beginning of a child's literacy learning – although different ones will be differently emphasised in various lessons and all four can be developed using a range of teaching methods.

This model provides a useful framework for weighing up and questioning the emphases of current classroom literacy curricula. It is arguable, for instance, that in the case of the NLS there is almost an exclusive emphasis on the code or functional aspects with virtually no attention devoted to the kind of critical aspects just described. This is because the NLS assumes a monocultural literacy; it is silent on issues of diversity. In practice a monocultural and functional literacy is much easier to measure, it lends itself to testing – it is the simple solution to a complex problem.

2.   *Stop Prescribing Literacy Pedagogy and Promote Culturally-Sensitive Pedagogies*

The fact of the matter is that one's first or home language is supported by one's biology and does not require overt instruction. Although all subsequent languages or literacies build on this vernacular, they do require cognitive and social support. Our genes do not help us to learn writing because writing came on the human evolutionary scene too late to be in our genes (Gee, 2000a). Novices of any literacy need contexts, props, examples, demonstrations, opportunities to behave as writers and readers do, to acquire those competencies – in a phrase they need 'situated practice' (Gee, 2000b). Those of us who are involved in literacy education need to be absolutely clear that when it comes to developing literacy competence a purely technical approach to pedagogy will not work. It is in ignoring this fact that the National Literacy Strategy shows its major weakness. Since literacy is bound up with the mind, body and soul, that is with one's sense of identity and sense of community, educators need to consider how school literacy interconnects with home and community literacy practices.

Literacy practices beyond school are extremely varied and often quite different from those in school but they always have a social purpose. People learn about these purposes, uses, strategies and values simultaneously and haphazardly through practice (Ivanic and Hamilton, 1989). They do not learn literacy competence through a neat, linear, objectives-driven programme. This is not to deny the importance of learning objectives or a structured programme to guide learning, or to deny that the NLS has a place, but to point out the futility of prescribing a series of set objectives that all should follow in the same sequence and to point out the weaknesses of the narrow perspective on literacy.

For many children the use of popular culture in the classroom can be a valuable way of recognising the cultural capital within their world. Given how pervasive popular culture is in the lives of all children, its use in the classroom seems eminently sensible. Some popular texts, for example comics, attract greater number of boys than girls and greater numbers of working class children than middle class children, thus highlighting their potential to extend the literacy skills of groups in society that are often under-achieving in literacy. Research by Ann Haas Dyson (1997; 1998) and by Jackie Marsh and Elaine Millard (2000) has demonstrated that the critical use of popular media to enhance children's literacy skills appears to work because it involves drawing on learners' values, passions and identifications – ones that emerge in home and community life.

Unfortunately teachers are often reluctant to incorporate popular media into the reading material of the classroom, seeing them as inferior and lacking in learning potential. Teachers need to be supported in understanding the bridging across literacies that this kind of work facilitates; it is a way of building on very real and distinctive lifeworld knowledge (Gee, 2000b) and of course they need to be skilled in developing pupils' critical engagement with such texts. This work is challenging for teachers; it can for instance meet with opposition from parents who are rightly concerned that their children master the codes of the culture of power (Au and Raphael, 2000). An emphasis on popular culture is often seen by parents as inconsistent with this. Teachers need to be able to communicate the links between such work and the acquisition of language registers valued by society.

At another level, Janet Maybin (2000) points out that the appropriation by the school of typically out-of-school texts runs the risk of removing the very meanings and functions that gave those texts their power and attraction in the first place. This is so because literacy activity is made meaningful through the ways in which it is intertwined with particular situated practices and relationships (Heath, 1983). Maybin advises that out-of-school activities require very skilful recontextualisation to become effective resources for learning. Clearly, the professional development needs of teachers in this regard are considerable.

What is absolutely crucial for equity in literacy is that we level the playing field in teaching and assessment so that children get to read and respond to all kinds of texts that are maximally relevant to their cultural heritage. One native Hawaiian literacy researcher, Kathy Au (1997b), tells how, as a primary pupil, she never encountered literature that reflected her culture – the texts available just did not feature any Asian-American people in them. At the time, she remembers, this led her to assume that books were supposed to represent worlds other than her own. While culturally-responsive pedagogy is certainly not precluded in current policy, neither is it given the status it merits in a policy that is currently located within a skills-based psychological and individualistic perspective on learning and literacy.

In summary, the policy on literacy pedagogy needs to be radically revised. I would recommend that we keep the national standards set for the curriculum, that is that we keep 'level descriptions' to use the national curriculum terminology, although their content would need to be modified in the light of the broader conception of literacy outlined here. I suggest that we keep national agreed standards, but that we let the pedagogic journey vary. In this way professionals can be more responsive to the cultural and linguistic diversity of their pupils. Treating everyone the same pedagogically is not the answer. We need to challenge the silences around identities, equity and diversity in current literacy policy. We need to encourage a pedagogy that is emancipatory and inclusive. Such a perspective has implications for the continuing professional development of teachers. One-off training days about a literacy programme are unlikely to equip teachers with the necessary sophistication, skill and expertise. This brings me to the third and final recommendation.

3. Recognise the Significance of the Teacher in Literacy Development

Reviews of the research on effective literacy teaching (Hiebert and Raphael, 1996; Hall, 2003b; Hall and Harding, 2003) which I draw on in more detail later show conclusively that a quality literacy programme is not merely about teaching materials and set procedures, but is primarily about the quality of the teachers who use those materials and procedures. The research is conclusive that the most critical element in building an effective reading programme is the teacher. Moreover, accomplished teachers are more significant in terms of their effects in high poverty than in low poverty schools (Taylor *et al*, 2000). This is not surprising when one considers that these children depend more on their school and their teachers to socialise them into school literacy practices.

Research on accomplished literacy teachers shows that they define themselves as powerful enablers whose task it is to understand what their learners already know and can do in various literacy contexts, to recognise what motivates and engages them, and to extend their literacy repertoires by building on their strengths. Becoming literate is implicitly defined as becoming increasingly adept at using literacy to do things for purposes that are valued by them and by their communities. These teachers are aware of their power. They are able to adapt teaching and learning environments to suit particular pupils, and groups of pupils. They are like ethnographers – always kid-watching. The evidence shows that they engage in evidence-informed practices, to use a fashionable phrase, and that this evidence is not only about literacy learning *per se* but, fundamentally, about specific children's literacy practices and dispositions. They appear to be more aware of what children bring to school and they are more aware of what learners are able to take from their schooling that may enhance the here-and-now of their lives.

To obtain this kind of knowledge and to apply a culturally-sensitive pedagogy, teachers need 'insider knowledge' of the communities in which they work. This socio-cultural take on literacy is asking them to use information or insights gained in one context (the home or the community) to inform the activities and routines in the classroom. Teachers are being asked to create a different kind of classroom dynamic in which these out-of-school activities would make a difference to pupils' learning.

What exactly is being asked of teachers here? Teachers do not usually live in the areas in which they teach so acquiring such understanding is not a simple matter. Proponents, practitioners and researchers of this approach, for example Luis Moll (2000) in the United States, acknowledge the challenge involved in doing this and it seems teachers need to be well supported through study groups involving themselves and teacher educators. It is in this context that scholars such as Hiebert and Raphael (1996) have argued that until teachers – usually white, female and middle class – can understand personally the role of culture in their own lives as literacy learners, they will struggle to understand it in the learning of their pupils.

There is no way of short-circuiting the professional development process, through by-passing or minimising initial teacher education or offering only inset training on literacy programmes. There needs to be substantial investment in the professional development of teachers, which needs to include a consideration of literacy aims, in the context of the kind of literate future our children will live. Currently there is an overarching emphasis on technique which in turn has the effect of technicising teaching, and almost no emphasis on literacy philosophy. Rather like the three workers in the cathedral, the technician says he is laying bricks, the craftsman says he is creating the north wall and the visionary says he is worshipping God. In literacy policy we have far too much of the technician's concern with phonemic awareness and far too little with the visionary's literacy aims and ultimate purposes.

The next chapter develops further the ideas about the significance of the teacher in the promotion of literacy. It narrows the focus yet further by describing the pedagogic changes that would be in line with the model of literacy outlined in this chapter.

Chapter 4

Outstanding Literacy Teachers and their Teaching:
Teachers not Packages!

Introduction

Previous chapters have shown how education policy in this country is preoccupied with 'standards', audits, league tables; in a word, with performativity. In the case of literacy this preoccupation has manifested itself in the form of prescriptive pedagogy, defined curricula, predetermined outcomes for every year of the primary school and print literacy. The assumption is that teachers can be given a blueprint for fostering literacy in their pupils and that 'one size fits all'. Yet, as the previous chapter stated, the evidence from research studies is that successful teachers tailor their teaching to suit individual circumstances, that they build up knowledge of their learners and use that knowledge to advance their learners' skills and understandings. This chapter will draw on a recently completed systematic review of literacy teaching in the 4 to 14 age range of mainstream schooling, a narrative review of evidence pertaining to the early years of school and several other reviews of and studies in the field in an attempt to understand the expertise of successful literacy teachers. A fuller understanding of expertise is facilitated through an examination of the teaching practices and perspectives of those teachers deemed to be most accomplished in promoting the literacy learning of their pupils. The body of evidence reviewed demonstrates the need to amend current literacy policy in a variety of specific ways and the final section of the chapter discusses some of these policy implications. The implications of the evidence cited in this chapter align with the arguments advanced in the previous one.

In the search for ways and means of improving the teaching of literacy, it is becoming increasingly acknowledged that the identification of teacher characteristics and teachers' ways of working is likely to be more productive than a reliance on and adherence to any particular package or materials. There is much evidence to show that a variety of packages and materials has been seen both to work and to fail depending upon the quality of the implementation (Allington, 2002). To improve literacy teaching, it is necessary to educate teachers well about literacy rather than to expect a panacea in the form of materials and equipment (Collins-Block and Pressley, 2000). How do we recognise successful or accomplished teachers of literacy? What do the best teachers of literacy do in their classrooms to promote the literacy achievements of their pupils?   These are the kinds of questions this chapter seeks to address.

Definitional and Research Methodological Issues

Attempts to understand the nature of 'effective' or 'successful' teaching go back quite a long way. In the late 1960s and early 1970s researchers began to document the teaching processes that occurred in classrooms. Their goal was to identify processes associated with high achievement, often reading achievement. This approach became known as the product-process approach because it was based upon the belief that educational outcomes (that is, products) could be understood as a function of educational inputs and processes. From the product-process research studies of the 1970s (Brophy, 1973; Dunkin and Biddle, 1974; Flanders, 1970) we learned that effective teachers maintain a clear academic focus in their classrooms, are consistently concerned to keep their pupils 'on task' and regularly rely on direct instruction. They set clear goals for their teaching and for pupils' learning, regularly monitor pupil understanding through questioning and give ample feedback about progress and achievement.

In the 1980s researchers like Duffy and Roehler and their colleagues (1987) helped our understanding of the cognitive processes used by effective teachers where, in the teaching of reading for example, they urged teachers to approach the task as a 'meaning getting' process. Emphasising a view of teaching as explanation they argued that by explaining and modelling how mature readers went about the task of making meaning from written texts such teachers would help their pupils to become more strategic, interpretative, meta-cognitive and thoughtful in their reading tasks. In a comprehension task, for example, an effective teacher would overtly explain and model how he or she would make predictions about what might develop in the text as it is read. The teacher would describe the kinds of questions that occurred to him or her as they read and would talk about the messages emerging from the text as it was being read. By letting pupils see skilled reading as a strategic activity and showing them how mature readers construct meaning and respond to text, such teaching would help pupils to become active themselves in the ways of skilled readers. Duffy and Roehler (1986, p.23) summarise their position as follows:

> Instruction is more than getting students on task and presenting content in organised ways. It is also a cognitive interaction between teacher and students, particularly when the goal is to develop conceptual understandings rather than automatised responses. Such instruction is much more subtle than earlier concepts of instructional effectiveness led us to believe and it requires much more substantive supervision.

In the late 1980s and the 1990s, as the previous chapters demonstrate, concerns about school and teacher effectiveness began to focus much more sharply on the area of teaching literacy. Although there is considerable research knowledge about how young children acquire literacy and develop as readers and writers and although there is much known about how to develop literacy (Adams, 1991; Geekie *et al*, 1999), there is still much to be learned about literacy pedagogy in different contexts and in different phases of schooling. Indeed the specific area of expertise in the promotion of literacy, however it is defined, has a short history. Writing with particular reference to the early years of schooling, as recently as 1998 Wharton McDonald *et al* wrote 'There is a lack of systematic study of effective literacy teachers, a lack of understanding of their practices and perspectives' (p.102).

Some of the existing research on successful literacy teaching has been in the previous chapter. In this chapter the focus is more specifically on some existing reviews in the field. Several reviews of different aspects of literacy teaching have been published over the past decade (Adams, 1991; Hiebert and Raphael, 1996; Beard, 1998; Lyon, 1998; Snow *et al*, 1998; National Reading Panel, (NRP) 2000; Kamil *et al*, 2000). It is of note that most reviews of literacy teaching conducted to date are narrative reviews. However the NRP study (2000) is a systematic review of the experimental and quasi-experimental research relevant to a set of topics on early reading. Correlational studies and ethnographic and qualitative research were, controversially, excluded from that analysis.

Unsurprisingly, very many studies of literacy have sought to determine which instructional methods are most effective for the development of literacy and the reviews have of course reflected this emphasis. Undoubtedly we now know a great deal about how literacy develops in children and how teachers can support that development. What emerges clearly from the literature is that there is no *one* best method of teaching literacy that works for all children. Summarising the reading research of the National Institute of Child Health and Development (NICHD) in the United States, in 1997, Lyon testified before the US Congress that:

> We have learned that no single method, approach, or philosophy for teaching reading is equally effective for all children ... The real question is which children need what, when, for how long, and with what type of instruction, in and what type of setting? (cited in Willis and Harris, 2000)

While considerable knowledge about literacy processes and about methods of teaching literacy has been accumulated and while a focus on instructional approaches or teaching methodology merits continued research to establish what works in specific contexts, it is likely that an exclusive emphasis on method is inadequate to determine effectiveness. Some highly influential literacy researchers in the US (Foorman *et al*, 1998) have been criticised for equating instructional method with teaching (Taylor *et al*, 2000). As Taylor *et al* point out, teachers' understanding of and commitment to particular teaching strategies are crucial and these, they argue, are significant factors and may well be equal to if not more important than the methods themselves. Drawing on general classroom research, these authors go on to argue that:

> ... teachers make a larger difference in students' growth as readers than do the methods those teachers are nominally using and that between-teacher variation has usually

proven to be greater than between-method variation, after taking account of variation in initial student characteristics. (p.21)

A major review of the evidence on the prevention of difficulties in early reading acknowledged the impact of the teacher, but did not give studies on this theme the same status in the reviewing process as it gave studies about methods (Snow *et al*, 1998). The Committee on the Prevention of Reading Difficulties in Young Children concluded their report as follows:

> Effective instruction includes artful teaching that transcends – and often makes up for – the constraints and limitations of specific instructional programs. Although we have not incorporated lessons from artful teaching practices with the same comprehensiveness as other topics in the conventional research on reading, we acknowledge their importance in conceptualizing effective reading instruction. (Snow *et al*, 1998, pp.314-5)

An emphasis on the centrality of teacher is timely. The extent to which the current state of the research base can offer descriptive characteristics of the unique features of outstanding literacy teachers and their teaching is especially timely and this is a theme that I have been working on with some colleagues for the past few years. Our recently completed reviews funded by the TTA and the United Kingdom Reading Association (now the United Kingdom Literacy Association, [UKLA]) are based mainly on case studies, many combining qualitative and quantitative research techniques. One is a systematic review of evidence of effective literacy teaching in the 4 to 14 age range of mainstream schooling (Hall and Harding, 2003) conducted with the support of the EPPI-Centre, while the other is a more conventional narrative review (Hall, 2003b).

A systematic review seeks to assemble and synthesise evidence in a way that is highly explicit. It is the explicitness in relation to the selection and reviewing of studies that distinguishes a systematic review from, say, a narrative one (see EPPI website for details). Our review question was: what are the professional characteristics, beliefs and classroom approaches of teachers of literacy in the 4-14 age range of mainstream schooling who have been nominated as effective? Embedded in that question was a concern to know more about how successful literacy teachers are recognised, what their classroom practices are like, and what professional knowledge and beliefs about literacy, learning and learners they bring to their classroom teaching. To answer the research question a protocol in which the main strategies for finding studies from the literature search and the methods to be employed for screening these studies to ascertain their inclusion or exclusion from the review were set out. Details of the systematic reviewing process are briefly summarised here but are published more fully in Hall and Harding (2003).

Three major databases were searched, key journals were 'hand' searched and web-sites were scrutinised. Using a set of explicit criteria, the titles and abstracts of the relevant studies were screened and the studies that met the criteria set out in the protocol were identified. These studies were then 'keyworded' or indexed. A 'mapping exercise' was conducted on the studies which met the selection criteria and a descriptive map helped to identify and describe the studies and build up an overall picture of the field. Over one thousand studies published in English after 1988 were identified as being of possible relevance to the review. Eighty studies satisfied the criteria for inclusion in the 'map' and a number of interesting patterns were detected amongst these studies.

The vast bulk (79%) of the studies were of American origin with only about one fifth from the United Kingdom. Whilst almost half of the studies were concerned with general literacy teaching, and one quarter focused on the teaching of reading, less than 10% were about the teaching of writing. The greater number of the studies was based upon the primary school years with only about one quarter focused on the middle and secondary school years. The research studies examined seem to suggest that by far the most popular and useful way to find out about effective literacy teaching is to observe teachers nominated as effective teachers and to talk to them about their teaching in interviews.

Space prevents a detailed account of the 'map' here but its development enabled the identification of a subset of 12 studies which were examined in an in-depth review. The in-depth analysis of these studies involved two stages. In the first stage each study was analysed carefully in terms of its contribution to answering the review question. The individual studies were given a 'high', 'medium' or 'low' weight of evidence score according to the extent to which they were judged to contribute to answering the research question.

The studies that were part of the systematic review will now be synthesised. Links with some themes emanating from the broader literature on literacy and literacy learning will be discussed. Other reviews and some of the broader scholarship on literacy teaching and learning will also be drawn on to take account of the diversity of learners in our schools.

Synthesising the Evidence for the Systematic Review

Twelve of the 80 studies were selected for in-depth systematic review. To aid analysis, these 12 studies were clustered as follows: a collection of seven studies, referred to as the 'Pressley' studies (Pressley *et al*, 1996; Pressley *et al*, 1997; Wharton McDonald *et al*, 1998; Pressley *et al*, 1998; Pressley *et al*, 2001; Collins-Block and Pressley, 2000; Collins-Block *et al*, 2002) since they collectively represent a substantial body of emerging research carried out by Michael Pressley and his associates and doctoral students; the CELA studies (Langer, 1999 and 2000) which consisted of two linked studies carried out at the National Research Center on English Learning and Achievement; one study (Taylor *et al*, 2000b) carried out at the Center for the Improvement of Early Reading Achievement (CIERA) stands alone; and two UK-based, linked studies (Medwell *et al*, 1998; Poulson *et al*, 2001) from the final cluster.

Because almost all of these 12 studies were based on case study methodology and incorporated quasi-ethnographic methods, a meta-analysis of a statistical nature was ruled out. However, it was possible to treat their findings as complementary and cumulative since the studies tended to incorporate a common theoretical – constructivist and socio-constructivist – and empirical literature base.

In addition, the 12 studies tended to refer to each other, to varying degrees. The Pressley studies, for example, were clearly building on each other and the CIERA study took account of the Pressley studies. The UK studies also referred to the US literature. This meant that there were common themes across most of the studies and these themes provided a logical basis for synthesising the substantive findings.

What do we know about Outstanding Literacy Teachers?

Caveat One: Scale of Evidence

The first thing to note in relation to the research base on effective teachers of literacy is the limited evidence that is grounded in England. Only two studies met the criteria for inclusion and these are linked studies, meaning that they derive from the same database. All the remaining ten studies describe teaching in the United States. One must be cautious therefore about applying the findings too rigidly to this country. In addition, the review itself, as is typical of its genre, is limited by the number of studies which were subjected to in-depth data extraction.

The review question sought information about teachers of pupils in the 4 to 14 age group. Only two studies (the 2 CELA studies) were devoted to the upper end of this age range. The majority of the studies, and all the studies allocated the highest rating for quality and weight of evidence, were focused on the younger end of that spectrum.

The vast majority (8) of the 12 studies relied exclusively on nominations of teacher effectiveness. Thus, teacher effectiveness was taken for granted rather than empirically investigated within the studies. A minority of studies relied on nominations only as a starting point and did empirically examine teacher effectiveness in considerable depth. However, the demands of doing this led to other issues to do with limited sampling, bearing on the scale of evidence available. The complexity of the research designs required for demonstrating actual effectiveness meant that typically those studies focused on a small number of teachers and schools, thus raising issues of generalisability. The majority of the studies then depend for their definition of effectiveness on teachers' reputed, as opposed to demonstrated, effectiveness. The following example from Pressley *et al* (1998, p.163) was the more usual approach to selection:

> In each district, the district-level language arts coordinator was asked to nominate teachers at the fourth- or fifth-grade level whom he or she believed were effective at helping students develop appropriate literacy skills and behaviours at their grade level. District A nominated 4 fifth-grade teachers ... *Specific criteria for ascertaining teacher effectiveness were left up to the language arts coordinators.* However, some of the most frequently cited criteria included students' year-end standardized test scores in reading and writing; students' written products; students' enthusiasm for reading and writing; teacher practices consistent with current thinking in the field ... and teacher creativity. (*Emphasis added*)

This mode of defining success or effectiveness would not be a problem if research showed that it is trustworthy, but this is not the case. When studies did incorporate empirical measures of literacy teacher effectiveness it was found that not all teachers nominated as exemplary were so (see Wharton McDonald *et al*, 1998; Taylor *et al*, 2000b) and incidentally, not all schools reputed to be exemplary proved to be so either (Stringfield *et al*, 1997). To illustrate, the final analysis in the study by Wharton McDonald (1998) was based on a subset of three teachers. Two of these teachers had been nominated as outstanding, one had been nominated as typical or average. Until we have many more studies, where literacy teacher exemplarity is defined empirically and validly, we cannot claim to have a very secure evidential base about what constitutes literacy teacher effectiveness across the range of mainstream schooling from 4-14.

Caveat Two: Methodological Limitations

There are limitations about the review process itself. We have, as a research field, limited methodologies for synthesising across qualitative studies. The over-emphasis on quantitative studies tends to privilege exploration and synthesis of problems that can be easily reduced to their subcomponents, such as recognising a letter-sound correspondence, or responding to text-based questions. Questions about outstanding literacy instruction cannot be easily reduced, so those studying this area use methodology appropriate to the complexities. Yet the methods for synthesising across such studies are limited, and this in turn limits the production of a synthesis of information in this field.

What do we Mean by 'Outstanding' or 'Effective'?

Despite the limited scale of studies and the methodological issues just noted, the substantive findings emerging from them (and from the 8 that did not actually test effectiveness) align in virtually all respects in terms of describing outstanding teachers and their teaching. An important starting point that emerges from the studies is how it was possible to identify and nominate those perceived to be effective teachers of literacy. A variety of different personnel in the studies including supervisors, head teachers, local authority inspectors and language arts specialists readily nominated teachers for inclusion in research studies and a common thread linking most such choices was that the teachers were recognised by the quality of their pupils' learning. The nominations across the studies were of teachers who were in some way 'adding value' or 'beating the odds' in that their expertise seemed to be associated with their students scoring highly on mandated tests as well as exhibiting generally high levels of literacy in their everyday school work. Most of the studies were based on the premise that the best way to find out about teaching expertise in literacy was to talk to the expert teachers and to observe their practice. By watching them in action and discussing their approaches and beliefs with them it was judged possible to build up a reliable picture of expertise in action.

The studies in this review represent hundreds of hours in which teachers were carefully observed and talked to about these observations. In this way the various researchers were able to construct their understanding of outstanding literacy teaching and to delineate its salient features. Scrutiny across the 12 studies in this review makes it apparent that effective literacy teachers share a number of important pedagogical practices and bring to their teaching a set of similar beliefs about the nature of children, literacy and its learning.

These common themes suggest the sorts of actions teachers and schools can consider taking to promote their pupils' literacy development.

Outstanding Literacy Teachers Balance Direct Skills Instruction with more
Holistic, Authentic, Contextually-grounded Literacy Activities

A key feature of all these studies is a view of the effective teacher of literacy as one who consciously and skilfully balances direct skills instruction with more holistic, authentic, contextually-grounded literacy activities. Effective teachers, it appears, manage to avoid distorting their teaching into bi-polar either/or choices but rather intelligently blend the teaching of skills like phonics, spelling and vocabulary with an immersion into literature (including non-fiction) and writing. Pressley (2001, p.49) puts it thus: 'Effective teachers combine practices that work well for them without regard for theoretical purity in their teaching'. The grounded theoretical nature of the research orientation used in this line of enquiry allowed the researchers to describe, in ways that have high 'relatability' for practitioners, how these teachers balanced different aspects:

> In addition to – and often as part of – explicit skills instruction, the high-achievement teachers provided many opportunities for students to engage in authentic reading and writing activities. Students in these classes read many books alone, in pairs, and with the teacher. They heard good literature read aloud. They used books to search for information on topics of interest. They wrote letters and notes, recorded plant growth in their gardens, and described the growth and development of the chicks hatching in their classrooms. All of these activities were meaningfully linked to ongoing themes and instruction in specific skills. (Wharton McDonald *et al*, 1998, p.114)

Effective literacy teaching in these studies is a complex interaction of many components, an intelligent weaving together of a lot of skills instruction with voluminous reading and writing. A number of studies suggest that this balance is much more sophisticated than mixing a little bit of a whole lot of approaches. Rather it is skilled and complex instructional balance.

Outstanding Literacy Teachers Integrate Language Modes and Curricular Areas

As well as blending skill instruction and holistic teaching, the effective teacher in the studies is a teacher who also integrates the various literacy modes so that children regularly and consistently talk and write about what they have been reading. Every literacy mode stimulates and supports the others. They regularly read and write with their teacher and for their teacher, with classroom helpers and for classroom helpers, with each other and for each other. Integration also occurs between literacy and the other areas of the curriculum. Literacy is not sealed off from other curricular activities but rather is woven skilfully, for example, into the science or history pursuits of the children. Clear and strong connections across the curriculum are a regular feature in the classrooms of effective teachers in many of these studies. Instruction was often seamless and overlapping. The strong connections between reading and writing and subject knowledge helped the children to develop a notion of literacy as a means to an end, a way of finding out, of getting things done.

Outstanding Literacy Teachers are Characterised by High Levels of Pupil Engagement and by Instructional Density

Most students in the classrooms of outstanding teachers were involved and engaged with their work most of the time. Students kept on task, their conversations were task oriented and there was little time wasting. Even when left unsupervised the children continued to be involved with their work. Also, the most effective teachers were distinguished by their ability to foster several aspects of learning in one short teaching episode. They were able to seize teaching opportunities as they arose and link them with planned teaching.

Outstanding Literacy Teachers Minimise Non-demanding Tasks

The most accomplished teachers in the studies were excellent managers of their classrooms. They managed to teach in a variety of effective ways and to make high demands on their students but did it within a strong management framework where children's behaviour and learning were effectively and efficiently supervised and where pupils and teachers collaborated about rules and routines. These rules and routines were then consistently and persistently applied. Classroom assistants, specialist teachers and helping parents were also used well and managed carefully and skilfully. Maximum time and opportunities were created for learning and time consuming, non-demanding tasks were minimised.

Outstanding Literacy Teachers Create a Positive, Reinforcing and Co-operative Environment

The classrooms of the most effective teachers were very positive places. Discipline problems were rare and they were dealt with positively and constructively, devoid of harsh, demeaning criticism and with minimal disruption to the class. Students received a lot of positive reinforcement for their efforts and accomplishments, both privately and publicly. Students were also consistently encouraged to work co-operatively. They were encouraged to aim high and a 'can do' approach was encouraged.

Outstanding Literacy Teachers Encourage Self-regulation

Effective literacy teachers promoted self-regulation in their classrooms. They helped students to use their time well and also to be organised and efficient in their work habits. They were taught, for example, to check their use of conventions like spelling and punctuation in their written work and to choose books which were within their reading capabilities. The teachers expected their students to work to their full capacity at all times; they did not accept work from them which was below par.

Outstanding Literacy Teachers Differentiate Instruction

Effective teachers made extensive use of 'scaffolding' and this contributed to the density of their instruction. They monitored their pupils' progress carefully and regularly and interacted with just enough help to facilitate learning but not so much that it would lessen their need to strive. These teachers were sensitive to students' literacy progress, they were skilled at matching task to ability and recognised the necessity to pace teaching in line with their students. Their teaching style was more akin to 'coaching' in which student understanding and skill development was prompted through the use of structuring comments, the probing of incorrect responses, the scaffolding of instruction and a readiness to seize opportunities and teach 'on the fly'. Their style of talking to their students was more conversational than interrogational. They grouped and re-grouped children for *instructional* purposes rather than created fixed *ability* groups. Small group teaching, one-to-one instructional conversations and whole class teaching were judiciously blended.

Outstanding Literacy Teachers Create Links with Parents and the Local Community

It is of note that in the most highly rated study in the review, which incorporated both school and teacher factors in its analysis of literacy teacher effectiveness (Taylor *et al*, 2000b), close links with parents and with the local community were highly significant. This particular study was based in 'low poverty' urban settings.

Teacher Beliefs

We also posed the question: what knowledge and beliefs about pupils, teaching and literacy do effective literacy teachers bring to their classroom tasks? Many of the effective teachers in the studies had a strong core of professional knowledge. They exhibited strong, coherent personal philosophies. They were able to relate their philosophies and beliefs to the individual needs of students. They had strong beliefs about their own effectiveness, believed that they could adapt instruction to meet individual student literacy needs and, as one study (Collins-Block and Pressley, 2000) described it, that no barrier to a student's literacy development was greater than their own professional competencies to overcome it. They were determined to communicate their own personal enthusiasm for literacy to their students. In addition the most accomplished literacy teachers appeared to be aware of how and why their teaching worked for individual pupils and for their class as a whole.

Professional Lives

The instructional potency of an individual teacher can be amplified if they are supported in their efforts by the professional contexts within which they operate (specifically, Taylor *et al*, 2000b). The school is an obvious source of such support. Schools can make teachers feel that their work is valued; they can offer teachers a sense of agency and help strengthen their commitment to their teaching tasks. Co-operation, collaboration and collegiality are the hallmarks of the supportive school. In addition, effective teachers are characterised by their continuing professional development.

Links with Other Studies and Other Reviews

Adopting a broader though less 'systematic' lens, other reviews (Hall, 2003b) and other studies (Knapp *et al*, 1995) support the above findings. With the exception of Taylor *et al*'s (2000b) study noted above, those in the review did not set out specifically or exclusively to examine high poverty catchments. However, further insights have been made available from a handful of studies on literacy which were based on low income catchments and with more ethnically diverse pupil populations (Au, 1997; Knapp *et al*, 1995). Again these insights are in line with the above but they bear further emphasis. One insight is the how effective teachers in low poverty areas are expert at seizing the teachable moment – they are not tightly bound by the 'scripted lesson' (Collins-Block and Pressley, 2000). Less expert teachers do not deviate from their intended plan to seize the teachable moment. More accomplished teachers appear to be expert differentiators – equipped to differentiate through their more in-depth knowledge of their pupils, not just as pupils, but as people from particular families and particular communities.

These teachers know how to build on the personal and cultural backgrounds of their pupils; teachers who are more effective with children from diverse cultural and linguistic groups are likely to know more about their pupils and their communities (McNaughton, 2001; Heath, 1983; Darling-Hammond, 1998). They spend more time than their less effective counterparts in small group teaching. Small group teaching affords them the opportunity to personalise the curriculum for pupils and to differentiate tasks and interaction according to pupil need. They also spend more time coaching and scaffolding their pupils' learning as opposed to more formal recitation or telling mode, a feature that distinguishes them from less successful teachers. They emphasise creativity and self-expression. All of this fits with a socio-cultural perspective on literacy and learning – these teachers embed knowledge and skills in their social and functional contexts and they do not separate cognitive and affective aspects of learning.

In terms of beliefs, the most accomplished teachers in low poverty catchments hold consistently high expectations for all their pupils. They see ability as something that is learnable as opposed to something that is innate or fixed.

So What Should Policy-makers Change?

Although we offer recommendations for policy and practice, we acknowledge the limitations of the database. The majority of studies reviewed are from the US and therefore may not be directly applicable to the school context in England. It is worth bearing in mind that children in England typically start formal schooling at a younger age than their counterparts in the US. This may mean that teachers in both countries have different expectations for pupils in the same age range. On the other hand, UK and US governments have implemented very similar educational reforms over the past fifteen years or so, leading to the specification of standards to be met, content to be covered and assessments to be carried out. Pedagogical guidance too has been a feature of reform in both places. In addition, literacy has been the major focus of curricular reform in both countries. All of this may suggest a convergence in educational priorities and practices, as pointed out in Chapter 1. Nevertheless, comparative researchers caution against 'uncritical borrowing' (Grant, 1999) so recommendations arising from the review must be considered in the light of the limited UK-based evidence.

The existing research base offers an account of what appears to be best practice at present. It is important that this knowledge is disseminated to teacher educators, student teachers and teachers. It is also important that it is shared with literacy advisors, literacy consultants and Ofsted inspectors. Teacher educators and student teachers might usefully be made aware of the strength of the evidence supporting the findings for the early years (up to age 8) and those findings could positively impact on their teaching of students and pupils respectively. What we currently know about best practice, as detailed in this review, should inform curricular policy in literacy. This evidence should provide the foundation for future experimental strategies and initiatives in literacy.

Outstanding literacy teachers have a detailed knowledge of their pupils' learning and they are adept at matching work to pupil need. This seems to be accomplished through small, instructional group work and one-to-one instructional conversations. Such differentiation seems to be a crucial aspect of effective teaching and may need to become much more common in classrooms. Our more diverse classroom populations and our national concern for inclusion suggest small group work and individual work with pupils should not be undermined.

The constant reviewing of the NLS is important in the light of the evidence about outstanding teachers of literacy. The recent emphasis of the policy-makers on the dialogic classroom – a theme developed in the next chapter – is to be welcomed in the light of the evidence about effective teachers' classroom interactional patterns outlined here. Also, the fact that effective literacy teachers do not just integrate the modes of language but also integrate literacy and other curriculum areas suggests that policy-makers might emphasise this feature to teachers and teacher educators.

In summary, policy-makers should consider the importance of the following in literacy development: the early years as a crucial time for literacy learning, differentiated instruction, authentic opportunities for reading, writing and talk, cross-curricular connections and careful monitoring.

It is very important that effective literacy teaching is seen as the sophisticated and complex practice that it is. It consists of a variety of characteristics which work in combination and it cannot be reduced to any one or two factors. Outstanding literacy teachers have a wide repertoire of varied practices and their skill lies in the ways in which they combine and integrate these in different ways and combinations to suit the different individual learning needs of pupils.

There is, according to the research evidence, a cluster of beliefs and practices like balancing skills teaching and more authentic literacy activities for meaningful purposes, integrating the language modes and making cross-curricular connections, scaffolding and differentiating teaching, promoting self-regulation, having high expectations for pupils, expertly managing the classroom, having a knowledge of their pupils' literacy learning, and so on. Student teachers need to know what is current best practice and they need experiences of all these practices as well as support in combining and blending them in the light of their monitoring of their pupils' learning. Given the complex nature of effective literacy teaching, teachers in training would need opportunities to reflect on their own and others' experience of teaching literacy in the light of the existing research base.

Two major issues stand out about effective literacy teachers. One is the twin emphasis on code and meaning, encapsulated by the word 'balance'. Effective literacy teachers foster their pupils' literacy learning through the use of contexts and activities that are meaningful to them in the here and now of their lives. The other issue is that they integrate the modes of language so that, for instance, talk and reading are developed in tandem. Also, literacy and the rest of the curriculum are integrated – effective teachers seize opportunities across the curriculum for literacy development. It is likely that student teachers and practising teachers would benefit from exposure to examples and experiences of the application of 'balance' and 'integration' in the literacy classroom.

The majority of the studies identified in this review were from the US. It is obvious that we need more high quality research in the UK on effective literacy in all phases of schooling. This is especially true of the middle years of schooling where concerns about literacy have been expressed most recently. Future research would benefit from a close focus on effectiveness in literacy teaching with reference to pupil outcomes. Whilst pupil outcomes as measured by valid assessment scores are clearly important, consideration should also be given to research on literacy teacher effectiveness to pupil interest and enthusiasm and how their motivation to learn might be enhanced in response to effective teaching. To focus only on the more readily measurable indicators of pupil progress, like test scores, would be inadequate. Such scores cannot be taken as indicators of pupils' levels of confidence in literacy, their attitude to learning or their commitment, as shown in their readiness to engage in literacy activities outside of school, as the recent Progress in International Reading Literacy Study (PIRLS) (Mullis *et al*, 2001) demonstrated. In the long run, such features may make a significant contribution to pupils' effectiveness in using literacy. What is essential is that nominations of literacy teaching effectiveness are accompanied by appropriate empirical validations of what effective literacy teachers think and do in their classrooms.

Research in the UK needs to examine more closely the links between effectiveness at the whole school level and the ways in which it can promote and support effective literacy teaching within individual classrooms. The synergy between school and classroom factors is worthy of further study. Taylor *et al*'s (2000b) trustworthy evidence is that a combination of school-level decisions as well as effective practices within individual classrooms is needed if low-income schools are to 'beat the odds' in literacy. This suggests that research is especially needed in contexts and settings that are associated with high levels of school disaffection. The more recent direction of research on effective literacy teaching in the US (see Taylor *et al*, 2002) has shifted to translating research on effective literacy teaching into practice and, particularly, to the professional development activities that are most effective in promoting changes in the teaching of literacy. This is also an area that merits study in the UK. Insofar as one might legitimately separate the modes of literacy, writing is more in need of further study than reading, at all phases, but especially in the primary and middle years.

Given the limitations pertaining to the existing research base, discussed above, it would seem that we need more studies about effective literacy teaching in which we can have high levels of trust. The best of the studies included in our review (Taylor *et al*, 2000b) depended on natural correlations between teaching factors and pupil achievements. Such studies are useful in directing us to what seems to work best in practice.

However, while we can learn much from the type of analyses described above, especially in terms of general pedagogic practice, the fact remains that it is futile to search for some 'holy grail' of outstanding teacher characteristics that will fit all situations. History has shown that different pedagogical practices and approaches, even different pedagogical orientations, have different effects for different pupils in different locations (see Comber, 2001). As Barbara Comber reminds us race, ethnicity, poverty, language, location and gender impact on pupils' educational success. This makes the case for local studies of literacy in practice taking account of the context of teachers' lives, political contexts and educational systems. As well as needing more UK-based studies of the kind described above, we also need studies that engage more directly with local realities such as those described in Barbara Comber and Anne Simpson (2001).

Conclusion

What is clear from the evidence – both through the systematic review above and the narrative reviews – is that literacy teaching cannot be packaged in teacher-proof scripts on the assumption that 'one size fits all'. There is no blueprint for outstanding teaching. A recurring theme in the studies is how outstanding teachers of literacy know their pupils well and have a strong sense of what their communities and families value. They use this understanding in interactions with their pupils and, moreover, the nature of their interaction appears to be more dialogic, democratic and pupil-led than monologic, authoritarian and teacher-led. Since the promotion of this type of interaction is an area that is fraught with difficulty, not least because of the NLS or perhaps the way the NLS is perceived, and since it is crucial for enhancing pupil engagement and control, the next chapter considers this theme further.

Much of the research base reviewed in this chapter underplays the importance of the socio-cultural context in which teaching and learning take place (see Hall, 2003b for a review) and does not engage with the impact of the subjectivity of the participants (Pollard, 1990). There is little emphasis on learners with reference to their responses to the social influences and teaching/learning situations in which they find themselves. The model of teaching could arguably be described as rather technical in which the teacher is in control and pupils comply with the tasks set for them. As Pollard and others have argued, while this line of enquiry is worthwhile and necessary, it is not sufficient and should be complemented by other work – work which is more informed by socio-cultural perspectives.

Chapter 5

From Monologic to Dialogic Classrooms

Introduction

One of the enduring messages of the studies on literacy – whatever research orientation is adopted – is the power of teachers to determine the life chances of their pupils. The existence of nationally prescribed norms, of curriculum mandates and assessment criteria leaves this intact. Many teachers and many researchers of literacy know, even if policy-makers choose not to, that it is easier to introduce new tools and procedures than it is to change relationships, attitudes or values – which lie at the heart of pedagogy. The implication of the debates and evidence in this book for improving primary practice, and literacy education more specifically, is not the technical fix that manifests itself in training in externally-prescribed curricula, but in professional opportunities for teachers to reflect on their own practice and to grapple with how their taken-for-granted practices impact on their pupils. It demands a radical rethink about literacy policy and about teacher development.

This chapter probes further the power of teachers in classrooms, with reference to their daily interactions with pupils. What different participation opportunities might teachers need to find to enhance literacy for all pupils? How can we create classroom participation structures where all children participate in the discourse? Before addressing such questions, it is worth considering what is omitted from current literacy policy in the form of the NLS. I suggest that the notion of culture or the ways in which children appropriate literacy within socio-cultural contexts is insufficiently recognised in the current policy. Studies of classroom interaction illustrate the ways in which teachers and pupils co-construct positions for themselves and each other and show how the type of interaction that is facilitated can empower or depower pupils. This chapter closes with a discussion of issues around the necessary shift from a monologic to a dialogic classroom.

Links with one's Lifeworld: A Socio-cultural Perspective

It is now a cliché to suggest that children learn better when that which they are being asked to learn is contextualised in their 'everyday' experiences. Learning something that is very distant from one's previous experiences or that is removed from one's lifeworld requires more effort to make the relevant connections and to construe the necessary concepts. James Gee talks about 'lifeworld' as 'the culturally distinctive ... ways of being, acting as, and talking as an "everyday", non-specialist person' (2000, p.66). He goes on to suggest that 'School-based, specialist, academic, and public-sphere forms of language often require us to exit our lifeworlds and construe contexts based on experiences we have had outside the lifeworld' (p.66). And '[w]hen we exit our lifeworlds, that is the worlds we all live in when we are being "everyday people" and not speaking out of some specialist domain or another, we leave "home", in a sense' (p.66). For many advantaged children this journey is not a problem, they do not have to leave home since plenty of rich bridges have been built over the years so that their lifeworlds are aligned with what the school is offering. They have been well inducted into the practices of several specialist domains. It seems who we become depends on the company we keep and what we do together (Wells, 1999). Many children are prepared for school literacy prior to coming to school by their exposure to books and by their experience of thousands of hours of being read to. Their schooling, being akin to a continuation of home life, does not ask them to deny or ignore their lifeworlds. For many other children, however, especially poor children and minority groups, what is on offer in school is very different to their lifeworlds and inadequate bridging occurs to link those two worlds for them. They are often expected, at best, to ignore and, at worst, to deny the value of their home culture. For example, the growth of supplementary schools in England is in many cases a direct response to the mis-alignment of school and home cultures for many children from ethnic minority backgrounds (Hall *et al*, 2002). But what can schools and teachers do to build richer bridges for pupils disadvantaged by not having the specialist knowledge valued by the school?

Four key principles suggested by James Gee (2000, pp.43-68) are summarised here in order to begin to address this question. First he suggests that poor children and those from ethnic minority groups should have 'situated practice'. This refers to first hand experience of social practices that are meaningful to them in the here-and-now of their lives, involving talk, texts, tools and technologies of the sort that help them imagine contexts that help to make sense of what is being taught. Second, overt instruction is important for these children. This includes scaffolding and coaching to help learners attend, in a critical and reflective way, to the salient features of the language being taught. Such features are likely to include the 'cognitively, socially, and historically important patterns and relationships in the language and practices being taught' (p.67). A similar point is powerfully made by Lisa Delpit in her book entitled *Other People's Children* (1995). Also, the notion of critical literacy noted in Chapter 3 links with this since to understand how language works to achieve certain effects requires attention to such issues as interests being served by a text, to implicit assumptions and taken-for-granted thinking about the way texts assume society works. Third, Gee suggests children have a right to 'critical framing' by which he means grasping how a subject being taught connects with other domains, whether specialist or non-specialist. This suggests a conscious and explicit integration and connecting of subject matter in the interests of clarifying for learners how knowledge domains are linked. Fourth, he suggests that learners need to be more than mere consumers of knowledge, they need to have opportunities to generate and transform it too. While children should, he suggests, 'master the standard "genres" of many school-based, specialist, academic and public-sphere forms of language and social practices' they should also 'know how to transform them, break them, and innovate new ones for their own social, cultural and political purposes' (p.68).

When one considers this line of thinking in the present policy context in England, two images come to mind. One foregrounds the significance of local and situational literacies, that skills need to be developed in context, that small group work matters, that children should engage and critique texts from a variety of points of view that reflect the diversity of their racial, social, cultural and linguistic backgrounds, and that teaching should be linked to community and local issues. Another image is one of competition where cultural differences are considered problematic (McCarthy *et al*, 2000). Unfortunately it is the second image that predominates in current policy and, indeed, in practice. The problem is that in reality teachers seem to be acquiescing and realigning their curricula in a manner that could be characterised as test-driven (Hall *et al*, 2004) and it is likely that our obsession with comparison across schools will fade in the near future.

Several researchers have demonstrated how children and families construct and use literacy in order to meet the demands and opportunities of their lives (for example Heath, 1983). Luis Moll for example describes how teachers, schools, and educational bureaucracies systematically misunderstand and discount the strengths of 'lifeworlds' (to use Gee's term) of poor, ethnically diverse children. Instead of recommending intervention programmes that further deny their out-of-school experiences, people like Moll (2000) and Kathy Au (1997a) have sought ways in which the lives of these groups can intervene in the practices of schooling by capitalising on the funds of knowledge that these children already possess. They start from the premise of situated practice, from the premise of contextualised notions of literacy practice. Their 'reverse interventions' (Shannon, 1996, p.441) seek to 'interrupt traditional teaching assumptions and practices' and seek instead to achieve academic success on the basis of existing expertise and strengths.

Au's work is interesting because it shows how class teachers can change their participation and interactional patterns to encourage greater involvement of pupils. One of several reasons advanced by Au for the under-achievement of some ethnic minority groups is what she terms 'cultural difference' (Au, 1997b). In this perspective the lack of school success of some ethnic minorities can be attributed at least partially to their preference for forms of interaction and language that conflict with the mainstream behaviours generally needed for success in school. Such preferences are the result of socialisation practices in the family and community, which in turn reflect cultural values. Au's premise is that non-mainstream students have difficulty learning in school because the teaching style on offer does not follow their particular community's cultural values and ways of interacting. She discovered, for example, that Native Hawaiian students performed poorly in literacy lessons when teachers conducted classes following the interactional rules of conventional classrooms – teacher asks a question, pupil responds and teacher evaluates the response. On the introduction of what she terms 'culturally responsive' practice these same students attended better to reading, they discussed more text ideas and made more sensible inferences about the texts in reading lessons where the teacher allowed the pupils to use interactional modes more in line with 'talk story' – a speech event in the Hawaiian community. 'Talk story' involves much collaboration in producing responses and involves much overlapping speech. In 'talk story' in the community, a story is co-narrated by more than one person, and the speech of the narrators is also over-lapped by others in the group. In this setting the skilled speaker is one who knows how to involve others in the conversation – this person does not dominate the conversation. Since they are familiar with this kind of speech event outside of school, the pupils introduce it into their story discussions in school. So the pupils work together to answer the teacher's questions. The teacher, appreciative and knowledgeable of the children's family and community culture, is willing to relax her control of turn-taking and allow more than one child to speak at a time as long as what is being said is relevant to the discussion. Au explains that in many Hawaiian families co-operation rather than competition is seen as important for the well-being of the extended family. Individual achievement is less highly prized than group contributions that benefit the family. In school lessons 'talk story' appears to be successful as it reflects this family emphasis on co-operation.

The fundamental principles on which her project is based are as relevant in England as they are in the United States. These are:

1. that ownership of literacy (that is that pupils value literacy and are willing to make it a part of their everyday lives) as well as the acquisition of meaning-making strategies and skills of literacy are important; and
2. that higher levels of literacy follow if literacy teaching happens in a culturally-responsive manner.

In justifying the first of these Au claims that people who experience ownership of literacy in school get the immediate rewards of schooling (Au, 1997b). The immediate, as opposed to the delayed, rewards of schooling are especially important for pupils from non-mainstream backgrounds since their families may not typically show connections among schooling, jobs and general life chances. The status attributed here to ownership is in line with socio-cultural theory in taking account of the relationship between motivation for schooling and family and community background.

Au's and Moll's assumption was that higher levels of literacy follow if literacy teaching is organised in a manner responsive to and accepting of children's home culture and language. Moll (2000, p.260) suggests that teachers create what he calls 'household analogs' where the aim is not so much to reproduce the household in the classroom but 'to recreate strategically those aspects of household life (for example social networks, funds of knowledge) that may lead to productive academic activities in the classroom'. What he calls 'funds of knowledge' are the bodies of knowledge that underlie household activities. He listed them under agriculture (to include ranching and farming, gardening, animal husbandry), economics (to include renting and selling, loans, accounting, trade and finance), construction (which included carpentry, roofing, masonry, design and architecture), religion (which included bible stories, catechism, liturgy and Sunday school) and Arts (which included music, lyrics, painting and sculpture). In documenting and using these funds of knowledge in classroom activities Moll seeks to make explicit the wealth of resources available within any single household or local community – resources that may not be so obvious to teachers or even to pupils themselves. So instead of attending to a community's deficits, attention shifts to the possibilities represented in the 'funds of knowledge'.

The major implication of a socio-cultural approach to literacy is the need to shift from a deficit model in which low achievement is located in inadequate or lacking home environments to a perspective which holds that schools succeed or fail according to how they connect with pupils' home cultures. The extent to which they are able to design culturally-response curricula will be a measure of their ability to reduce the disparity between school and community literacy experiences and in turn an indicator of their commitment to reduce the disparity between the 'haves' and 'have-nots' in literacy. Socio-cultural approaches to literacy (see Hall, 2003a for a discussion of this and other perspectives on literacy) are characterised by interactive, dialogic and reciprocal styles of participation.

Classroom Discourse in England

One of the learner's major aims in school must be to become accomplished in the use of the culture's most important tools. The tool of all person-made tools is surely language, as Bruner reminds us (1996). Language is the primary symbol system that allows us to shape meaning – it gives our thoughts shape and expression, yet it also shapes our very thoughts in the process. Cole (1994 cited in Wells, 1999) refers to language as 'the master tool' – the tool that mediates the learning of all others.

Classroom language or pedagogical discourse, therefore, shapes learning opportunities for learners. Discourse positions participants as they engage moment-by-moment with others. The messages the teacher is supplying in the course of interacting with pupils about how learning should be done and who is doing it well are of major significance. By adopting a socio-cultural perspective on literacy one can make explicit the identities available to pupils and teachers in classroom interaction, to show what is available to be learned, and *inter alia* to demonstrate what counts as valuable knowledge. Another assumption of a socio-cultural take on literacy learning, indeed on learning more generally, is that being a member of a particular classroom leads to a particular way of being a pupil, to the construction and development of particular types of knowledge and competencies. Furthermore, having an understanding of these processes is assumed to be important for changing and improving pedagogical practices. Drawing on Kress (1989) one can use the notion of subject position to suggest that all participants in an interaction are acting subjects. People also act on the basis of others' expectations of how they should act or take up different positions depending on unequal power relations (Kress, 1989). It is well established that classroom discourse tends to promote pupil achievement when it actively involves them in the production of knowledge and when the discourse is highly interactive (Nystrand *et al,* 2001).

Previous research has sought to describe the way teachers have accommodated the demands of the NLS, particularly with reference to the recommendations by policy-makers (DfEE, 1998) for 'interactive whole class teaching' (Mroz *et al*, 2000). Reynolds (1998) describes the latter as involving rapid question and answer sessions designed to establish what pupils know and followed by slower paced, higher order questioning designed to promote reflection and higher levels of pupil thinking. The policy-makers assert that this type of interaction plays a vital role in raising literacy standards. It was this assumption that led Mroz *et al* (2000) to investigate whether the Literacy Hour was indeed promoting higher order questioning. Their findings indicate a strong adherence to traditional practices of whole class teaching and teacher-led recitation and it seems the Literacy Hour does not promote high quality interaction between pupils and teacher.   Their work confirms the more extensive research by Galton *et al* (1999, p.67) which concluded that '[t]oday's teachers devote even more of their time to telling pupils facts and ideas or to giving directions than their counterparts of twenty years ago'. It seems pupils are playing an even less active role in classroom interaction than they did in the past.

Other research suggests that the NLS offers contradictory pedagogical advice to teachers on 'interactive teaching' (English *et al*, 2002). These authors refer specifically to what they see as a contradiction in official thinking about what constitutes successful teaching. *The NLS Framework for Teaching* (DfEE, 1998, p.8) describes successful teaching as:

- discursive – characterised by high quality oral work;
- interactive – pupils' contributions are encouraged, expected and extended;
- well-paced – there is a sense of urgency, driven by the need to make progress and succeed;
- confident – teachers have a clear understanding of the objectives;
- ambitious – there is optimism about, and high expectations of, success.

As English *et al* point out the first two elements above seem to be in tension with the third. Of note also in this regard is the series of videos of NLS practice produced to demonstrate effective practice (Ofsted, 1997). These videos show teachers engaged in 'quick fire' question and answer sessions. English *et al* found that over half of their 30 participating teachers were aware of and confused by this conflict.   It seems their teachers typically prioritise pace and the objectives of the lesson over extending pupil responses and facilitating higher order interaction. The line of enquiry pursued by these researchers helps us to better understand why there is still such a strong emphasis on teacher talk and control in classrooms – a point revisited below.

The notion of pace is well developed in the seminal work of Alexander (2000). He rightly argues that the critical issue is the relationship of interactive pace to cognition and learning and convincingly demonstrates that 'a fast pace in teaching is not necessarily a virtue' (p.418). Whole class teaching too, he suggests, is not itself a virtue, in contrast to the assumption of Ofsted and UK governments over the 1990s. He writes '[w]hole class teaching may yield interaction that positively scintillates with cognitive demand, or it may be mind-numbingly pedestrian' (p.394).

The work of the Russian scholar, Bakhtin (1981; Haworth, 1999), is relevant and illuminating and fits squarely within a socio-cultural perspective. Bakhtin distinguishes between 'monologic' and 'dialogic' discourse. When 'monologism' characterises interaction he suggests that:

> the genuine interaction of consciousness is impossible, and thus genuine dialogue is impossible as well. In essence idealism knows only a single mode of cognitive interaction among consciousness: someone who knows and possesses the truth instructs someone who is ignorant of it and in error; that is, it is the interaction of a teacher and a pupil, which, it follows, can only be a pedagogical dialogue. (Bakhtin, 1981, p.81)

Applied to the classroom this kind of interaction provides little or no space for learners to participate actively in the construction of knowledge; they are denied the opportunity to make meaningful contributions on their terms. When interaction is dialogic, on the other hand, the balance of discourse is more symmetrical and in the classroom the teacher's voice is 'but one voice among many' (Nystrand *et al*, 2001, p.6). What kind of interaction might be the NLS encourage and in particular does it encourage the kind of interaction that would invite learners to construct their own knowledge?

As explained in Chapter 3, the NLS, with its accompanying daily Literacy Hour, was introduced into all primary schools in England in 1999 and aims to enhance literacy standards. It prescribes in precise detail the content, objectives and classroom organisational strategies that teachers should use (Hall, 2001). Of interest here is the nature of interaction in the Literacy Hour and the extent to which it coincides with contemporary theory on classroom learning discourse. This section of the chapter is based on a collaborative micro-analysis of observational data from two poetry lessons conducted within the Literacy Hour in two Year 6 classrooms in two different suburban schools in a city in the north of England and was part of collaborative research project conducted with colleagues in 2002 at Leeds Metropolitan University (see Hall *et al*, 2003).

The approach in that project was not dissimilar to the one adopted by researchers like Mroz *et al* above in that it sought to portray the nature of interaction in classrooms and to explain it. It was different to some of the empirical studies of practice just noted above in that it tackled the issue from an overtly socio-cultural stance. The identities or subjectivities of teachers and pupils were of interest. By making these, as well as the assumptions about what knowledge and skills were valued, explicit one can offer complementary and fresh insights that would help explain the prevalence of recitation in classrooms. Eventually, such insights may help change this emphasis to one where pupils participate more actively, at least in the case of some teachers.

One further concept – literary stance – had particular relevance for the analysis of the poetry lessons which were observed and analysed. The idea of literary stance was introduced by the literary theorist Louise Rosenblatt (1985; 1991) who developed a transactional theory of reading. She proposed the idea that one reads from one or two stances. One stance she called 'aesthetic' which occurs when the reader is focused on what she is living through during the reading event – the reader is attending to the words and to the qualitative overtones of the ideas, images, situations and characters that are being evoked in her as she reads the text. The oft-quoted phrase Rosenblatt used to characterise the aesthetic stance is 'lived through experience' where the thoughts and feelings of the poet or a story's characters are vicariously experienced. The second stance Rosenblatt described is 'efferent'. This is a stance concerned with the information the reader takes away from the text. These two stances are not mutually exclusive but, according to Rosenblatt, when reading imaginative literature the predominant stance should be aesthetic. That is, literature should be read primarily for the enjoyment of the experience. Approaching literature from an efferent stance, she says, gives the impression that it should be read for facts and analysis. For this reason she urges teachers to dwell in the experience of reading and to prolong the aesthetic experience through activities like drawing, writing, drama, dance and discussion.

Other stances are also worth noting. One is a critical/analytic stance (Wade *et al*, 1994) and this stance suggests a focus on a major issue or dilemma or problem facing a character in a story or posed by the author or poet. Adopting this stance could involve a consideration of reasons for different courses of action and appeals to the text for evidence (Chinn *et al*, 2001). Another stance is a critical literacy or socio-political stance (Chapter 3 and Hall, 1998; 2003a) which involves learners in a discussion about whose interests are being served by a text, whose voices are included or excluded. This is a stance that helps learners understand how texts have power, how that power is exercised, how it works to privilege particular knowledges, beliefs, attitudes and values, and to marginalise and silence others. As noted earlier in this chapter, it asks learners to question taken-for-granted or 'natural' assumptions about the world. Discussions could of course adopt a mixture of stances, possibly with one stance predominating.

The Project

Teachers in two schools gave permission to the research team (Hall *et al*, 2003) to observe their practice, to interview them about their teaching and to talk to a sample of their pupils. The team explained that it was interested in how the teacher and pupils operated the Literacy Hour as well as how they taught other subjects. Permission was obtained to audio record our observations and to collect lesson plans, school policy documents and to talk to pupils about their learning experiences. This section is based on just two lessons by two different teachers, one in each school of the project.

The first teacher, Sarah (not her real name), was nominated as effective in her delivery of the Literacy Hour by a literacy advisor, while Robert (not his real name), the second teacher, was rated by the deputy head teacher as an effective science teacher. To enhance the reliability and validity of the data collected, three members of the research team observed and took detailed fieldnotes of the same lessons. In addition, the full team engaged in the analysis of data – this involved prior individual reading and annotation of the transcripts, then meetings to share and discuss interpretations, followed by further detailed analysis of types and numbers of questions and statements, a content analysis of the interaction and an exploration of non-verbal interaction as evidenced from fieldnotes and recall of the shared observations. The team recognised that the attribution of meaning to discursive acts is far from a neutral activity since all aspects of meaning-making are acts of construction (Jaworski and Coupland, 1999; Moje, 1997) and, in this case, the fieldnotes and the audio-recordings already filtered or mediated what took place. The dual observations reflect this – they seek to maximise confidence and trustworthiness in relation to the claims made about the data.

What follows is an account, drawn from multiple fieldnotes and transcripts of audio-recordings of two poetry lessons.

Poetry Lesson One: 'We have picked these poems to bits'

Sarah is teaching a poetry lesson to her Year 6, mixed ability class of all white pupils. This is the Literacy Hour in action in June 2002, that is post SATs (the externally imposed standard assessment tests are taken by Year 6 pupils in English, Mathematics and Science). Sarah is relaxed and friendly with her pupils; she is a well-organised and confident teacher; and her pupils clearly like and respect her. Following some slight confusion about books and who is paired with whom, the class settles and Sarah clearly and with good humour explains what the pupils have to do: 'What I would like you to do is to have a look at the poems, read them through with your partner and then we'll talk about them ... Scan through those poems and see what they have in common.'

In pairs the children have just read three poems about families which have been reproduced for them on a double page spread with some questions attached. Sarah poses several questions, for example, 'So at first glance, what do you notice? What do you notice about the poems? Helen ... who's written the poem?'; 'What clue did you pick up that told you it must be a little girl, Kirsty?'; 'How do you think the writer feels about this lady?'; 'What gives you that clue, Zoe?' Short sentences, phrases or one word answers are offered by pupils, such as, 'They're all about grown ups'; 'They're all short rhymes'. Sarah draws their attention to metaphors and similes. (One of the classroom walls has a chart defining metaphors and similes and giving many examples of each.)

Sarah then explains that she is going to select people to read the poems aloud. Several volunteers raise their hands but Sarah says, 'Put your hand down now because I need to tell you what you need to do and think about why you are doing this. You need to read them in a clear voice and you need to put expression in your voice.' A volunteer (girl) is chosen from a show of hands to read one of the poems aloud. She struggles a little but gets to the end of the poem chosen. 'Thanks, Maria' says Sarah, 'that was quite a hard poem to read, wasn't it? There were some interesting words there that were hard to get the tongue round.' Two other girls read the other poems.

This is followed by further teacher-led questioning and answers such as, 'Which word in the poem suggests he's old?' One of the poems 'My Sparrow Gran' is selected by the teacher for more detailed study. It has been reproduced on an overhead projector. Sarah leads the activity, drawing pupils' attention to the text on the OHP: 'My Sparrow Gran, so let's have a look at the clues in this text to support the idea that Gran is like a sparrow.' James is invited to come out in front of the class and ask other children to call out the words in the poem that suggest Gran is like a bird. Pupils raise their hands as if he is the teacher. He finds their responses in the poem and underlines them. Sarah thanks him and tells him to 'Have a rest now.' She adds, 'These words convey the idea that she is like a sparrow. There is another way that the poet has given us the impression that Gran is a sparrow. The movement of a sparrow. How has she conveyed that idea? ... How is the poem a metaphor? Can you find a simile there?'

A lengthy question and answer session follows about what similes and metaphors are, examples are sought from the class. Some responses are affirmed, some ignored, some rejected, some taken up and embellished, but all the while Sarah leads, directs, evaluates responses; she establishes that they do know this terminology. The teacher knows the answers to the questions she poses, she has a particular response in mind and she chases after it. Next pupils are asked to work in pairs again: 'I want you to work with your partner now and what I would like you to do is complete this (worksheet) and it is not something that you both need to write on, one of you needs to write and this you have to agree with your partner, and you have to agree who's going to share with the rest of the group when we come back as a big group. So three poems, the titles are on here and you've got to write how the poet feels about every person in the poem and the words and phrases that tell you, and we've sorted some of that already haven't we, so it shouldn't take you too long to get started ...'

The plenary session consists of pupils sharing their responses to the task in question/answer format again, much like the previous part of the lesson. The lesson finishes with reminders about metaphors and similes. Sarah recaps: 'We've picked out ... we have picked these poems to bits really, haven't we, backwards and forwards, picking them to bits and we have noticed the use of metaphors and similes. And we've reminded ourselves what metaphors and similes are. Let's see if you remember.' More definitions and more examples follow. Pupils collect the books and put them away neatly. This Literacy Hour is over.

Poetry Lesson Two: 'A bit of a poem'

England beat Nigeria in a match in the World Cup earlier this morning. It is now 9.30 am and Robert and his eight 'lower ability' Year 6 pupils (seven boys and one girl) are in their sparsely furnished and rather bleak classroom in a large school in the middle of a council estate. Tanya, the only girl, is accompanied by a female classroom assistant. She sucks her thumb and does not look comfortable in this male-dominated setting. It is noisy as construction work goes on nearby in another classroom. Robert, a little nervous being observed by two researchers, tells his *small gathering they are going to have a poetry lesson, that they are going to watch a video of Michael Rosen reading some of his poems, that they are going to talk a bit about the last one they will hear.*

The poem is called 'The washing machine'. They have heard it before, he reminds them that they like it, how they especially liked the 'washing machine bit' before. The video is played. All children join in, clearly enjoying the sounds, the rhythm and the expressive voice of the poet reading his own poetry. Robert stops the video and asks them: 'In what way is that a poem, what makes it a poem?' A boy suggests it is the 'rhymes' which leads to a brief exchange about other poems they've read that rhymed. Another boy says 'rhythm' and this leads into some questions about how the rhythmic effects in Rosen's poem were created. They are invited to 'have a go' at doing 'train rhythms' and following some promptings, most do have a go. They repeat lines from the poem, they clearly have fun with exaggerating and moving to the rhythms: 'tickets and railcards please, tickets and railcards please'.

Robert plays the video again and this time they all join in saying the poem. He questions them about the rhythms and what the poem is about; he asks many questions and they supply the answers. But they are excited as they respond and, while Robert controls the sequence of questions and the interaction overall, they are engaged with the task. He crouches down to hear their responses, he encourages and elaborates on their offerings. He talks more than the children but all pupils get a turn and all are eager to have their say – they sometimes raise their hands and he sometimes nominates someone to answer, but mostly they talk out without being individually invited and there is much overlapping speech. They do not speak to each other – all their responses are directed to their teacher. Although the mode of interaction is recitation-like (teacher poses question, pupil responds and teacher evaluates) the style is informal, engaging and pupils' ideas are genuinely elicited.

Robert does not always have a pre-set answer in mind for his questions. Now a task is set: 'I want you to write a thing a bit like this but not to do with a train,' Robert says. 'Now you see with this, it's important that you choose things that have got some sort of rhythm like we saw on the video "tickets and railcards please" or "mum can I have a sandwich?". Now, little phrases and sentences like that. Now you're going to do your poem about things that people might say at a football match. So things that people might shout out or say to each other at the match, while the match is going on.' Pupils start to offer suggestions immediately: 'Get your hotdogs here' says one boy and Robert says, 'That sounds like an idea Paul ... somebody might be shouting out "get your hotdogs here, get your hotdogs", alright that's a good one, anybody else got a good one? Think about those people at that match this morning what they may have been calling out in the match as England supporters.' A boy suggests, 'Like come on England, come on England.' Tanya, no longer thumb-sucking, adds, 'We're on the ball, we're on the ball.' Pupils are interested, involved and motivated to participate. Robert gives each pair a piece of paper and asks them to work in pairs: 'Think of things like that that people might say at a football match, like "come on England" and stuff like that.

And then we're gong to try and turn them into a bit of a poem that we can say either in pairs or all together.'

Pupils work in pairs, but Tanya and her partner work alone, either she or her partner being reluctant co-workers. Robert sits with each pair, advising and listening and encouraging: 'You don't have to have things in the order you might use them in eventually' ... 'You have to decide eventually how you're going to put it together', 'Oh, that's a good one, that's a great one' ... 'That's great, I like that.' Tanya recites hers enthusiastically on her own, so does the boy who was meant to be her working partner. The pairs have to decide how to put all the 'bits' together. There is little time left and it is getting very noisy, but all are immersed in the task. Robert tells them they have only two more minutes and then they must be ready to recite their poem. 'It's going to be a performance remember, so practise it.'

At last 'It's performance time, you've planned it well, it works, so now the skill is in performing it as well as you can,' enthuses Robert. The pairs recite their creations to the group with varying degrees of gusto; there is much applause and many superlatives, not just from Robert but from some of the children themselves: 'Fantastic', 'Brilliant'. Robert tells them they will get to write them down 'nicely' another day, but for now they can finish the lesson by returning to recite Michael Rosen's poem once more. The Literacy Hour is over.

As an analytic technique the notion of stance (described above) is helpful in explicating what knowledge is most valued in the two poetry lessons. In the first lesson the stance is undoubtedly 'efferent' with very little, if any, indication of other stances, including the 'aesthetic' – the latter one might have been expected, given the text. Sarah does not really encourage a personal response to the poem from her pupils, although she does ask them what they think. They are not, for instance, invited to link the poem with their own lives or their own families, although the poems arguably lend themselves to such connections. There is some attempt to elicit emotional identification with the characters in the poems but the overarching emphasis is on clarification of descriptions, understanding of technique, particularly similes and metaphors. Indeed one could reasonably argue that the poems themselves and engagement with their themes are subservient to the inculcation in pupils of knowledge about language. What is really valued here is information that is to be found in the text itself. Of less significance is text-to-life connections or what they bring to the text. Pupils are introduced to the poems to find out things, the stance adopted is almost entirely efferent.

Robert's lesson, on the other hand, is a mix of 'efferent' and 'aesthetic' stances, with the latter predominating. In this lesson Rosen's poem is to be experienced, not merely read or listened to. And it is not just a cognitive experience that is on offer but an embodied and sensory one – pupils move as they chorus the rhythmic sounds of the poem, for example. While 'knowing that' is important as evident by the teacher's line of questioning to ascertain that they knew the meaning of certain words in the poem (like 'buffet') 'knowing how' or the application of knowledge is privileged. Pupils get to appreciate the role of rhythm by creating their own poems, by performing them and by listening to the performances of their peers. Rosenblatt's 'lived through experience' is what seems to matter. Such a stance to literacy is not so easily expressed in learning objectives or learning outcomes that are measurable and perhaps that explains why Robert did not refer to any objectives in his lesson introduction or conclusion.

In summary, Robert's pupils are invited to engage imaginatively with the poem while Sarah's pupils maintain a critical detachment from their poems. As I will demonstrate, the kinds of roles, responsibilities and expectations exercised in both settings are in line with these identified literary stances.

Subject Positions for Pupils and Teachers

What are the roles, responsibilities and norms of and for both pupils and teachers in the two settings? In both settings it is argued that pupils and teachers are co-constructors of the lesson. A teacher who manages to be highly authoritarian and authoritative cannot be so unless pupils are highly compliant, obedient and passive (even if reluctantly so). Even in such a scenario (which describes neither lesson above) the pupils and teacher co-construct the event.

In the first lesson above there is a very clear distinction throughout between Sarah's position and the position of her pupils. Sarah positions herself as director of the show, she is definitely the boss. She is instructor ('so let's look at the clues in this text to support the idea that Gran is like a sparrow'), commander ('put your hand down'), interrogator ('which bit in the poem tells you that?'), teller ('simile says that something is like something else, so for example, the winter wind cuts through you like a knife'), possessor of knowledge (she asks questions to which she knows the answers), judge ('that's right'), assessor and arbiter ('yes and what else?' and 'that's an interesting one, that wasn't one that I had thought about' and 'I'm not saying that you're wrong Jane, I'm just saying ...'), commentator ('some people did that first column for each poet ... some people did it that way because ...'), and task-setter ('have a look at them .. read them through with your partner' and 'I'm looking for ideas, so don't get hung up on spellings'). But she is also a sympathiser ('Thanks, Joanne, that was quite a hard poem to read, wasn't it ... words ... hard to get the tongue round'), helper ('underline it, that will make it a lot easier for us'), and a person with likes and desires ('that's what I like about these particular books').

Most of these subject positions are not available to pupils. The subject positions that are available to pupils include those of listener, recipient of knowledge, answerer of teacher-set questions, rememberer ('let's see if you remember') text detective, text analyser, and testee.

How are these teacher and pupil positionings accomplished? The main way is the conventional 'Initiation Response Evaluation' (IRE) format (Sinclair and Coulthard, 1975) so commonly found in whole class teaching. This, in combination with whole class teaching, maximises Sarah's control over the proceedings and minimise pupil-pupil interaction. The boundaries for what may happen in this lesson are strongly influenced by a more or less predetermined instructional frame (Green *et al*, 1988). She constantly scans the room, making eye contact with everyone, to ensure maximum attention to the task. She controls both the topics for talk and the turns for talking by asking all the questions and by nominating pupils to respond. Pupils relate to her as expert, submitting their responses to her for approval.

The discourse features that Sarah and her pupils use are worth highlighting here since they reflect the various roles being played out. For example, Sarah typically repeats or embellishes pupils' utterances, securing her agency and status, but pupils themselves are not so privileged. One pupil offers the response 'they are all one family' to a question about what the poems have in common to which she offers the counter response 'somebody has actually mentioned that already'. Also pupils are expected to adhere closely in their responses to the business in hand – there is no expectation that they can deviate from the task. This is reflected in their typical use of noun clauses and her use of first person pronouns and verb forms. She allows herself to deviate from the task when pupils are suggesting examples of similes and metaphors, offering the aside: 'I don't have a bath, I always have a shower. But I love it when you take the towel off the radiator and wrap yourself up in it'. She permits herself a personal perspective on several occasions in the lesson but there is no evidence of pupils so doing. In this sense the dominant identity available to pupils is one of pupil. While she is definitely teacher, she is also an individual with likes and desires and a life outside of school as the previous utterance indicates.

However, some caveats have to be added here. There are moments when some children do manage to deviate from the pupil identity and negotiate or have conferred upon them different positions. For example we saw above how one pupil, a boy, is invited out to the white board and gets to decide which pupils can contribute responses. He is momentarily in teacher role. Also, during pair work, while Sarah and the classroom assistant are moving around the room checking that all are on task and offering supportive comments, Sarah notices two boys who are not discussing the poems as requested. She walks towards them, she briefly joins in a conversation with them, laughs with them and momentarily all three have equal status. As she leaves them she says 'you stay focused on this poem and you can talk about trains as much as you like at playtime'. They return to their task. On the other hand, just as the lesson is coming to an end one pupil, a girl, gets up too early and Sarah fixes her eyes on her and the girl hastily sits down again, looking embarrassed. Could it be that boys are permitted a wider range of identities than girls in this classroom, girls needing to position themselves and to be positioned as ever hard working, while boys 'have another life' and are perceived perhaps as not as suited as girls to these literacy tasks? This is beyond the scope of the evidence available but it does suggest the need to view subject positions as dynamic and differentially available and desirable and suggests a theme that merits further investigation.

In the second poetry lesson subject positions are more fluid and less bounded than the ones just described in Sarah's lesson. In Robert's lesson pupils are listeners and answerers of teacher-posed questions. Like their counterparts in Sarah's lesson, they are obliged to offer the right answers to the teacher's questions. But they are not just the recipients of the poet's text or deferential to Robert as expert and knower, they are positioned as poets, authors and performers such that they too are credited with expertise, knowledge and skill. They are not just pupils, they are also positioned as people with interests (football), prior histories and fun-loving. There is an expectation that they will enjoy school, that school is meant to be meaningful in the here-and-now of their lives. The particular poem that is chosen for the lesson, albeit by the teacher, together with the theme for their own text productions draw on real life experiences to which all can relate. Poetry is about real life and real life is about things outside school, especially popular culture. The explicit recognition of pupils' out-of-school experiences in this lesson extends subjectivities beyond that of being a pupil. The teacher has multiple roles in the lesson. When an efferent stance is being taken he is in more traditional teacher role, asking questions to which he knows the answer; here we see him as evaluator, teller and organiser. When the stance is aesthetic, however, which it is for the vast majority of the lesson, he is negotiator, facilitator, helper and performer. For much of the lesson pupils are applying their knowledge.

These pupil and teacher positionings are accomplished through the use of several different linguistic devices, through the activity itself and through the size and composition of the group.

The Initiation Response Evaluation format is evident throughout the lesson but especially at the beginning, and it is noteworthy that when Robert is involved in the discussion with the whole group (of eight pupils) he is front and centre – he talks to the group, they talk to him; they do not typically address each other. Yet this is not the conventional recitation mode that we saw in Sarah's lesson with the whole class. The interaction facilitated in Robert's lesson is more dialogic, there is more negotiation, there is more overlapping speech, there is more tentativeness (Robert to pupil about his poem 'yes, it can be short ones [phrases] like that, can't it? So that would be better, wouldn't it?'). Everyone talks and the pupils' frame of reference is more strongly prioritised. He positions pupils as having expertise in relation to the topic (football) while positioning himself as lacking expertise, for example he says 'Don't they do "we are the champions", don't they? Have you ever heard that? I don't know much about football, but I know that one'. The interaction has a more natural and less didactic quality because interpretative authority lies not exclusively with him as teacher, but is shared with the learners. For example a pupil asks a question of Robert about another boy's rendering of his poem: 'would it sound better if he did more than two "he scores"?', then he demonstrates saying 'he scores' three times. There are at least some opportunities for pupils to question.

While Robert talks more than the pupils, he does not control who speaks and for how long. The impression is not of compliant and obedient pupils but of pupils who are absorbed by the activity, who are intrinsically motivated by the activity set for them (for example one boy says 'I'm going to do a really good one'). Humour is used to effect equality of status: with reference to the task set, Jake says 'I've got it, I've got it' to which Robert responds 'He's almost got it', and Jake comes back with 'I've actually got it'. This exchange also shows Jake's excitement as he composes his lines. Pupils had considerable opportunity to collaborate and share experience here.

What is also worth noting in this lesson is that the pupils were described as 'low ability'. Previous research suggests that the pattern of authentic questioning and other bids for dialogue is 'dramatically less likely to occur' in such classes (Nystrand *et al*, 2001). These authors suggest that 'In low-track classes ... neither teachers nor students tend to offer dialogic bids, and hence monologic forms of discourse predominate to an even greater degree than in other tracks' (p.37). To a large extent the more dialogic character of this lesson can be attributed to the fact that it occurred in a small group. Previous research has shown that small group work allows the teacher to adopt a more informal role in discussion, to hand over more control to learners (Hall, 2002), essentially to move from a monologic to dialogic mode of interaction (Bakhtin, 1981).

Moving from Monologic to Dialogic Discourse

In both lessons described above interaction sometimes prioritised the recall and display of bits of information and the reportage of what was already known. While the traditional recitation format or IRE pattern resulting in monologic interaction is strongly evident in both lessons one can see how interpretative authority (Dillon, 1990) rests more with the pupils in the second lesson. In the first it is located in the poetic texts under study and with the teacher herself. We can reasonably conclude that Bakhtin's monologism is a stronger feature of lesson one and that dialogism is a stronger feature of lesson two.

What specific contexts are associated with the emergence of dialogic discourse? On the basis of the exploratory evidence presented here, other research on interaction in classrooms (Nystrand *et al*, 2001), and the studies reviewed in the previous chapter, one can speculate that the following factors matter: the size of the group, the nature of the tasks set, the learning objectives and teacher awareness of language as a medium of learning. (The wider policy context is discussed in a moment.) Previous research based on an in-depth study of one teacher over five months (Hall, 2002) shows that while recitation characterises even small group work and is ubiquitous in whole class teaching, the small group seems to offer greater potential for dialogic interaction than the whole class. The evidence above is in line with that finding. The reasons for this are straightforwardly practical – the teacher, being less concerned about classroom management and order, is able to loosen her hold on the discursive reins and confer more freedom and agency to pupils. Secondly, where the set tasks are requiring pupils to construct their own knowledge (such as collaboratively writing verse) dialogue would seem to be an important means towards that construction. Thirdly, where teachers are quite strictly bound by pre-determined learning objectives and where coverage of curricular content are accorded high status (such as recognising similes and metaphors) such tight planning may constrain dialogue; it may even be seen as time-wasting. The latter, especially, is a feature of the Literacy Hour. Robin Alexander (2000) sums up the constraints well when he says '... the organisational context is extremely important, because among the reasons why the discourse of classrooms is so unlike everyday conversation is that it is framed and shaped not only by its pedagogical purposes and power differential between teacher and taught, but also by the no less pervasive power of the clock and the crowd' (pp.392-3).

However in the project the team argued that teachers may be generally quite unaware of the power of language as a medium of learning. Certainly pupils are unaware of this (Hall, 1995). Teachers are highly aware of the organisational and pedagogical strategies and decisions that they use and make as they teach (such as whether and how to group, tasks to set, the resources they need, how to assess, and how to differentiate, etc). They are far less knowledgeable, however, about the way their discourse impacts on the learning opportunities on offer.

Understanding the role of classroom discourse, specifically the notions of literacy stance, interpretative authority, the control of turn-taking, and the control of the topic, is likely to enhance teachers in moving away from recitation as a main mode of classroom interaction. In the field of literacy there are several examples of alternative interactional styles that teachers have been trained to apply successfully. These include collaborative reasoning (Chinn *et al*, 2001; Waggoner *et al*, 1995) experience-text-relationship (ETR) (Au, 1979) and Book Club (Raphael and McMahon, 1994). Recitation and Book Club fall at extreme ends of a continuum in terms of pupil control while the collaborative reasoning and ETR fall in between. If teachers got the opportunity to study and reflect on alternative formats to recitation it is likely that they would be more likely to adjust their classroom interactional patterns for the betterment of their pupils' learning.

It will be recalled from the previous chapter that one of the salient features of accomplished teachers is their scaffolding of children's learning, their 'coaching' of pupils in a way which does not depend on a recitation script. The notion of 'instructional conversation' (Tharp and Gallimore, 1988, p.111), it seems, characterises their interaction. Instructional conversation is:

> Discourse in which expert and apprentices weave together spoken and written language with previous understandings appears in several guises ... The concept itself contains a paradox: 'instruction' and 'conversation' appear contrary, the one implying authority and planning, the other equality and responsiveness. The task of teaching is to resolve this paradox. To most truly teach, one must converse; to truly converse is to teach.

Gordon Wells talks about instructional conversation in the context of what he calls 'an inquiry classroom' (Wells, 1999, p.125). Here it is not only the teacher who is the expert, but pupils too or a group of pupils may hold the role of expert. Teachers who consciously do this appear to be aware of their power over and with learners. In the end teachers do have considerable discretion in deciding how to enact the policies set down in the day-to-day events that make up their programmes. As Wells observes, it is teachers who decide whether to have children working collaboratively in groups or to have them mostly listening to them in whole class teaching:

> whether to value conjectures, supported by argument, or 'correct answers', as defined by the textbook; whether to attempt to get all students to achieve the same outcomes at the same time, or to recognise the various forms of diversity in the student community

and to tailor expectations to take account of these differences, by negotiating appropriate challenges for each individual and providing the assistance that each needs in order to meet them. (p.263)

However, it would be naïve to suggest that teachers in England currently have complete control over the kind of discourse they facilitate in their classrooms. Teachers now have less control over curriculum and pedagogy than they had in the more recent past, as explained in Chapter 3, and therefore they feel less encouraged to be reflective about their practices or to make the kinds of pedagogic adjustments that would allow all children to participate actively in their learning. Indeed research conducted recently with colleagues at the Open University testifies to the narrowing of the curriculum as a result of the external testing regime, more specifically the Standard Assessment Tests in Year 6 classrooms. That project sought to understand inclusive school cultures (Hall *et al*, 2004; Benjamin *et al*, 2003; Nind *et al*, in press) and the way school and classroom practices help or hinder all children to participate fully in their learning. The conclusion drawn was that the SATs-dictated versions of being a pupil massively hinder inclusion. Children did not enjoy equality of respect since their worth seemed to depend so much on their varying ability and willingness to achieve in SATs. The message carried by the culture in the two schools in that study and clearly delivered to and received by pupils was that the major incentive for learning, for working hard to learn, for coming to school, etc, is not the satisfaction of understanding or coming to know; it was not to become a more fulfilled person; it was the reward of 'high numbers' in SATs. The recitation script was predominant in our observational evidence and pupil identities were prescribed according to what we called 'versions of pupildom' that were related to SATs.

In such a scenario education is reworked as a commodity (Ball, 1990; Arnot and Barton, 1992; Apple, 1995; Kenway, 1995; Gewirtz, 2000) and children are commodified as part of that process. Gewirtz, for example, tells how children are recast as commodities which are differentially valued. She says '[n]ow schools and teachers are being encouraged to value students according to what these children can offer the school financially and in terms of image and examination performance' (Gewirtz, 2000, p.361). Our evidence supported the same conclusion. From the perspective of the theme of this chapter, the point being emphasised is that the quality of the interaction in the classroom, which is not beyond the control of the teacher, would, unsurprisingly, appear to be heavily influenced by the broader policy context.

Chapter 6

What Kind of Future?
A Road to Better Things

Discourses and Voices

It is sadly ironic that whilst successive governments since at least the 1980s have sought to raise educational standards and to make schools and teachers more responsible, accountable and professional, they have in reality managed to create a teaching workforce that is more demoralised, bitter, anxious, frustrated, overloaded and keen to leave teaching. Although there is general acknowledgement of the value of many of the educational changes which have been witnessed under governments of both persuasions, many teachers appear to feel that they have lost most of their professional autonomy and control. They are still not seen as trustworthy and they suffer from a surfeit of prescription and regulation and an accompanying loss of professional creativity, fulfilment and satisfaction. It should not come as any surprise, least of all to politicians, that the supply of teachers is becoming a growing problem in terms of both recruitment and retention. Essentially 'top down' approaches by governments have been concerned primarily with structural change and there is a pressing need to acknowledge the necessity of cultural changes within schools related to enhancing teacher development and their involvement in school processes. External government approaches need to acknowledge the centrality of the school community's own internal views and aspirations if a vigorous and genuine renewal is to occur. Both external and internal agency is necessary; change can never simply be mandated from the centre. Direction and impetus for change can and should come from all constituencies within the educational enterprise and this should be welcomed, encouraged and supported by central government which should invite rather than command, and seek to stimulate rather than impose curricular and pedagogic improvements.

Two distinct discourses occur within the current educational system. One is dominant whilst the other is very much subordinate (Ball, 1999). The former encompasses the 'reformed' teacher who, in response to initiatives emanating from central government has been 'colonised', is now much more accountable and is primarily directed in her/his work by performance indicators, competition and comparison. S/he works in a performative institution where her/his professional activity is structured and constrained by external requirements and specified targets which have been set down and determined by politicians. The second, under-valued and under-stated, discourse encompasses the 'authentic' teacher who absorbs but is not fundamentally remade by government reforms. This discourse resents the way governments persist in telling teachers what to do and rather would want them to encourage and support teachers as they indulge in ongoing professional reflection, dialogue and debate about the best and most moral way to teach in our uncertain and constantly changing times. Ball (1999) argues that the current concerns about the low morale of teachers and the associated problems of teacher recruitment and retention may well be, at least partly, associated with the teachers' sense of having had to abandon their authentic commitments to and beliefs about teaching in the face of government reforms. This is not an argument about turning back the clock; much reform was necessary but now may well be the time for both discourses to be heard and for all parties to consider collectively what it means to teach and to be a teacher in today's and tomorrow's world.

The relationship between the narrative of renewal and that of reform is surely dialectical. The gap between the rich and the poor is wide, poverty blights the lives of too many citizens and violence, racism and intolerance are facts of everyday life. Whilst it is right and proper that governments should concern themselves with stimulating and maintaining economic growth and improving educational standards as part of this process, they must also encourage and support teachers as they also address the cultural and social failures of our society. Social justice and economic success can and should go together. Governments need to generate policies concerned with increasing people's capacity to influence and determine their own lives, to be more tolerant and to respect human dignity. Students must leave our schools ready for high skill, high pay work but also with a more robust understanding of the value of diversity, a stronger sense of belonging and active participation in our communities. It is time for an ambitious, imaginative agenda that seeks to empower individuals and communities, values pluralism and promotes a participatory democratic state (Hallgarten, 2000). Education policy needs to recognise the potential which schools can have for serving a wider purpose in their communities rather than simply the educational achievements of their pupils. Schools must be encouraged and supported in their determined efforts to forge links with their communities and prospective teachers need to be trained in such a way that they embrace this new broader role for themselves. Indeed, it might be possible for all professionals working with children, including teachers, social workers and youth workers, to undergo some common multi-agency training and to create and maintain mutually supportive networks.

There is and always will be a need to heed both the voice of reform and that of renewal. There is a serious imbalance between the case for education associated with renewal, social justice and equity and a view of education as little more than a preparation for economic life. One is a view of education as an extension of market forces that helps to prepare students for employment opportunities: teachers are providers, students are consumers; teaching is described in terms of inputs and achievements are measured as outputs. In a competing view, education is seen as a democratising force that helps to prepare students to participate actively in all aspects of democratic life by helping them to develop a sense of efficacy, the ability to think critically, a commitment to compassionate action as well as the basic abilities to read, write and be competent with numbers. A new consensus or *rapprochement* is required which draws upon both viewpoints and this will necessitate changes in the thinking and practices of all those actors involved in the educational enterprise – policy-makers, teachers, parents and pupils. As Hartley (1997) says, the 'truth' about education can no longer be imposed; it will need to be negotiated and the space for such a dialogue needs to be open to all.

There is a need for systemic changes in educational policy and practices so as to address the needs of children growing up in modern society and as far as possible to make these compatible with, but not dominated by, the economic needs of that society. The changes must focus on all aspects of school life from the aims and purposes of the curriculum to its implementation and assessment.

If education really is to be the key to economic prosperity then perhaps what is needed is a fresh look at what we are discovering about learning and how it might be promoted in schools. Teachers must have a role in such an appraisal that must re-examine the didacticism and prescription of some of the approaches contained in national initiatives. If we are to embrace 21st century aims and goals for our educational system then perhaps we also need to have 21st century pedagogies for achieving such aims. A genuine dialogue between those who make policy and those who are expected to implement it is overdue. If there is will and commitment on both sides, we can simultaneously generate *personal* goals for education leading to fulfilment, self-improvement and mastery, *economic* goals leading to marketable knowledge, skills and competences as well as *social* goals leading to greater civic participation and engagement. A strong and determined imagination needs to be brought to bear upon such important issues so that educational goals can be re-formulated and creatively associated with a reconsidered and expanded set of educational practices and procedures. It will no longer be acceptable for a one-way (top down) traffic to continue where those who formulate policy are distant from those who are expected uncritically to implement it. Initiatives for change and improvement can surely come from the bottom up as well as from the top down; the commitment and creativity of teachers needs to be released and begin to replace the colonisation of teachers by central policy-makers.

All initiatives, from wherever they emerge, must be subjected to open discussion; governments should not fear constructive criticism from teachers and ought to see its creative potential. Major initiatives ought to be subjected to independent and constructive evaluation and a 'many voices' approach should replace the quick fix solutions approach currently too common (Coffield, 1999).

Major Issues

The remainder of this chapter sets out to offer some exploratory ideas around which a shared agenda for educational renewal might be constructed. Dialogue between the government and its educators might be structured around a number of key issues. These can be expressed as seemingly simple questions like:

Issue One

What do we know about human learning capabilities and how might such knowledge be used in the formulation of educational goals and the associated reconfiguration of educational practices and procedures?

Issue Two

What is it that we want our students to learn? Is it possible to specify a knowledge content or set of skills and dispositions which will be of benefit to students themselves and also useful to the wider society?

Issue Three

When and where and under what circumstances do we envisage that learning will occur?

Issue Four

What purposes and whose purposes do we expect to be served by the educational system? Why do we want our young people to learn in a certain way?

On the basis of these four issues, a further issue can be raised about the implications for teacher and teacher professionalism. Within which fora and with what support can teachers regain control over their professionalism? Can teachers regain their 'voice' in educational dialogue and can that voice be strengthened though alliances with parents, teacher educators and others? An attempt is made to address these questions in some detail.

Issue One: What Is Known About Human Learning Capabilities?

The quest to understand human learning has undergone dramatic change. Once a matter of philosophical argument, the workings of the human mind and brain are now subject to powerful research tools and from that research a science of learning is emerging. Such a science has important implications for the design of curricula, teaching methods and learning environments as well as suggesting that some existing school practices are inconsistent with what is coming to be known about effective learning.

In the last 25 years or so quite enormous strides have been made in our understanding of the human brain, intelligence and the process of learning. Such thinking will need to be made available to teachers in such a way that it will inform their thinking and professional practices. Whilst intelligence has previously been seen as an individual trait and has prompted the use of systematic, direct instruction followed by supervised practice as a central teaching approach, there is now access to a constructivist model of learning in which the mind is seen as constructing knowledge and understanding through its adaptive capacity to change cognitive structures. Education, within such a viewpoint, is a learner-centred process that involves the provision of an environment that stimulates the construction of knowledge and promotes reflection upon that process. A guided discovery approach is now seen as preferable to direct instruction with learners engaged in inquiry and interaction and teachers acting as guides, mentors and stimulators of the process.

The capabilities of the human brain are no longer seen as being fixed at birth but as being capable of growth and maturity as a consequence of engaging with a stimulating physical and social environment.   Childhood, from conception to adolescence, is seen as a particularly optimal time for neural development and 'exuberant connectivity' (Diamond and Hopson, 1998, p.289). The human brain can and does function on many levels and in many ways at the same time. In parallel fashion, it can engage with thought, emotions, imagination, pre-dispositions and physiological processes: a truly phenomenal human possession.

We now know that the brain is a social brain continuously changing in response to engagement with other people and that it is innately purposeful, constantly searching for patterns and meaning and making sense of experiences. Such sense-making is strongly influenced by emotions; fear inhibits learning whilst challenge and strong self-esteem enhance it.

Our growing knowledge of the complex, multi-faceted brain can be used to inform a renewed appraisal and re-appraisal of educational practices and procedures for the classroom. Howard Gardner's book *Frames of Mind* (1983) is indicative of a sea change in our understanding of what constitutes intelligence in a post-industrial society. In this book he argues against a unitary idea of intelligence as represented by the IQ tradition and instead outlines a theory of multiple intelligences, numbering among them linguistic, musical, logical and mathematical, spatial, bodily-kinaesthetic and personal intelligence. We now know that learners have multiple ways of knowing (Gardner, 1983) and thus benefit from the provision of multiple learning and assessment approaches. A varied pedagogy needs to be accompanied by a supportive emotional climate that is indispensable to effective learning. It is no longer appropriate for students to have teacher interpretations imposed upon them. Rather, they ought to be helped to formulate their own understanding in terms of a range of experiences. Learning how to learn and how to remember can be even more important than what is actually to be learned and remembered.

From theorists like Vygotsky (1978) , Luria (1976), Lave and Wenger (1991) and Rogoff (1991) we more fully understand how knowledge is the creation of social groups and learning is a process of being initiated into the group and learning to use the language, artefacts and tools of the group. Notions like 'cognitive apprenticeship' suggest that apprentice-like learning settings allow students to 'learn by doing' as the processes of particular activities like, say, reading or writing are made visible and demonstrable by more expert others. Cognitive apprenticeship makes processes like problem solving and critical thinking visible to students. They see key elements of the learning process modelled by their teachers who, in turn, show skill in recognising the processes of a task and in demonstrating them in authentic situations. Part of the attractiveness apprenticeship approaches is the way they seek to end the familiar discontinuity between school and the outside world; it is important that schooling at all stages keeps an eye on the outside world including the world of work.

Of course it is important to acknowledge that new ideas and approaches to teaching and learning might clash with the taken-for-granted understandings of teachers and students on these matters. The influence of research on educational practice has been weak for a variety of reasons. Educators generally do not look to research for guidance. The concern of researchers for the validity and robustness of their work, as well as their focus on underlying constructs that explain learning, often differ from the focus of teachers on the applicability of those constructs in real classroom settings with many students, restricted time, and a variety of demands. Even the language used by researchers is very different from that familiar to teachers. Additionally, the full timetables of many teachers leave them with little time to identify and read relevant research. These factors contribute to the feeling voiced by many teachers that research has largely been irrelevant to their work. The new will thus have to compete with, adjust to and even replace the old. Old ideas may be used as starting points however – they might form the basis, in a particular school for example, of a community of learners learning about learning, teachers' own learning as well as that of their pupils. Certainly if the newly accumulating knowledge about human capability is seriously addressed, then a new perspective on effective classroom practice should emerge. Pupils are more likely to participate in learning and to succeed in it if they are allowed a degree of learner independence and choice. There should be an appeal to their intrinsic motivation and their curiosity as, in collaboration with others, they construct knowledge and understanding for themselves through active learning and real-world tasks. The climate of the classroom should acknowledge the importance of emotional well-being and of satisfying social relationships so that high challenges are set and threats are avoided. Complex and holistic thinking abilities should be nurtured through multi-sensory engagement in learning tasks which are situated in the context of practice.

Issue Two: What Do We Want Our Students To Learn?

A second set of questions to be considered in any reform/renewal dialogue will need to be concerned with the content of the curriculum in our schools and the skills and competences which are to be developed ˄s a consequence of engaging intellectually with that particular content.

In the past, when information and knowledge were relatively scarce, it fell upon the school to codify, guard and transmit such knowledge to its pupils. Now, in a time of information abundance, there is a need to rethink the role of the school and its staff and to see the job of teachers as being much more concerned with helping pupils choose wisely from the wide array of knowledge sources that exist (libraries, cd-roms, the internet, multimedia, etc) and to help them to find ways of collecting, collating and utilising that information. Rather than seeing themselves primarily as providers of information teachers might increasingly see their role as being concerned with helping their pupils to organise, manage, analyse, verify, apply and give meaning to information.

Since the world is increasingly complex, ambiguous and uncertain it is important that schools seek to help pupils develop 'habits of mind' appropriate to such complexity and uncertainty. Pupils will need to learn that 'simple solutions' and 'the right answer' are increasingly rare and that life and learning are increasingly more 'messy' than hitherto. A readiness to accept complexity, temporary resolutions and non-algorithmic thinking can, it might be argued, be developed through an emphasis upon inquiry and project-based approaches to learning where it is acceptable, indeed necessary, to be reflective, tentative and suspicious of formulaic solutions. If teachers can cease to be knowledge-disseminators and act more like cognitive and meta-cognitive coaches then pupils are likely to get better as problem-solvers and decision-makers. This, it could be argued, would enhance their motivation and sense of empowerment. They would see a relevance to their studies in schools and they would be prompted to think critically and creatively instead of playing a guessing game where they seek to 'please' teacher by giving the 'right' answers. Their meta-cognitive skills would be enhanced and self-regulated behaviour would be promoted.

The curriculum of our schools, as prescribed in the National Curriculum, is one in which the traditional academic disciplines or subjects predominate as the organising framework. Such a curriculum is based upon the belief that the disciplines represent the major bodies of what is known and that they contain within them the major means of knowing and verification. Certainly, there needs to be a consideration of whether the study of subjects and disciplines will produce the kinds of critical and creative thinking abilities required for life and work in the 21st century. It may well be that we need to start considering subjects not as ends in themselves but as the contexts through which teachers can stimulate, promote and sustain analytical and analogical thinking, problem solving, decision-making and creative skills. Discussing the 'recovery of the comprehensive ideal' Holt (1999) suggests a loosely defined curriculum structure that would allow the school to build and assess its pupils through its own model of the curriculum. Sensitively monitored with externally moderated assessment such a curriculum could entail the construction of interdisciplinary entities that would honour the conceptual structures of their component subjects whilst promoting thematic enquiry and raising civic, economic, moral, social and other important issues.

Pupils cannot simply be given these skills and abilities through a reliance on transmissional teaching. Their acquisition and the associated empowerment of pupils will require a particular approach to learning and teaching – what might be called a new progressivism. It is not enough to develop critical and creative thinking skills in our pupils; simply having certain skills with which learning can effectively occur does not mean that it will occur. Indeed, research indicates that pupils often do not use the thinking skills which they have been taught. They often have the ability to think well but fail to do so – they lack the *dispositions* to think well (Perkins and Tishman, 1998). Teachers will need to give much more serious consideration to the affective and attitudinal dimensions of high level thinking. Pupil motivations, attitudes, values and habits of mind, although they are barely mentioned in National Curriculum, demand much more recognition. It is these dispositions that play a key role in good thinking and to a large extent determine whether thinking skills will actually be used when they are needed (Tishman and Andrade, 1995).

Thinking dispositions are tendencies towards particular patterns of intellectual behaviour. Research associated with Project Zero at Harvard University (for example Perkins, 1995a; 1995b) suggests that such dispositions have three components which can be described as: sensitivity (the perception of the appropriateness of a particular behaviour like detecting bias when reading newspapers); inclination (the felt impetus towards a behaviour like actually looking to detect such bias); and ability (the basic capacity to follow through with the behaviour and detect bias, distortion, etc). Whilst some writers argue that there really is only one overall general disposition to thinking well – what Ellen Langer (1998) calls 'mindfulness'– the team at Harvard outline seven major dispositions which, they argue, teachers might develop in their pupils.

1. Pupils can be encouraged and helped to become broad and adventurous in their thinking: they can be helped to be open-minded, alert to narrow thinking, able to generate multiple options and ready to explore and consider alternative views.
2. Pupils can to be helped to sustain intellectual curiosity; they can be helped to wonder about things, to probe the detail of situations, to observe closely and be ready and able to pose questions.
3. Pupils can be helped to seek connections, to build conceptualisations and to seek explanations for things.
4. Pupils can be encouraged to be strategic in their thinking; they might be taught to set goals for their learning, to make plans and anticipate outcomes. They can be trained to detect a lack or loss of direction in their work.
5. Pupils can be taught to be intellectually careful in their work, to be alert to error and inaccuracy as well as developing precision, organisation and thoroughness in their studies.
6. Pupils can to be taught to evaluate the reasons for things. Being alert to the need for evidence, showing an ability to weigh up and assess reasons as well as regularly questioning such reasons are all desirable classroom (and life) habits.
7. Pupils can to be taught to be meta-cognitive; they can be taught to be aware of and monitor the flow of their thinking. Being able to exert control over their mental processes can be encouraged by teachers as a desirable state of affairs.

Research like that of Project Zero points to intelligence as learnable. Perkins (1995a and 1995b) recognises that whilst research still has some way to go, there are sufficient grounds to believe that pupils can be helped to 'outsmart IQ' and learn to think better in a range of contexts both in and out of school. Examining the research associated with a variety of teaching and learning initiatives associated with the learnability of thinking dispositions, Perkins concludes that pupils can learn to be more intelligent in a number of ways. They can learn, as noted above, to be more reflective, to provide more reasons and explanations, to seek more alternatives and to be more imaginative. Research indicates that gains in these areas persist over a number of years, and some research also indicates that these gains are reflected in modest gains in IQ scores – if that is still a relevant concept. Of course, researchers in the 'thinking skills movement' are not simply concerned with imparting thinking skills so that pupils can do better in tests. The hope is to teach pupils to transfer and internalise the thinking skills they learn so that they will be better thinkers on their own, in a variety of contexts in and outside of school.

Perkins' work and the work from Project Zero at Harvard generally give a sound rationale for teachers to aspire to help pupils to develop strong and stable thinking dispositions. Work by Tishman, Perkins and Jay (1992) has explored possible teaching approaches which might help to develop thinking dispositions. Their view is based on the idea that thinking dispositions are learned through a process of enculturation rather than direct transmission. Thinking dispositions, they argue, like many human character traits, develop in response to a particular cultural milieu. They maintain that the cultural milieu that best teaches thinking dispositions is a culture of thinking – an environment that reinforces good thinking in a variety of both tacit and explicit ways. Such a classroom provides models of good reasoning behaviour. Through exemplars from both in and out of school and through teacher modelling, pupils can see what good thinking looks like. The teacher in such an environment makes explicit what good reasoning is. Pupils are helped to understand why good reasoning is important, what counts as evidence in different contexts, how to formulate and test hypotheses, and how to justify positions. Pupils need to be given explicit opportunity to practise methods of seeking and testing evidence, constructing hypotheses and so on. The classroom environment should be one in which there are plenty of opportunities for peer interaction about reasoning. Good thinking grows when it is embedded in meaningful contexts where pupils are encouraged to talk about their own reasoning and the reasoning of peers. They should be encouraged to discuss, for example, the likelihood of events described in a story and to give reasons why they accept or reject a particular aspect of the narrative. Such reasoning should be open to comment from peers in an atmosphere of exploration and mutual tolerance. There should be regular formal and informal feedback about thinking and reasoning. Teacher feedback, peer feedback and self-feedback are all ways of strengthening and shaping the developing thinking dispositions (Hall and Burke, in press). A readiness to share one's thoughts, ideas and lines of thinking ought to be supported, encouraged and valued.

A classroom where transmission teaching dominates, where most of the work is outcomes-driven and where teaching to the test is commonplace is not likely to be a productive breeding ground for the thinking skills so needed both in and out of school. Indeed, many of the characteristics of so called 'progressive' classrooms, castigated so fiercely by often ill-informed critics, would seem to be more appropriate as environments where the development of thinking skills could occur. It may well be that what is required in schools is a 'new progressivism' and a socio-constructivist pedagogy rooted in recent research on the way children learn and the best ways of ensuring that they do so.

Krechevsky and Stork (2000) discuss the ways in which much educational practice and thinking are in need of re-assessment in the light of what we are discovering about teaching and learning. Exhortations about preparing for the challenging world into which our young people are growing contain very little consideration about the way schools might also make changes. If children are to be prepared for full, meaningful and productive lives in the post-industrial world then perhaps they need to have that preparation in schools about which many of our currently widely held assumptions have been rigorously challenged. From their Project Zero starting point, and drawing on recent cross-cultural research, Krechevsky and Stork use the example of the municipal pre-schools and infant-toddler centres of Reggio Emilia, in Italy, to challenge these assumptions and suggest alternative ways for imagining classrooms of the future. Although they ground much of their discussion in early childhood, they believe that the images found in Reggio Emilia can inform education well beyond the pre-school years.

They identify several key assumptions about teaching and learning which they think need to be re-evaluated in looking towards a curriculum of the future. The first erroneous assumption is that learning is solely an individual activity. Learning, they argue, needs to be seen as both a group activity and an individual achievement brought about by shared activity. Whilst children in schools are seldom out of some group or other, in most classrooms there is a focus on individual performance and achievement. Teachers tend to plan work and assess it with individuals in mind and scant emphasis is placed on true collaboration as a critical way to build intellectual understanding. Krechevsky and Stork suggest that learning in a group fosters a kind of emotional and intellectual learning that is qualitatively different from that which results from individuals working alone. A kind of 'distributed cognition' occurs and learning in groups enables individuals to construct new knowledge and understanding by using the learning strategies and outcomes of others. Individuals grow by confronting and accepting viewpoints different from their own. Each child in a group brings their own unique perspective and way of thinking and, as they communicate with each other, they make their thinking 'visible' and available to each other. Individuals need not get lost or swamped in a group, rather they can have their intellectual functioning supported and enhanced.

A second erroneous assumption is the idea that teachers are consumers rather than makers of theory. Experience at Reggio Emilia suggests that teachers do not rely exclusively on theory generated elsewhere and imported into the classroom. Rather, by reflecting on their own practices and pondering, speculating and examining documentary evidence by and about children's learning, teachers can make theory for themselves and extend their own professionalism. They can begin to see themselves as theory builders as well as theory consumers.

Another assumption these authors question is that testing improves educational outcomes. In documenting evidence of children's learning Krechevsky and Stork warn against the almost obsessive concern in modern education systems with tests and testing. They argue that too much time and energy is devoted in schools to judging, testing and measuring outcomes whilst more emphasis ought to be placed upon knowing more about how children learn and the contexts and processes in which that learning occurs. Research in Year 6 classrooms in England shows how pervasive the testing regime is and how identities are dictated by the perceived demands of the external tests (Hall *et al*, in press). A combination of educational products and processes is required in order to provide the best evidence upon which future curricular and pedagogical decisions can be made. Teachers will be better placed to find the 'zone of proximal development' for each child by knowing about them as fully as possible; how they learn, in what contexts their best learning occurs and with what support and help it happens. In making learning plans for children teachers are urged to avoid a total concentration on the cognitive. They are advised to adopt a broad view of learning incorporating cognitive, emotional, aesthetical and ethical aspects (Gardner, 1983) and they should seek to promote an approach to learning that incorporates wonder, amazement and a sense of adventure.

As long as knowledge acquisition remains the major preoccupation of our school system there is the danger of pupils indulging in 'surface learning' as they attempt to cope with increasing amounts of knowledge and wider, more packed curricula like the National Curriculum. They risk ending up learning less about more things. Langer (1998) describes the process as 'mindless learning' with pupils on 'automatic pilot' during most of their school years. Studies which promote 'deep' thinking are required with the focus shifting to a concern with using subject knowledge for the development of thinking skills and dispositions.

Another important point which educators will need to consider is the way in which schooling is assumed to be a preparation for life but, in fact, is quite insulated from many of life's important issues. The curriculum has little to say explicitly about important issues like the world of work, the nature of the economy, parenting, poverty, ageing and many other important topics which are absent or marginal in the National Curriculum. Life's practicalities and its moral and social dimensions appear to be left to take care of themselves and many young people are remarkably ill-informed about such things. Perhaps it is time for value laden issues like abortion, pollution, racism, human rights, poverty and inequality, as well as activities like mediation, conflict reduction, values analysis and clarification and active enquiry to be brought into the centre of the school curriculum. The importation into the school curriculum of contentious issues would, of course, raise questions about worth, value and desirability and would inevitably provoke discussion about relativist and universal value systems.

In its report *Our Global Neighbourhood*, the United Nations (1995) urges such debates and, whilst acknowledging the sovereignty of nations, proposes a core of values which, it suggests, represents a global civic ethic. Global citizenship is based on the ideal of a citizen whose primary loyalty is to human beings throughout the world and whose national, local and group loyalties are considered secondary in importance. The report's implications for schools are that 'educated' pupils are those who engage in a critical examination of themselves, their traditions and their actions through inquiry and debate ruled by reason and fact. They will also be helped to cultivate their humanity by seeking to understand other cultures, traditions and points of view. Without opening their minds in this way the pupils' concept of global citizenship would remain a hollow and abstract one.

Issue Three: What are the Optimal Circumstances within which Successful Learning Occurs?

This issue is concerned with the ways in which people can and do learn and when and where such learning can best take place. It prompts teachers to consider the places, spaces, time-slots, contexts and learning processes and styles through which learners can be helped to be successful and productive.

Traditionally schools have generated a dominant form of learning involving the reception, memorisation and recitation of content usually in verbal or in written form and a form of teaching, as noted in the previous chapter, of teacher dominated talk and questioning. Some pupils, of course, learn well within this approach although research mounts an increasingly clear challenge to the idea that there exists one dominant mode of learning and strongly suggests that learners have a larger set of learning preferences and strategies available to them (Gardner, 1983; Perkins, 1995b). Such variety, it is argued, necessitates a reconceptualising of curricula and teaching strategies in order to provide multiple contexts and means through which diverse learners with multiple learning preferences can engage with content using a varied range of different learning strategies and intelligences.

In places as different as the developed USA and developing Malaysia, for example, Smart Schools (Perkins, 1995b) have been developed to transform education away from memory-based learning to education that stimulates thinking, creativity and caring in all children (Vision 2020 Malaysia: The Way Forward). According to Perkins (1995b), such schools are based on two guiding principles:

1. Learning is a consequence of thinking, and good thinking is learnable by all pupils.
2. Learning should involve deep understanding and involve the flexible, active use of knowledge.

These beliefs generate key ideas in a Smart School which, for example, urges that the choice of disciplinary and inter-disciplinary subject matter be based upon a prime consideration about whether it has the potential to provide deep thinking. Such thinking, it is suggested, is available to all children when it is stimulated, championed and scaffolded by teachers in such a way that it boosts pupils' views on their own abilities. When the emphasis is upon deep understanding and the teacher helps to build bridges from what is known to new contexts then significant learning can occur. Pupils also need to be involved in teacher-pupil, pupil-pupil and self-assessment and to see assessment as an opportunity to reflect upon and discuss their present understanding and to contemplate the next steps in their learning.

Central to many interpretations of the Smart School concept is the regular deployment of information and communication technology (ICT) as an enabler of the learning process. The recognition of the diversity of learning styles and the need for more varied models of the learning process are evident in on-line education where learning occurs within an electronic and virtual context that is asynchronous in time, learner-centred and unbound by limitations of space and distance. Clearly ICT can have a very profound influence on the quality of teaching and learning if the appropriate training and resources are in place. New information technologies and the learning highways that they create can bring learning and expertise to pupils and teachers and can mean that pupils and teachers can learn anytime, anyplace and with 'virtually' anybody. They provide what Perkins (1995a) refers to as a 'person plus' system of learning, the person plus the mediating tools and technologies which can amplify the mind.

What can emerge with the skilled use of ICT is a pupil-centred learning system in which various providers of content, tools and learning processes can augment or even replace the school as the major source of learning for many. This is especially true for those outside the formal educational system who can now study a huge range of high quality courses and materials that can be adapted to suit individual preferences. Rather than the principle of 'one size fits all' it is now the case that technology in all its forms can allow much more of a tailor made approach to individual learning needs. By using technology a learner can interact with a wider range of teachers and other learners. Content can be presented in a wide range of forms and the learner can often proceed in a self-directed manner and pace often with immediate and 'just in time' feedback for corrective action. Teachers can shift their professional emphasis from the repetitive process of dispensing information to the much more professional role of facilitating analysis, critique and synthesis.

For the most part schools have not yet fully grasped the potential of ICT in their curriculum and pedagogic practices. It has been powerfully argued that much effort and change are required if schools are to harness fully the potential of ICT in their curricula (Buckingham and Macfarlane, 2001). Pupils must be taught digital literacy as well as conventional literacies and must be empowered to understand and critically participate in the digital culture which surrounds them. The aim must be to produce informed, critical, active users of digital media who can become both creative producers and critical consumers of digital media (Chapter 3). They must be able, for example, to create intelligent and useful web pages of their own as well as to use critically those of other people. Notions of digital literacy will require a willingness to think beyond the narrow confines of the current National Literacy Strategy.

Issue Four: What and Whose Purposes ought to be Served by the Education System?

It may be time to reconsider the seemingly simple question 'why learn?'. Our education system is likely to benefit from a frank exchange of views between those who see the purposes of education as being rooted in a concern for individual development and growth and those who see individual learning as being subsumed within a stronger, more pressing concern for the development of the nation and its competitive advantage in the global economy. For some, the purposes of the educational system are concerned with the induction of individuals into the norms and values of society and the acceptance of civic responsibilities. Issues are raised about whether the growth and development of the person (represented most strongly in the child-centred model of education) is compatible with a view of education as a process for the acquisition of competitive competences, that is the knowledge, dispositions and skills deemed by the government and others to be critical for making the country internationally competitive.

Many would argue that core competences like problem solving capacity, decision-making skills, communication and computational skills, computer literacy and a resilient attitude to change should lie at the heart of any school curriculum. International, comparative assessments like those in mathematics and science by the International Assessment of Educational Progress (IAEP) and the International Association for the Evolution of Educational Achievement (IEA) consortia are often used to berate teachers and to accuse schools of ineffectiveness and lack of clear focus. It is strongly argued that the engine of growth in the economy in the information age resides increasingly in education. Certainly the OECD has made strong suggestions to its members to shape their policies so as to strengthen the connections between the economy and the aspirations of the educational system. Economic growth is seen as being directly dependent upon education. Maintaining a country's competitive edge requires a deepening and enlarging of its intellectual capacity and requires that creative intelligence be placed at the top of the education system's list of objectives. A 'theory of human capital', or rather an over-simplified version of it, derived from the writings of Schultz (1961) and Becker (1975) is confidently and seductively sloganised by politicians, the media and representatives of the business world who, ignoring the detail and intricacies of the theory, posit a simple and uncomplicated relationship between improvements in educational standards and the economic well-being of society. Coffield (1999, p.482) explains how such a simplified 'set of unquestioned articles of faith' is used to claim that individuals, communities and whole nations are poor, or risk being poor, because they have not had their human capital developed. Such simplifications divert attention away from structural failures and injustices and blame victims for their poverty. The simplification of the theory ignores the social capital requirements for effective development. Trust, shared values and supportive networks are necessary as well as individual effort. Applying human capital theory in a naïve way runs the risk of creating a new moral economy where some individuals are treated as more 'desirable' than others. If, for example, people are valued according to their likely contribution to the economy then there is not likely to be much room in such an economy (or in many schools for that matter) for people with learning difficulties. Advocacy for a simplified version of human capital theory permits politicians to blame schools and teachers for many of society's claimed problems. Politicians in this scenario appear to be taking action and 'doing something about the problems' which they couch in terms of 'quick fixes' that will support political careers based on four or five year cycles.

Simplifications and quick fixes merely divert attention away from the economic and social reforms that are critical for any real effect on the more tractable problems like low levels of investment.

It is time to re-examine the shortcomings of the dominant utilitarian discourse and to acknowledge the dangers of over-promoting business values in school. Alternative perspectives need to be heard and the role of the school in promoting a just and fair society explored.

Teachers and their Professionalism

On the basis of the four issues raised above and on the basis of the arguments in the preceding chapters, how might teachers re-assert their professionalism?

It is indeed ironic that at a time when there is tighter surveillance and external control of teachers' professional practices, another growing pressure from recent developments in cognitive science is urging a new look at curriculum and pedagogy and placing learning how to learn and reflective practice on the top of the list of educational aims. These two pressures – external control of teachers' practices and an emphasis on autonomy and self-reflection – appear to be somewhat difficult to reconcile. Whilst government initiatives appear to result in a lowering of professionalism and a technicist status for teachers, the new theories of learning are calling for highly sophisticated classroom facilitation by teachers and a strong knowledge base. The situation becomes even more complicated and demanding if we consider the increasingly diverse cultures, values, expectations and life conditions which pupils bring to school with them. Day (1997) outlines a challenging scenario within which teachers for the 21st century are working. Our classrooms are populated by pupils from a wide range of cultural and ethnic backgrounds. They stay within the school system in greater numbers for a longer period of time. Increasingly more pupils with special educational needs are taught in ordinary classrooms in mainstream schools. Many children grow up in poverty and endure a multiplicity of stresses that may often exhibit themselves in behavioural and learning difficulties in school. Bullying is a worrying feature of life in many schools and truancy is a growing problem amongst the school population. Today's teachers are indeed faced with the breathtaking challenges of trying to meet government demands for rising standards, adopt a pedagogy which is in tune with modern knowledge of the nature of pupils and their learning in an environment characterised by social, economic, educational and cultural diversity. Simple formulaic responses are totally inadequate to the task – small wonder there are considerable problems in teacher recruitment and retention. Nothing short of a professional renewal can possibly help teachers to cope with such challenges.

The challenges facing teachers present themselves in specific forms concerned as they are with specific pupils in specific schools. It is at the level of individual school that such problems will even have a chance of being resolved. A renewed and reformed professionalism derived from the study of such problems represents a possible way forward.

Etzioni (1969) has outlined what teachers require if they are truly to be a profession. They need a *technical culture* (a set of highly polished classroom skills), a *service ethic* (a commitment to meeting their pupils' needs), a *professional autonomy* (collegiate control over their profession and its practices) and a clear *professional identity* (which commits teachers to each other). Teachers, it would appear, have much to do if they are to rebuild their professionalism. The progressive stripping away of their professionalism and the increasingly technicist nature of their work leaves them far from satisfying Etzioni's requirements for true professionalism. They will need spaces, occasions and the impetus to reflect critically upon their practice in order to fashion new knowledge and beliefs about ways and means of meeting their professional challenges. It will simply not do for a government to attempt audaciously to tell teachers everything which they require. The way forward is not systemic top down missives, diktats and requirements. Neither is it a wholesale reliance on the TTA and its particular brand of professional wisdom. The answer lies perhaps in local school-level capacity-building policies which view professional knowledge as constructed by practitioners for use in their own immediate contexts. The government's job is to encourage, support and enable professional development activities rather than specify what they ought to be. School staff must be encouraged and supported as they restructure their habits and practices so as to further the learning of teachers and pupils. The government must see its role as creating a climate, the incentives and the resources for school or local collaborations of schools to reform and renew themselves. The government's penchant for 'one size fits all' just will not do; it simply misses the point. Old models of 'in-service' and 'staff development' delivered after school and at weekends at sites away from the school are inadequate. Top down support is required for bottom up reform (Day, 1997). Local initiatives can be guided by newly emerging paradigms of professional development (Darling-Hammond, 1993) and may require liaison with higher education institutions or other consultants and 'critical friends'. They need to be grounded, however, in notions of 'situated cognition' and the embedding of teacher development in their everyday activities. Teachers are ill served by 'how to' type prescriptions emitted away from the context of the their work; they are likely to learn best from doing, reading, consulting, reflecting and collaborating with the focus provided by their own work and that of their pupils. Schools need to be better structured so that theory and practice rub together and both provide a basis from which professional growth and development can grow. It goes without saying that teachers need time to benefit from such synergy.

The government must recognise that improved teaching skills, although obviously important, are not enough of themselves. Teacher idealism, which lies at the heart of all good teaching, needs to be re-kindled. The narrow technicist focus that characterises much that has emanated from government initiatives through the work of the TTA needs to be changed. All teachers need much more than subject knowledge and classroom skills; they need to think deeply about educational aims and values and to consider critically matters of curriculum content and pedagogy. It is not acceptable that the lion's share of in-service education has concentrated upon bringing teachers up-to-date with the latest government top down initiative or package. Such a narrow focus has hindered personal development and the continuing development of teaching practices and strategies. The notion of teachers as technicians in which teachers receive and then implement policies developed by outsiders away from the context of need is symptomatic of the managerialist oriented focus of the TTA and is inappropriate for the true professional. What is required is an approach to professional development which is born out of self-study based upon the engagement with, and the reflection upon, real professional issues (Dadds, 2001).

How can teachers find opportunities for such reflection? Certain schools in Australia, even in the face of 'the effects of so-called educational reforms and re-structuring, allegedly aimed at converting them into front-line warriors engaged in the restoration of sagging international competitiveness' (Smyth *et al*, 1997 p.1; Loughran, 1999) have managed to create 'dialogic space'. It is in such spaces that pedagogical conversations can occur around issues of teaching and learning and in which teachers can interrogate the current tendencies of individualism and hopelessness bred by an increasingly marketised view of the school. The research reveals that in some schools at least teachers still find ways of keeping dialogue about what works in classrooms alive. They manage to continue to craft, analyse and test their own local theories about pedagogy and school and classroom organisation. Using a 'voiced research' approach the researchers indulged in 'purposeful conversations' with teachers on the assumption that teachers have important stories to tell about their work, the context of schooling and what supports and inhibits teaching and learning (Smyth *et al*, 1997). Through these conversations the researchers came to understand the ways that teachers in some schools managed to harness the structures of their schools to make them work for pupils in more inclusive and democratic ways. They regarded themselves as interpretative communities which engaged parents, pupils and teachers in discussions about sustaining a culture of learning. Three school factors seemed to be especially important in dialogic schools communities: a) basing the school's work upon democratic practices and policies; b) maintaining a coherent support system for teachers; and c) ongoing discourse about teaching and learning.

Four further features stand out about such schools:

- they know where they want to go and have a clear set of beliefs, ideas and values which they hold about schooling, theory, curriculum and pedagogy;
- they create an administrative framework and set of practices which allow them to enact their vision;
- they are aware of opposition to their approach and confront and deal with it whether it is within the school or within the community they serve; and
- they act strategically through effective leadership which engages all of the members of the community in socially-just education for all.

In country after country in recent decades the work of schools and teachers has been dramatically changed in ways that have overtly excluded teachers from discussions about what is feasible and desirable. This, at a time when schools are struggling to cope on a day-to-day basis with the effects of poverty, family fragmentation and disintegration and an increasingly diverse pupil population. Whilst any mention of social justice seems to have been expunged from the discourse of the education system it is very much alive in those 'dialogic' schools struggling to enhance the life chances of large numbers of pupils. Through debate and critique about what is happening to education, through experimentation, shared risk-taking and distributive forms of leadership they refuse to succumb to the fear which dismissive criticism, league tables and the policing of their activities instil. They manage to address their daily challenges constructively and creatively.

The comments of Mahony and Hextall (1997) are interesting here as they describe how the conception of what constitutes the 'effective teacher' is being reshaped by the TTA in line with particular responses to demands for the United Kingdom to become more competitive in the global economy. Teachers' responsibilities in relation to social justice are evaluated as the 'true purposes of schooling' and the need for 'effective teachers' is redefined. If concerns for social justice are about trying to bring the best things in society like a good education to the many rather than to the few then there is little said about such aspirations in the documentation of the TTA. The ways in which educational progress and success can be inhibited by factors associated with social class, gender, race, sexuality and disability seem to be ignored within the reconstruction of teachers and teaching. The Agency seems unaware or uncaring about the ways that schools exist and are structured by social inequalities. There seems to be no real connection between the pedagogy and curriculum discussed by the TTA and the sophisticated skills required of teachers to cope effectively with such pupil diversity and the opportunities and challenges presented by such diversity. It is surely time for teachers to re-assert their professionalism and resist its disintegration. They must have a stronger say in the debates about what constitutes relevant and desirable professional knowledge and practice; they need to be key participants in helping to determine the goals, processes, content and conditions of their own professional training and also the learning of their pupils in schools and colleges.

One possible way forward for teachers might be to forge new and more meaningful alliances with parents and the local communities which schools serve. Exhortations about the value of building strong relationships between the home and the school have a long history in England and date back at least to the Plowden Report (1967). Unfortunately, however, there remains quite a gap between the rhetoric and the reality. Frequently used metaphors like 'open' schools and parent-teacher 'partnerships' appear regularly in the speeches and writing of politicians of all persuasions. However, as reported in earlier chapters, the reality would seem to be that middle class parents reap a disproportionate amount of the rewards of education. If meaningful partnerships are to be developed between teachers and parents then both parties must see the mutual value of such pairings. Changed behaviour by both parties, together with a strong leap of faith, is required. Teachers must change their ways and genuinely recognise the integral part they can play in the development and educational support of children. It will simply not be enough for schools to keep parents at a distance from real decision-making and relegating them to being 'useful' in raising funds, providing transport or carrying out educational support in, say, literacy and numeracy activities where they are strictly managed and monitored by teachers with no real input of their own. At the same time parents will need to be convinced of the value of a stronger participation in the life and work of the school and how they have much skill and expertise that they can bring to children's learning. They need to see themselves as complementary to teachers rather than their adversaries.

Since the 1980s a view of parents as consumers has developed and legislation has given parents new rights over their children's schooling. Most important amongst these are the right to choose the school that their child will attend, the right to be involved in school management through a governing body and the right to an array of information about the school including its pupils' achievements. Schools which can demonstrate effective practices and policies in teaching and learning will, it is claimed, flourish through high enrolments whilst less satisfactory schools will need to reform or go to the wall. Of course one must always be cautious when evaluating parental impact and influence upon the running of a school. Writers like Vincent (2001) have shown how a school's parents do not constitute a homogeneous group, especially in urban, pluralist contexts and how parental influence upon a school is likely to vary along ethnic, social class and gender lines.

Governors in schools have been given considerable statutory responsibilities over a range of school matters like staffing, curriculum and discipline. Research, however, indicates that their activities tend to be governed by the high regard with which they tend to hold the knowledge and expertise of head teachers whom they seldom challenge (Munn, 1993). Supporting the school and its policies seem to be regarded by governors as their principal role; generally they make few attempts at initiating or formulating school policy. Parents, it would seem, have not been involved as policy participants and partners in the key issues of schooling. Arising out of their explorations of parental 'voice' in a sample of schools, Vincent and Martin (1999, p.19) state that 'to be a citizen is to fulfill a largely passive role. Engaging in processes of deliberation and participation with regard to public sector institutions is an unfamiliar concept for most people'.

It would appear that there is no strong tradition of parents participating and taking part in collaborative action with teachers about important and critical matters in schools. In only a few schools it seems that there are 'collective spaces' being opened up where participatory approaches to decision-making might take place. In some schools Vincent and Martin did find spaces that had been opened up (albeit by the school and to some extent on the school's terms) and within these spaces they witnessed modes of association where all had the right to articulate their point of view. The authors conclude that increasing parental participation in school decision-making is a project worth pursuing and that since parental voice is so fragile, limited and generally tentative, teachers should ensure that they do not deflect parental energies and silence their voices. They should see parents and help parents to see themselves as valuable partners in decision-making. There needs to be an end to the lay/professional divide. Governments need to replace their fine-sounding rhetoric about home and school partnerships with specific proposals and policies designed to facilitate home-school deliberation and debate. What is needed is a vision of schools as community-based democracies in which parents not only have a voice but are actually listened to.

Education Action Zones (EAZs) were part of New Labour's policy to improve standards in schools and reduce social exclusion. It was envisaged that they would be more inclusive than previous government, LEA and teacher-led alliances; part of their aim was a communitarian intention to empower communities by engaging local people in the development and delivery of policies. They were intended to be seen as part of a wider effort to shift the nature of educational governance by reducing the power of historic partners like LEAs and teachers in favour of parents, community organisations and the private sector. Research, however, questions whether the Forums at the governing centres of EAZs are currently fulfilling government's hopes at empowering parents and local communities. Forums are not as inclusive as had been hoped; indeed their composition and operation reflects still further consolidation of professional and managerial interests. Although EAZ policy was supposedly to capture grass roots initiatives, research by Theakston, Robinson and Bangs (2001) explored evidence collected from NUT members and other sources and showed that, by and large, teachers felt excluded from the development of zones. It was head teachers who were more likely to be involved although the better head teachers did involve their staff by acting as conduits between them and the zone managers.

Power and Gewirtz (2001) examined a collection of bids for EAZ status and suggest that they were flawed from the outset in that they appeared to have an insufficiently comprehensive grasp of the nature of social exclusion and disadvantage. They suggest that the bids appear to contain misconceptions about the nature of the difficulties being experienced by the populations they are designed to help and also about the resolution of these difficulties. They acknowledge that economic injustices within the zones are recognized and that the poverty and economic disadvantage are well described. However, they maintain that there is scant appreciation of the insidious injustices associated with people being disrespected, stereotyped and not having their own culture acknowledged (cultural injustice). Additionally, they note the lack of appreciation of circumstances which prevent people from participating fully in decisions which affect their lives (associational injustice). The approach adopted in the EAZs is one which appears to pathologise the supposed beneficiaries of the EAZ initiatives and an aggressive, militaristic feel suffuses the bids. For example, there is reference to the need for 'rapid response teams' to 'isolate and eliminate disruptive behaviour' and deal with aggressive parents. Parents tend to be mentioned in terms of 'weaknesses and challenges' and never in terms of 'strengths and opportunities'. They found practically nothing in the bids about increasing parental involvement in school decision-making and parents, pupils and even teachers are not especially well represented in the Education Action Forums which were to run the EAZ. The constitutions of the Forums suggest that they are clearly not designed to foster the widespread democratic participation of pupils, parents and teachers. The researchers conclude that if social justice and inclusion are to be fostered there must be a more sophisticated understanding of the complexity of the injustices in operation and of the nature and scope of the remedies needed to address them.

Both parents and teachers need to recognise their own passive roles and likewise to acknowledge that hitherto and at present they themselves have, for the most part, relegated the pupils, supposedly at the heart of the educational process, to the status of voiceless, opinion-less and passive objects to be processed. Parents and teachers alike need to guard against being seen by pupils as mounting a 'conspiracy of elders' (Heywood-Everett, 1999, p.7) and must encourage and support pupil voice and agency. It is quite surprising that in a climate where there is so much talk of markets and consumers the pupils in schools have not been seen as worth consulting. Only quite recently are we beginning to take account of the voices of pupils. They can provide reliable accounts of their school experiences and being listened to is likely to increase their commitment to learning and to boost their achievements. Of course, adopting an open stance to the views of pupils is not meant to suggest that their ideas should be the final and conclusive word in how schools need to change. To accept their views as the sole guide in school improvement is 'to accept a romantic view of students that is just as partial and condescending as excluding them completely from the discussions' (Nieto, 1994, p.398). If there is to be a reassertion of a view of education as helping young people not just to be employable but to grow into active, informed, critical and responsible citizens, then they must have experiences of making decisions about their school and their own learning. As Hodgkin and Newall (1998, p.11) say 'democracy is not something which is taught. It is something which is practised'.

Pupils are capable of getting involved in democratic decision-making about issues relating to school policy and practice. Macbeth (1984) reminds us that other countries like Denmark already have such process partnerships built around the learner in which school councils exist for pupils to discuss policy and practice. As things stand at the moment in England parents, teachers and pupils are placed at some considerable distance from real decision-making in education. Teachers have had their roles centrally prescribed for them, pupils generally have no voice at all and parents have been 'used' and manipulated from the centre. The Conservative government constructed parents as 'consumers' of a product which they had no say in creating. More recently parents have had their sphere of influence narrowed down in the New Labour government's home-school agreements pertaining largely to issues about punctuality, regular attendance, discipline and homework. In no sense can parents be seen as being invited to become joint decision-makers in the life and work of their schools; at best they are accountable extras.

For real partnership to come into being teachers and parents will need to assemble a common agenda rooted in national guidelines and frameworks but centred on the educational needs of the actual children in their particular school. They will need to articulate their aims and values and create a plan of action through which such aims can be achieved. This will require a deeper involvement of parents in school governance and a broader base of parental influence through parent associations. Consensus will not be easy or automatic; the recognition and resolution of conflict through the joint efforts of all those involved in the community life of the school will be necessary if partnership is to be more than a programmatic metaphor, a political gesture.

It is unfortunate although perhaps understandable that teachers, feeling that central governments have increasingly denied them their professional autonomy, have not always showed a strong commitment to building meaningful home and school relationships. Finding a way in which all parents in a school and not just the active and unrepresentative few can have a real stake in the life and work of their school is a daunting task. Macbeth (1989) outlines a four stage progression in the growth of home-school partnerships which depends upon teachers' acceptance of a new form of their professionalism. The 'Self Contained School' (Stage One) is characterised by guarded teacher autonomy with only a very limited and formalised contact with parents, little or no parental consultation or choice and curriculum and pedagogy very much seen as the teacher's domain. A second stage occurs when schools begin to make tentative experiments in home and school relationships, although teachers still want to restrict parental influence and tend to blame parents for poor pupil achievement and bad behaviour. It is likely that most schools in England are at either Stage One or Stage Two. Happily there will be some schools in which there is a growing and strengthening commitment to strong home and school relationships (Stage Three) where close liaison and regular consultation with parents is encouraged. Such schools genuinely recognise the value of home teaching and encourage parents to get involved fully with school issues. These schools make vigorous attempts to adapt themselves to include parental voices. Macbeth describes a fourth stage where the home and the school represent a strong concordat.

Finally, teacher recruitment and retention need to be addressed. The mounting seriousness about the recruitment and retention of teachers presents an opportunity for some straight talking amongst all members of the education community about what has led to this crisis and how collectively those who govern and those who are governed might generate possible solutions. The government needs to acknowledge that, despite the considerable successes of many of their reforms, there is a crisis within the teaching profession where morale has never been so low. The problems of recruitment and wastage will only be reduced, according to a study conducted by the Institute of Public Policy Research (IPPR) (Johnson and Hallgarten, 2002), if there are significant improvements in the job itself. Currently teaching is regarded as unattractive and dissatisfying by many teachers because of the unnecessary and excessive workload, poor pupil behaviour, poor management and the loss of opportunities for creativity and professional autonomy which offer satisfaction (Johnson and Hallgarten, 2002). Research findings like those of Spear *et al* (2000) clarify the sources of job satisfaction and dissatisfaction and indicate clearly that the intrinsic features of the job of teaching are without doubt the most important. They indicate that government needs to give very careful consideration to the roles which teachers are currently expected to fulfill; it is the nature and content of the job which is producing teacher frustration and unhappiness. Extrinsic factors like pay and conditions of work are less important than the intrinsic characteristics of the profession like working with young people, collaborating with colleagues and being more creative and autonomous than is currently permissible. There appears to be a widespread belief amongst teachers that they are constantly under attack. Many feel that in the name of accountability they are required to complete an unnecessary amount of paperwork which contributes little to pupil performance.

PriceWaterhouseCoopers (2001) concluded that many primary teachers are often required by their head teachers to produce detailed lesson plans and evaluations which represent a workload that may be disproportionate to the value it adds. It seems that teachers do not object to the work *per se* but feel that much of the workload is not contained in the work itself but rather in the production of written accounts of it. The teachers find that much of this imposed rather than self-generated paperwork is irksome, unnecessary and unproductive. Teachers consistently report that they enjoy the core work of the classroom and want the responsibility and freedom to determine the course of events in the classroom. Applying their own initiative and creative skills to curriculum content and pedagogy is preferred to central prescription and incessant accountability demands which weaken professional confidence. There is no way that government aspirations will be delivered and sustained whilst the teachers, those who must 'deliver the goods', are demoralised, frustrated and keen to leave the profession. The time is ripe for a re-appraisal – a coming together of all parties with the purpose of taking stock and restating shared intentions and aspirations.

Government is well aware of the scale of the recruitment and retention problem and the threat that this poses to its commitment to raising standards in schools. It is attempting to market the profession aggressively, appealing to the PIT (Pool of Inoperative Teachers) to return to teaching and devising a range of 'golden hellos' and other financial inducements. Whilst almost anything that might improve the number and quality of those entering the profession is welcome, it seems doubtful that high quality teachers will be recruited until the government seriously addresses the issue of teacher morale and esteem. Only by improving teacher morale, self-esteem and their sense of ownership of their work will high quality candidates enter and stay in teaching. Better advertising, improved salaries and accelerated career progression may be important, but they are doomed to fail unless the government begins to trust teachers. Policies are required which will deal with those factors that produce dissatisfaction for teachers, like their increasing workload, poor pupil behaviour, poor over-asking management and a sense of being publicly criticised; the positive features of the job must also be promoted and enhanced.

Conclusion

Government approaches for the last quarter of a century or more have seemed to stifle the very things which may be needed in our uncertain future – creativity, imagination, daring and risk taking even. Instead of continually telling teachers what to do and increasingly how to do it, government policy needs to begin to play a major part in articulating the nation's vision for the future of the educational system. Schools and their staff need to be allowed to raise their sights much higher than merely satisfying the next Ofsted inspection and maintaining an acceptable position in the league tables. Whilstever schools feel the need to be constantly looking over their shoulders for Ofsted rejections and public shaming they will never become vibrant institutions in which teachers and pupils engage their minds and also their hearts in teaching and learning. Feelings of fear and anxiety can be replaced by those of optimism and commitment. Positive emotions, so seldom mentioned in government documentation, can fuel and sustain activity and release energy and expertise. The notion that enjoyment is the birthright of every child, proclaimed by the Secretary of State for Education and Skills, Charles Clarke, represents a recent exception (Clarke, 2003). Whilst central government could provide a broad framework of guidance within which schools can operate, teachers in individual schools must be allowed, rather encouraged, to contextualise and operationalise such a broad framework to suit its particular locality and community. Top-down prescriptions may reassure politicians and some members of the public that the government is in control and is guaranteeing accountability but they do not recognise or respond to the complexity and diversity of local situations and circumstances. What is required is not central diktat, expressed in macho tones, but rather encouragement and support which help to build local capacity to analyse local problems. Within central frameworks policy and practice are best realised in schools and localities which take collective action with such issues. Time, space and resources need to be made available so that a co-operative and collaborative culture can flourish in schools and their wider communities. Instead of seeking to 'script' teachers' practices for them, central government should support them by creating conditions for change and expectations so that teachers feel that they can change and actually want to do so. The newly created General Teaching Council might help teachers to become a self-regulating profession and Ofsted could change its emphasis to become more of a 'critical friend' than an enemy and seek to assist schools to monitor their performances and review their successes and failures. The most recent suggestion from Ofsted that it is time 'to trust schools more' and 'to draw on the professionalism of teachers' (Ofsted, 2004, p.8) is certainly a step in the right direction. At the centre of the educational system must be schools which are learning and teaching institutions and where co-operation, collaboration and community become watchwords. In such communities collective aspiration can be set free and teachers may connect with their pupils and their parents in mutually respecting and supportive ways. Reform from the outside has been tried and it has failed; now it is time for renewal from the inside.

Bibliography

Adams, M.J. (1991), *Beginning to Read: Thinking and Learning about Print*, Cambridge, MA, MIT Press.

Adey, P., Fairbrother, R. and Wiliam, D. (1999), *A Review of Research Related to Learning Styles and Strategies*, London, King's College Centre for the Advancement of Thinking.

Alexander, R. (2000), *Culture and Pedagogy: International comparisons in primary education*, Oxford, Blackwell.

Alexander, R. *et al* (1993), *Education - Putting the Record Straight*, Network Education Press.

Allington, R.L. (2002), 'What I've Learned About Effective Reading Instruction from a Decade of Studying Exemplary Elementary Classroom Teachers', *Phi Delta Kappan*, 83,10, pp. 740-47.

Angus, L. (1993), 'The sociology of school effectiveness', *British Journal of Sociology of Education*, 14, 3, pp. 333-345.

Angus, L. (1994), 'Sociological Analysis and Education Management: the social context of the self-managing School', *British Journal of Sociology of Education*, 15, 1, pp. 79-91.

Apple, M. (1992), Review of 'Education and the Economy in a Changing Society', Comparative Education Review, 36, 1, pp. 127-129.

Apple, M. (1995), *Education and Power*, New York, Routledge.

Apple, M.W. (1996), *Cultural Politics and Education*, Buckingham, Open University Press.

Arnot, M. and Barton, L. (Eds) (1992), *Voicing Concerns: sociological perspectives on contemporary educational reforms*, Wallingford, Triangle Books.

Au, K. (1979), 'Using the Experience-Text-Relationship method with minority children', *The Reading Teacher*, 32, 6, pp. 677-679.

Au, K. (1993), *Literacy Instruction in Multicultural Settings*, Fort Worth, TX, Harcourt Brace.

Au, K. (1997a), 'A sociocultural model of reading instruction: the Kamehameha Elementary Education Program', In *Instructional Models in Reading*, (Ed) S.A. Stahl, pp. 181-202, New Jersey, Lawrence Erlbaum.

Au, K. (1997b), 'Ownership, literacy achievement, and students of diverse cultural backgrounds', In *Reading Engagement: Motivating Readers through Integrated Instruction*, (Eds) J.T. Guthrie and A. Wigfield, pp. 168-182, Newark, DE, International Reading Association.

Au, K. and Raphael, T. (2000), 'Equity and literacy in the next millennium', *Reading Research Quarterly*, 35, 1, pp. 170-188.

Bakhtin, M. (1981), *The Dialogic Imagination*, Austin, University of Texas Press.

Ball, S. (1990), 'Discipline and Chaos: the New Right and Discourses of Derision', In *Politics and Policy-Making in Education: Explorations in Policy Sociology*, London, Routledge.

Ball, S. (1994), *Education Reform: A Critical and Post-Structural Approach*, Buckingham, OUP.

Ball, S.J. (1990), *Politics and Policy-making in Education; explorations in policy sociology*, London, Routledge.

Ball, S.J. (1999), 'Global trends in educational reform and the struggle for the soul of the teacher!' Paper presented at the British Educational Research Association Annual Conference, University of Sussex at Brighton, September.

Barber, M. (1996), *The Learning Game: Arguments for an Education Revolution*, London, Gollancz.

Barlow, M. and Robertson, H. (1994), *Class Warfare*, Toronto, Key Porter.

Baron, D. (1999), 'From pencils to pixels: the stages of literacy technologies', In *Passions, Pedagogies and 21st Century Technologies*, (Eds) G.E. Hawisher and C. Selfe,. Utah State University Press/National Council of Teachers of English.

Barton, D. (1994), *Literacy: An Introduction to the Ecology of Written Language*, Oxford, Blackwell.

Beard, R. (1998), *National Literacy Strategy: Review of Research and other Related Evidence*, London, DfEE.

Becker, G.S. (1975), *Human Capital: a theoretical and empirical analysis, with special reference to education*, Chicago, IL, University of Chicago Press.

Benjamin, S., Nind, M., Hall, K., Collins, J. and Sheehy, K. (2003), 'Moments of Inclusion and Exclusion: Pupils negotiating classroom contexts', *British Journal of Sociology of Education*, 24, 5, pp. 547-558.

Berliner, D.C. and Biddle, B.J. (1995), *The Manufactured Crisis: myths, frauds, and the attack on America's public schools*, Reading, MA, Addison Wesley.

Blair, T. (1998a), *The Third Way*, London, Fabian Society.

Blair, T. (1998b), quoted in Department of Education and Employment *The Learning Age: a renaissance for a new Britain*, London, Stationery Office, Cm 3790, 0.

Blair, T. (1999), available at www.number-10.gov.uk (February).

Blair, T. (2001), Extracts from Blair's undelivered TUC speech, *Guardian*, 12 September.

Blunkett, D. (1997), *The General Teaching Council*, DfEE Press Release, 27 November.

Bottery, M. (1998), 'The Challenge to Professionals from the New Public Management: implications for the teaching profession', *Oxford Review of Education*, 22, 2, pp. 179-197.

Bottery, M. (2000), *Education, Policy and Ethics*, London, Continuum.

Brehony, K.J. (1992), 'Active Citizens': the case of school governors', *International Studies in the Sociology of Education*, 2, 2, pp. 199-217.

Brighouse, T. (2001), 'New Labour on education: could do better', *Political Quarterly*, 72, pp. 19-29.

Brimblecombe, N., Ormston, M. and Shaw, M. (1996), 'Teachers' perceptions of inspections', In *Ofsted Inspections: The Early Experience*, (Eds) J. Ouston, P. Earley and B. Fidler, London, Fulton.

Broadfoot, P. (1996), *Education, Assessment and Society*, Buckingham, OUP.

Broadfoot, P., Osborn, M., Planel, C. and Sharpe, K. (2000), *Promoting Quality in Learning: Does England Have the Answer? Findings from the Quest Project*, London, Cassell.

Brooks, G. (1998), 'Trends in standards of literacy in the United Kingdom 1948-1996', *TOPIC*, 19, Spring, Item 1.

Brophy, J. (1973), 'Stability of teacher effectiveness', *American Educational Research Journal*, 10, pp. 245-252.

Bruner, J. (1996), *The Culture of Education*, Cambridge MA, Harvard University Press.

Buckingham, D. and Macfarlane, A. (2001), *A Digitally Driven Curriculum?* London: IPPR.

Byers, S. (1997), 'Engine of change in motion', *Times Educational Supplement*, 25 July, p. 15.

Callaghan, J. (1976), 'Towards a National Debate', Speech at Ruskin College, Oxford, 18 October.

Campbell, J. and Husbands, C. (2000), 'On the reliability of Ofsted inspection of initial teacher training: a case study', *British Educational Research Journal*, 26, 1, pp. 39-48.

Carr, W. and Hartnett, A. (1996), *Education and the Struggle for Democracy*, Buckingham, Open University Press.

Chinn, C.A., Anderson, R.C. and Waggoner, M.A. (2001), 'Patterns of discourse in two kinds of literature discussion', *Reading Research Quarterly*, 36, 4, pp. 378-411.

Chubb, J. and Moe, T. (1990), *Politics, Markets and America's Schools*, Washington DC, Brookings Institute.

Clarke, C. (2003), *Forward to Excellence and Enjoyment*, London, DfES.

Coffield, F. (1999), 'Breaking the consensus: Lifelong learning as social control', *British Educational Research Journal*, 25, 4, pp. 479-499.

Collins, R. (1979), *The Credential Society: A Historical Sociology of Education and Stratification*, New York, Academic Press.

Collins-Block, C. and Pressley, M. (2000), 'It's not scripted lessons but challenging and personalised interactions that distinguish effective from less effective classrooms', Paper presented at National Reading Conference, Scottsdale AZ, USA, December.

Collins-Block, C., Oakar, M. and Hurt, N. (2002), 'The Expertise of Literacy Teachers: A Continuum from Preschool to Grade 5', *Reading Research Quarterly* 37, 2, pp. 178-206.

Comber, B. (2001a), 'Critical literacies and location action: teacher knowledge and "new" research agenda', In *Negotiating Critical Literacies in Classrooms*, (Eds) B. Comber and A. Simpson, pp. 271-282, Mahwah, NJ, Lawrence Erlbaum Associates.

Comber, B. (2001b), 'Critical literacy: power and pleasure with language in the early years', *Australian Journal of Language and Literacy*, 24, 3, pp. 168-181.

Cope, B. and Kalantzis, M. (2000), (Eds) *Multiliteracies: Literacy Learning and the Design of Social Futures*, London, Routledge.

Cope, P. and I'Anson, J. (2003), 'Forms of exchange: education, economics and the neglect of social contingency', *British Journal of Educational Studies*, 51, 3, pp. 219-232.

Corson, D. (2000), 'The eclipse of liberal education in the twenty-first century', *Educational Review*, 52, 2, pp. 111-113.

Croll, P. (2002), 'Social deprivation, school-level achievement and special educational needs', *Educational Research*, 44, 1, pp. 43-53.

Cross Commission (1888), *Royal Commission on the working of the Elementary Education Acts*, HMSO, 1888.

Dadds, M. (2001), 'The Politics of Pedagogy, *Teachers and Teaching*, 7, 1, pp. 43-58.

Darling-Hammond, L. (1993), 'Reframing the school reform agenda: developing capacity for school transformation', *Phi Delta Kappan*, 74, 10, pp. 753-761.

Darling-Hammond, L. (1998), 'Teachers and teaching: testing policy hypotheses, from a National Commission report', *Educational Researcher* 27, 1, pp. 5-15.

Davies, M. and Edwards, G. (1999), 'Will the curriculum caterpillar ever learn to fly?', *Cambridge Journal of Education*, 29, 2, pp. 265-275.

Davies, S. and Guppy, N. (1997), 'Globalization and educational reforms in Anglo-American democracies', *Comparative Education Review*, 41, 4, pp. 435-459.

Day, C. (1997), 'Teachers in the twenty-first century: time to renew the vision', In *Beyond Educational Reform: Bringing teachers back in*, (Eds) A. Hargreaves and R. Evans, pp. 44-61, Buckingham, Open University Press.

de Grouchy, N. (1997), 'Teaching Council model looks feeble', *Times Educational Supplement*, 1 August, p. 14.

Dearing, R. (1994), *The National Curriculum and its Assessment: Final Report*, London, SCAA.

Deem, R. (1996), 'The school, the parent, the banker and the local politician: what can we learn from the English experience of involving lay people in the site based management of schools?' 55-70, In *Reshaping Education in the 1990s: Perspectives on Secondary Schooling*, (Eds) C.J. Pole and R. Chawla-Duggan.

Delpit, L. (1995), *Other People's Children: Cultural Conflict in the Classroom*, New York, The New Press.

Department for Education and Employment (1997a), *Excellence in Schools: White Paper*, London, DfEE.

Department for Education and Employment (1997b), *The Implementation of the National Literacy Strategy*, London, HMSO.

Department for Education and Employment (1998), *The Learning Age: Green Paper*, London, DfEE.

Department for Education and Employment (1998a), *The National Literacy Strategy: A Framework for Teaching*, London, HMSO.

Department for Education and Employment (1998b), *The National Literacy Strategy: Training Pack*, London, HMSO.

Department for Education and Employment (2001a), *Citizenship Education*, see www.dfes.gov.uk.

Department for Education and Employment (2001b), *Building on Success*, London, DfEE.

Department of Trade and Industry (1998), *Our Competitive Future: Building the Knowledge Driven Economy, White Paper*, http://www.dti.gov.uk/comp/competitive/main.htm.

Diamond, M. and Hopson, J. (1998), *Magic Trees of the Mind*, USA, Penguin.

Dillon, J.T. (1990), *The Practice of Questioning*, London, Routledge.

Duffy, G.G. and Roehler, L.R. (1986), 'The Subtleties of Instructional Mediation', *Educational Leadership*, 43, pp. 23-27.

Duffy, G.G., Roehler, L.R., Sivan, E., Rackliffe, G., Book, C., Meloth, M.S., Vavrus, L.G., Wesselman, R., Putnam, J., and Bassiri, D. (1987), 'Effects of explaining the reasoning associated with using reading strategies', *Reading Research Quarterly*, 20, pp. 347-368.

Dunkin, M., and Biddle, B. (1974), *The Study of Teaching*, New York, Holt, Rinehart and Winston.

Dyson, A.H. (1997), *Writing superheroes: Contemporary childhood, popular culture, and classroom literacy*, New York, Teachers College Press.

Dyson, A.H. (1998), 'Folk processes and media creatures: reflections on popular culture for literacy educators', *The Reading Teacher*, 51, 5, pp. 392-402.

Earley, P., Fidler, B. and Ouston, J. (Eds) (1996), *Improvement Through Inspection? Complementary Approaches to School Development*, London, David Fulton.

English, E., Hargreaves, L. and Hislam, J. (2002), 'Pedagogical dilemmas in the National Literacy Strategy: primary teachers' perceptions, reflections and classroom behaviour', *Cambridge Journal of Education*, 32, p. 1.

Etzioni, A. (1969), *The Semi-Professions and Their Organization*, New York, Free Press.

Ferguson, N., Earley, P., Fidler, B. and Ouston, J. (2000), *Improving Schools and* spection: the Self-Inspecting School, London, Paul Chapman.

on, N., Earley, P., Ouston, J. and Fidler, B. (1999), 'New heads, Ofsted inspections nd the prospects for school improvement', *Educational Research*, 41, 3, pp. 241-249.

, C., Greenstreet, D., Kusel, K. and Parsons, C. (1998), 'Ofsted inspection reports and the language of educational improvement', *Evaluation and Research in Education*, 12, 3, pp. 125-139.

:-Gibbon, C.T. (1997), 'Monitoring with feedback: the democratisation of data', In *Quality in Education*, (Eds) K. Watson et al, London, Cassell.

tz-Gibbon, C.T. (1998), 'Ofsted: time to go?', *Managing Schools Today*, 7, 6, pp. 22-25.

Flanders, N. (1970), *Analyzing Teacher Behavior*, Reading MA, USA, Addison-Wesley.

Flood, J. and Lapp, D. (1995), 'Broadening the lens: towards an expanded conceptualization of literacy', In *Perspectives on Literacy Research and Practice 44th Yearbook of the National Reading Conference (NRC)*, Chicago, NRC.

Foorman, B., Fletcher, J. and Francis, D. (1998), 'Preventing reading failure by ensuring effective reading instruction', In *The Keys to Literacy*, (Eds) S. Patton and M. Holmes, pp. 29-39, Washington DC, Council for Basic Education.

Foster, P. and Hammersley, M. (1998), 'A review of reviews: structure and function in reviews of educational research', *British Educational Research Journal*, 24, 5, pp. 609-628.

Foucault, M. (1977), *Discipline and Punish*, London, Penguin.

Galton, M., Hargreaves, L., Comber, C. and Wall, D. (1999), *Inside the Primary Classroom: 20 years on*, London, Routledge.

Gardner, H. (1983), *Frames of Mind*, New York, Basic Books.

Gee, J.P. (1999), 'Critical issues: reading and the new literacy studies: reframing the national academy of sciences report on reading', *Journal of Research on Literacy*, 31, 3, pp. 355-374.

Gee, J.P. (2000a), 'New people in new worlds: networks, the new capitalism and schools', In *Multiliteracies: Literacy Learning and the Design of Social Futures*, (Eds) B. Cope and M. Kalantzis, pp. 43-68, London, Routledge.

Gee, J.P. (2000b), 'The New Literacy Studies: from 'socially situated' to the work of the social', pp. 180-196, In *Situated Literacies: Reading and Writing in Context*, (Eds) D. Barton, M. Hamilton and R. Ivanic, London, Routledge/Falmer.

Gee, J.P. and Green, J.L. (1997), 'Discourse Analysis, Learning and Social Practice: a methodological study', *Review of Research in Education*, 23, pp. 119-169.

Gee, J.P., Hull, G. and Lankshear, C. (1996), *The New Work Order: Behind the Language of the New Capitalism*, Sydney, Allen and Unwin.

Geekie, P., Cambourne, B., Fitzsimmons, P. (1999), *Understanding Literacy Development*, Stoke on Trent, Trentham.

Gewirtz, S. (1997), 'Post-welfarism and the reconstruction of teachers' work in the UK', *Journal of Education Policy*, 12, 4, pp. 217-231.

Gerwitz, S. (2000), 'Bringing the politics back in: a critical analysis of quality discourses in education', *British Journal of Educational Studies*, 48, 4, pp. 352-370.

Gewirtz, S., Ball, S. and Bowe, R. (1995), *Markets, Choice and Equity in Education*, Buckingham, OUP.

Giddens, A. (1994), *Beyond Left and Right: The Future of Radical Politics*, Cambridge, Polity Press.

Gillborn, D. and Gipps, C. (1996), *Recent Research on the Achievement of Ethnic Minority Pupils*, London, HMSO.

Gillborn, D. and Youdell, D. (2000), *Rationing Education*, Maidenhead, Berkshire, Open University Press.

Gilroy, P. (1998), 'New Labour and Teacher Education in England and Wales: the first 500 days', *Journal of Education for Teaching*, 24, 3, pp. 221-231.

Ginsburg, M.B. (1997), 'Professionalism or politics as a model for educators' engagement with/in communities', *Journal of Education Policy*, 12, 1/2, pp. 5-12.

Goodson, I. (1991), 'Nations at Risk' and 'national curriculum': ideology and identity, pp. 219-232, In *The Politics of Curriculum and Testing*, (Eds) S.H. Fuhrman and B. Malen, London, Falmer.

Goody, J. (1977), *The Domestication of the Savage Mind*, Cambridge, MA, Cambridge University Press.

Grant, N. (1999), 'Comparing educational systems', In *An Introduction to the Study of Education*, (Eds) D. Matheson and I. Grosvenor, London, David Fulton.

Gray, J. (1998), *False Dawn: The Delusions of Global Capitalism*, London, Granta Books.

Gray, J. (2000), *Causing Concern but Improving: A review of schools' experiences*, London, DfEE (Research Report RR188).

Gray, J. (2001), Interview 'Start the week', Radio 4, 2 October.

Green, A. (1999), 'Education and globalization in Europe and East Asia: convergent and divergent trends', *Journal of Education Policy*, 14, 1, pp. 55-72.

Green, A., Wolf, A. and Leney, T. (1999), *Convergence and Divergence in European Education and Training Systems*, Bedford Way Papers, Institute of Education, London.

Green, J. and Dixon, C. (1996), 'Language of literacy dialogues: facing the future or reproducing the past', *Journal of Literacy Research* 28, 2, pp. 290-301.

Green, J.L., Weade, R. and Graham, K. (1988), 'Lesson construction and student participation: a sociolinguistic analysis', In *Multiple Perspective Analysis of Classroom Discourse*, (Eds) J.L. Green and J.O. Harker, pp. 11-47, Norwood, NJ, Ablex.

Greene, M. (1971), 'Curriculum and Consciousness', *Teachers College Record*, 73, 2, pp. 253-269.

Hall, K. (1995), 'Learning Modes: An Investigation of Pupils in Five Kent Classrooms', *Educational Research*, 37, 1, pp. 21-32.

Hall, K. (1998), 'Critical literacy and the case for it in the early years of school', *Language, Culture and Curriculum*, 11, 2, pp. 183-194.

Hall, K. (1999), 'Standards and Initial Teacher Training: Current Policy and Critical Issues', *Capability: Journal of Autonomous Learning for Life and Work* 4, 2, pp. 12-16.

Hall, K. (2001), 'An analysis of literacy policy in England using Barthes' notion of "readerly" and "writerly" texts', *Journal of Early Childhood Literacy*, 1, 2, pp. 153-165.

Hall, K. (2002), 'Co-constructing subjectivities and knowledge in literacy class: an ethnographic-sociocultural perspective', *Language and Education*, 16, 3, pp. 178-194.

Hall, K. (2003a), *Listening to Stephen read: Multiple Perspectives on Literacy*, Buckingham, Open University Press.

Hall, K. (2003b), 'Effective literacy teaching in the early years of school: a review of evidence', In *Handbook of Early Childhood Literacy Research*, (Eds) N. Hall, J. Larson and J Marsh, pp. 315-326, London, Sage.

Hall, K. and Burke, W. (2003), *Making Formative Assessment Work: Effective Practice in the Primary Classroom*, Buckingham, Open University Press.

Hall, K. and Harding, A. (1999), 'Teacher Assessment of seven year olds in England: a study of its summative function', *Early Years International Journal of Research and Development*, 20, p. 2.

Hall, K. and Harding, A. (2002), 'Level Descriptions and Teacher Assessment: Towards a Community of Assessment Practice', *Educational Research*, 40, 1, pp. 1-16.

Hall, K. and Harding, A. (2003), 'A systematic review of effective literacy teaching in the 4-14 age range of mainstream schooling', In *Research Evidence in Education Library*, London, EPPI-Centre, Social Science Research Unit, Institute of Education.

Hall, K., Allan, C., Dean, J. and Warren, S. (2003), 'Classroom Discourse in the Literacy Hour in England', *Language, Culture and Curriculum*, 16, 3, pp. 284-297.

Hall, K., Collins, J., Benjamin, S., Nind, M. and Sheehy, K. (2004), 'SATurated Models of Pupildom: Assessment and Inclusion/Exclusion', *British Educational Research Journal*, 30, 6.

Hall, K., Zulfiqar, M., Ozerk, K. and Tan, J. (2002), '"This is our school": provision, purpose and pedagogy of supplementary schooling in Leeds and Oslo', *British Educational Research Journal*, 28, 3, pp. 399-418.

Hallgarten, J. (2000), *Parents Exist, OK! Issues and visions for parent-school relations*, London, IPPR.

Halpern, D. and Mikosz, D. (1998), *The Third Way: summary of the Nexus on-line discussion*, London, Nexus.

Hamilton, D. and Weiner, G. (2000), 'Subjects, not subjects: Curriculum pathways, pedagogies and practices in the United Kingdom', Paper presented at the *Internationalisation of Curriculum Studies Conference*, Louisiana State University, USA.

Hargreaves, A. and Evans, R. (Eds) (1997), *Beyond Educational Reform: Bringing Teachers Back In*, Buckingham, Open University Press.

Hartley, D. (1997), *Re-schooling Society*, London, Falmer.

Hartley, D. (1998), 'Repeat prescription: the national curriculum for initial teacher training', *British Journal of Educational Studies*, 46, 1, pp. 68-84.

Haverman, R. and Wolfe, B. (1995), 'The determinants of children's attainments: a review of methods and findings', *Journal of Economic Literature*, 33, pp. 1829-1878.

Haworth, A. (1999), 'Bakhtin in the classroom: what constitutes a dialogic text? Some lessons from small group interaction', *Language and Education*, 13, 2, pp. 99-117.

Heath, S.B. (1983), *Ways with Words: Language, Life and Work in Communities and Classrooms*, Cambridge, CUP.

Hertz, N. (2001), *The Silent Takeover: Global Capitalism and the Death of Democracy*, London, Heinemann.

Hextall, I. and Mahony, P. (1999a), '"Modernising" the Teacher', Paper presented at the European Conference on Educational Research, Lahti, Finland, 22-25 September.

Hextall, I. and Mahony, P. (1999b), 'Representation and accountability in the formation of policy on teacher education: the GTC (England)', *Larutbildning och Forskning i Umea*, 6, pp. 7-25.

Hextall, I. and Mahony, P. (2000), 'Consultation and the management of consent: standards for qualified teacher status', *British Educational Research Journal*, 26, 3, pp. 323-332.

Heywood-Everett, G. (1999), 'The business of learning: parents as full, unwilling or sleeping partners', *International Studies in Sociology of Education*, 9, 3, pp. 267-278.

Hiebert, E.H. and Raphael, T.E. (1996), 'Psychological Perspectives on Literacy and Extensions to Educational Practice', In *Handbook of Educational Psychology*, (Eds) David C. Berliner and Robert C. Calfree, pp. 550-602, New York, Macmillan.

Hobsbawm, E. (1994), *Age of Extremes: The Short Twentieth Century 1914-1991*, London, Michael Joseph.

Hodgkin, R. and Newall, P. (1998), *The Implementation Handbook for the Convention on the Rights of the Child*, UN Children's Fund Geneva, UNICEF.

Hoggett, P. (1996), 'New Modes of Control in the Public Service', *Public Administration*, 74, Spring, pp. 9-32.

Holt, M. (1999), 'Recovering of the comprehensive ideal', *Teacher Development*, 3, 3, pp. 329-340.

House of Commons Select Committee on Education and Employment (1999), *The Work of Ofsted: 4th Report of the Education and Employment Committee, H.C. Papers 62-I, session 1998-1999*, London, The Stationery Office.

Howson, J. (1999), 'A case of slipping standards', *Times Educational Supplement*, 1 January.

Hoyle, E. (1974), 'Professionality, professionalism and control in teaching', *London Education Review*, 3, 2, http://www.readingonline.org/critical/shanahan/panel.htm.

Huckman, L. and Fletcher, J. (1996), 'A question of costs: budget management in secondary schools', In *Reshaping Education in the 1990s: Perspectives on Secondary Schooling*, (Eds) C.J. Pole and R. Chawla-Duggan, pp. 130-148.

Instance, D. (1997), 'Education and social exclusion', *The OECD Observer*, 208, Oct/Nov.

International Reading Association (IRA) (2000), *Making a Difference Means Making it Different*, Newark, DE, IRA.

Ivanic, R. and Hamilton, M. (1989), 'Literacy beyond schooling', In *Emerging Partnerships in Language and Literacy*, (Ed) D. Wray, Clevedon, Multilingual Matters.

Jaworski, A. and Coupland, N. (Eds), (1999), *The Discourse Reader*, London, Routledge.

Jeffrey, B. and Woods, P. (1996), 'Feeling deprofessionalised: the social construction of emotions during an Ofsted inspection', *Cambridge Journal of Education*, 26, 3, pp. 325-343.

Jeffrey, B. and Woods, P. (1998), *Testing Teachers: the effects of school inspections on primary teachers*, London, Falmer Press.

Jeffrey, B. and Woods, P. (2002), 'The reconstruction of primary teachers' identities', *British Journal of Sociology of Education*, 23, 1, pp. 89-106.

Johnson, M. and Hallgarten, J. (Eds) (2002), *From Victims of Change to Agents of Change: the future of the teaching profession*, London, Institute of Public Policy Research (IPPR).

Joseph Rowntree Foundation (2001), *Monitoring Poverty and Social Exclusion*, London, JRF.

Kamil, M.L., Mosenthal, P.B., Pearson, P.D, and Barr, R. (Eds) (2000), *Handbook of Reading Research*, 3, Mahwah, NJ, Lawrence Erlbaum.

Kenway, J. (Ed) (1995), *Marketing Education: some critical issues*, Victoria, Deakin University Press.

Kirk, G. (2000), 'The General Teaching Council for England', *School Leadership and Management*, 20, 2, pp. 235-246.

Knapp, M.S. and Associates (1995), *Teaching for Meaning in High-Poverty Classrooms*, New York, Teachers' College Press.

Krechevsky, M. and Stork, J. (2000), 'Challenging educational assumptions: lessons from an Italian-American Collaboration', *Cambridge Journal of Education*, 30, 1, pp. 57-74.

Kress, G. (1989), *Linguistic Processes in Sociocultural Practice*, Oxford, Oxford University Press.

Kress, G. (2000), 'Multimodality', In *Multiliteracies: Literacy Learning and the Design of Social Futures*, (Eds) B. Cope and M. Kalantzis, pp. 182-202, London, Routledge.

Labour Party (1994), *Opening Doors to a Learning Society: a policy statement on Education*, London, Labour Party.

Labour Party (1995), *Excellence for Everyone: Labour's Crusade to Raise Standards*, London, Labour Party.

Labour Party (2001), *Realising the Talent of All*, Labour Party, London.

Langer, E.J. (1998), *Mindfulness*, Massachusetts, Addison-Wesley.

Langer, J. (1999), *Excellence in English in Middle and High School: How Teachers' Professional Lives Support Student Achievement*, CELA Research Report 12002, The National Research Center on English Learning and Achievement, The University at Albany State University of New York.

Langer, J.A. (2000), *Beating the Odds: Teaching Middle and High School Students To Read and Write Well*, CELA Research Report 12014, The National Research Center on English Learning and Achievement, University at Albany State University of New York.

Lave, J. and Wenger, E. (1991) *Situated Learning: Legitimate Peripheral Participation*, New York, Cambridge University Press.

Lawn, M. (1996), *Modern Times? Work, Professionalism and Citizenship in Teaching*, London, Falmer.

Lawton, D. (1989), 'The National Curriculum', In *The Education Reform Act: Choice and Control*, (Ed) D. Lawton, pp. 27-43, London, Hodder and Stoughton.

Lawton, S.B. (1992), 'Why restructure? An international survey of the roots of reform', *Journal of Education Policy*, 7, 2, pp. 139-154.

Learmonth, J. (2001), *Inspection: What's in it for schools?* London, Routledge/Falmer.

Lemke, J.L. (1998), 'Metamedia literacy: transforming media and meanings', In *Literacy for the 21st Century: Technological Transformation in a Post-typographic World*, (Eds) D. Reinking, L. Labbo, M. McKenna and R. Kiefer (Eds), pp. 283-301, Erlbaum.

Levin, B. (1997), 'The lessons of international education reform', *Journal of Education Policy*, 12, 4, pp. 253-266.

Levin, B. (2001), *Reforming Education: From Origins to Outcomes*, London, Routledge Falmer.

Livingstone, D. (1995), 'Popular beliefs about Canada's schools', In *Social Change and Education in Canada*, (Eds) R. Ghosh and D. Ray, pp. 16-44, 3rd edition, Toronto, Harcourt Brace.

Lonsdale, P. and Parsons, C. (1998), 'Inspection and the school improvement hoax', In *School Improvement After Inspection*, (Ed) P. Earley, London, Chapman.

Loughran, J. (Ed) (1999), *Researching Teaching: methodologies and practices for understanding pedagogy*, London, RoutledgeFalmer.

Luke, A. and Freebody, P. (1999), 'Further notes on the four resources model', *Reading Online*, readingonline.org/research/lukefreebody.html.

Luke, A., Lingard, R., Green, B., and Comber, B. (1999), 'The abuses of literacy: Educational policy and the construction of crisis', In *Educational Policy*, (Eds) J. Marshall and M. Peters, pp. 1-25, London, Edward Elgar.

Luria, A.R. (1976) *Cognitive development: its cultural and social transformations*. Cambridge, MA, Harvard University Press.

Lynch, K. (1999), *Equality in Education*, Dublin, Gill and Macmillan.

Lyon, G.R. (1998), 'Overview of reading and literacy research', In *The Keys to Literacy*, (Eds) S. Patton and M. Holmes, pp. 1-15, Washington DC, Council for Basic Education.

MacBeath, J. (1999), *Schools Must Speak for Themselves: the Case for School Self-evaluation*, London, Routledge.

Macbeth, A. (1984), *The Child Between: Report on School-Family Relations in the Countries of the European Community*, Education Series 13 Brussels, Commission of the European Communities.

Macbeth, A. (1989), *Involving Parents*, Oxford, Heinemann.

Maclure, S. (1988), *Education Re-Formed*, London, Hodder and Stoughton.

Maddaus, J. (1990), 'Parental choice of school: what parents think and do', In *Review of Research in Education*, (Ed) C. Cazden, pp. 267-95, 16, Washington, AERA.

Maguire, M. and Ball, S. (1994), 'Discourses of education reform in the United Kingdom and the USA and the work of teachers', *Journal of In-Service Education*, 20, 1, pp. 5-16.

Mahony, P. and Hextall, I. (1997), 'Problems of accountability and reinvented government: a case study of the Teacher Training Agency', *Journal of Education Policy*, 12, 4, pp. 267-284.

Mahony, P. and Hextall, I. (2000), *The Reconstruction of Teaching*, London, Falmer.

Marchant, P. and Hall, K. (2003), 'Explaining Differences in Key Stage 2 Pupil Attainments: a multilevel analysis', *London Review of Education*, 1, 2, pp. 141-151.

Marsh, J. and Millard, E. (2000), *Literacy and Popular Culture: Using children's culture in the classroom*, London, Sage/PCP.

Maybin, J. (2000), 'Response to Gemma Moss: literacy and the social organisation of knowledge in and outside school', *Virtual Seminar 2: International Association of Applied Linguistics*, http://education.leeds.ac.uk/AILA/virtsem2.ma.

McCarthy, S.J., Dressman, M., Smolkin, L., McGill-Franzen, A. and Harris, V.J. (2000), 'How will diversity affect literacy in the next millennium?', *Reading Research Quarterly*, 35, 4, pp. 548-552.

McNaughton, S. (2001), 'Co-constructing expertise: the development of parents' and teachers' ideas about literacy practices and the transition to school', *Journal of Early Childhood Literacy*, 1, 1, pp. 40-58.

Medwell, J., Wray, D., Poulson, L. and Fox, R. (1998), *Effective Teachers of Literacy: A Report for the Teacher Training Agency (TTA)*, London, TTA.

Mishra, R. (1999), *Globalization and the Welfare State*, Cheltenham, Edward Elgar.

Moje, E.B. (1997), 'Exploring discourse, subjectivity and knowledge in chemistry class', *Journal of Classroom Interaction*, 32, 2, pp. 35-44.

Moll, L.C. (2000), 'Inspired by Vygotksy: ethnographic experiments in education', In *Vygotskian Perspectives on Literacy Research*, (Eds) C.D. Lee and P. Smagorinsky, pp. 256-268, Cambridge, CUP.

Morgan, W. with Gilbert, P., Lankshear, C., Werba, S. and Williams, L. (1996), *Critical Literacy: Readings and Resources*, Norwood, Australian Association for the Teaching of English.

Mortimore, P. and Goldstein, H. (1996), *The teaching of reading in 45 inner London Primary Schools: a critical examination of Ofsted research*, London, Institute of Education.

Mortimore, P. and Whitty, G. (1997), *Can School Improvement Overcome the Effects of Disadvantage?*, London, University of London Institute of Education.

Mroz, M., Smith, F. and Hardman, F. (2000), 'The Discourse of the Literacy Hour', *Cambridge Journal of Education*, 30, 3, pp. 379-390.

Mullis, I.V., Martin, M.O., Gonzalez, E.J. and Kennedy, A.M. (2001), *PIRLS 2001 International Report: IEA's Study of Reading Literacy Achievement in Primary School in 35 Countries*, International Association for the Evaluation of Educational Achievement, International Study Centre, Boston College.

Munn, P. (Ed) (1993), *Parents and Schools: Customs, Managers and Partners*, London, Routledge.

National Commission on Education (1993), *Learning to Succeed: A Radical Look at Education Today and a Strategy for the Future*, London, Heinemann.

National Commission on Excellence in Education (1983), *A Nation at Risk: The Imperative for Educational Reform, A Report to the Nation and the Secretary of Education United States*, Department of Education.

National Reading Panel (2000), *Teaching Children to Read: an evidence-based assessment of the scientific research literature on reading and its implications for reading instruction*, Washington DC, NICHD. available at http://www.readingonline.org/critical/shanahan/panel.htm (accessed 14 November 2001).

Nieto, S. (1994), 'Lessons from students on creating a chance to dream', *Harvard Educational Review*, 64, 4, pp. 392-446.

Nind, M., Benjamin, S., Sheehy, K., Collins, J. and Hall, K. (in press), 'Methodological challenges in researching inclusive school cultures', *Educational Review*.

Nystrand, M., Wu, L.L., Gamoran, A., Zeiser, S. and Long, D. (2001), 'Questions in Time: investigating the structure and dynamics of unfolding classroom discourse', Report 14005 from the Center on English Learning and Achievement (CELA) http:cela.albany.edu/nystrand01-5/main.html 05/03/02.

O'Hear, A. (1988), *Who Teaches the Teachers?*, London, Social Affairs Unit.

O'Neill, O. (2002), 'Trust and Transparency', Reith Lectures, BBC Radio 4 April.

OECD (1989), *Decentralization and School Improvement*, Paris, OECD.

Office for Standards in Education (1995a), *Corporate Plan 1995*, London, Ofsted.

Office for Standards in Education (1995b), *Class size and the quality of education*, Ofsted Publication Centre, London.

Office for Standards in Education (1996), *The Teaching of Reading in 45 Inner London Primary Schools: A Report of Her Majesty's Inspectors in Collaboration with the LEAs of Islington, Southwark and Tower Hamlets*, London, Crown Copyright.

Office for Standards in Education (1997), *Literacy Matters*, London, Ofsted.

Office for Standards in Education (1998), *School Evaluation Matters*, London, Ofsted.

Office for Standards in Education (1999a), *Inspecting Schools: Handbook for Inspecting Secondary Schools*, London, HMSO.

Office for Standards in Education (1999b), *Handbook for Inspecting Primary and Nursery Schools with Guidance on Self-evaluation (Inspecting Schools)*, London, The Stationery Office.

Office for Standards in Education (2003), *Handbook for Inspecting Secondary Schools with Guidance on Self-evaluation (Inspecting Schools)*, London, The Stationery Office.

Office for Standards in Education (2004), *The Future of Inspection: A Consultation Paper*, London, The Stationery Office.

Office for Standards in Education and Teacher Training Agency (1996), *Framework for the Assessment of Quality and Standards in Initial Teacher Training 1996/97*, London, Ofsted and TTA.

Office for Standards in Inspection (Ofstin) (1996), *Improving School Inspection: An Account of the Ofstin Conference, New College, Oxford, July*, Hexham, Northumberland, The Office For Standards in Inspection.

Office for Standards in Inspection (Ofstin) (1997), *A Better System of Inspection?* Hexham, Northumberland, The Office For Standards in Inspection.

Olson, D.R. (1977), 'From utterance to text: the bias of language in speech and writing', *Harvard Educational Review*, 47, pp. 257-281.

Paterson, L. (2003), 'The three educational ideologies of the British Labour Party 1997-2001', *Oxford Review of Education*, 29, 2, pp. 165-186.

Perkins, D. (1995a), *Outsmarting IQ: the emerging science of learnable intelligence*, New York, The Free Press.

Perkins, D. (1995b), *Smart Schools: From training memories to educating minds*, New York, Touchstone Books.

Perkins, D. and Tishman, S. (1998), *Dispositional Aspects of Intelligence*, available at http://www.learnweb.harvard.edu/alps/thinking/docs/plymouth.pdf.

Peters, M. (2001), 'National education policy constructions of the "knowledge economy": towards a critique', *Journal of Educational Enquiry*, 2, 1, pp. 1-22.

Pierson, C. (1998), 'The new governance of education: the Conservatives and education 1988-1997', *Oxford Review of Education*, 24, 1, pp. 131-142.

Plowden Report (1967), *Children and Their Primary Schools*, London, Central Advisory Council.

Pollard, A. (1990), 'Towards a sociology of learning in primary schools', *British Journal of Sociology of Education*, 11, 3, pp. 241-257.

Popkewitz, T.P. (1988), 'Educational reform: rhetoric, ritual, and social interest', *Educational Theory*, 38, 1, pp. 77-93.

Postman, N. (1970), 'Illiteracy in America: position papers', *Harvard Educational Review*, 40, 2, pp. 244-252.

Poulson, L., Avramidis, E., Fox, R., Medwell, J., Wray, D. (2001), 'The theoretical beliefs of effective teachers of literacy in primary schools: an exploratory study of orientations to reading and writing', *Research Papers in Education* 16, 3, pp. 271-292.

Power, S. and Gewirtz, S. (2001), 'Reading Education Action Zones', *Journal of Education Policy*, 16, 1, pp. 39-51.

Power, S. and Whitty, G. (1999), 'New Labour's education policy, first, second or third way?' *Journal of Education Policy*, 14, 5, pp. 535-546.

Power, S., Halpin, D. and Fitz, J. (1996), 'The grant maintained schools policy: the English experience of educational self-governance', In *Reshaping Education in the 1990s: Perspectives on Secondary Schooling*, (Eds) C.J. Pole and R. Chawla-Duggan, pp. 105-115.

Pressley, M. (2001), 'Effective Beginning Reading Instruction: A Paper Commissioned by the National Reading Conference', Chicago, IL, National Reading Conference.

Pressley, M., Rankin, J. and Yokai, L. (1996), 'A Survey of Instructional Practices of Primary Teachers Nominated as Effective in Promoting Literacy', *Elementary School Journal*, 96, 4, pp. 363-84.

Pressley, M., Wharton McDonald, R., Allington, M., Collins-Block, C., Morrow, L., Tracey, D., Baker, K., Brooks, G., Cronin, J., Nelson, E. and Woo, D. (2001), 'A study of effective first grade literacy instruction', *Scientific Studies of Reading* 15, 1, pp. 35-58.

Pressley, M., Wharton McDonald, R., Mistretta-Hampson, J. and Echevarria, M. (1998), 'Literacy instruction in 10 fourth and fifth grade classrooms in upstate New York', *Scientific Studies of Reading*, 2, 2, pp. 159-194.

Pressley, M., Yokoi, L., Rankin, J., Wharton McDonald, R. and Mistretta, J. (1997), 'A survey of the instructional practices of grade 5 teachers', *Scientific Studies of Reading*, 1, 2, pp. 145-160.

PriceWaterhouseCoopers (2001), *Teacher Workload Study: Final Report*, London, PWC.

Raphael, T. and McMahon, S.I. (1994), 'Book Club: an alternative framework for reading instruction', *The Reading Teacher*, 48, pp. 102-116.

Rassool, N. (1999), *Literacy for Sustainable Development in the Age of Information*, Clevedon, Multilingual Matters.

Reich, R. (1991), *The Work of Nations*, New York, Vintage.

Reynolds, D. (1998), 'Schooling for literacy: a review of research on teacher effectiveness and school effectiveness and its implications for contemporary educational policies', *Educational Review*, 50, 2, pp. 147-162.

Reynolds, D. and Farrell, D. (1996), *Worlds Apart? A Review of International Surveys of Educational Achievement Involving England*, London, Ofsted.

Reynolds, M. (1999), 'Standards and professional practice: the Teacher Training Agency and Initial Teacher Training', *British Journal of Educational Studies*, 47, 3, pp. 247-261.

Riley, R. (1999), 'New challenges: a new resolve: moving American education into the 21st century', available at http://www.ed.gov/Speeches/02-1999/9902/b.html.

Rosenblatt, L. (1985), 'The transactional theory of the literary work: implications for research', In *Researching Response to Literature and the Teaching of Literature: Points of Departure*, (Ed) C.R. Cooper, pp. 33-53, Norwood, NJ, Ablex.

Rosenblatt, L. (1991), 'Literature: S.O.S!', *Language Arts*, 68, 6, pp. 444-448.

Rudd, P. and Davies, D. (2000), 'Evaluating School Self-Evaluation', Presentation at the British Educational Research Association Annual Conference, Cardiff University, September.

Sachs, J. (1997), 'Reclaiming the agenda of teacher professionalism: an Australian experience', *Journal of Education for Teaching*, 23, 3, pp. 263-275.

Sachs, J. (2001), 'Teacher professional identity: competing discourses, competing outcomes', *Journal of Education Policy*, 16, 2, pp. 149-161.

Sammons, P., Thomas, S. and Mortimore, P. (1994), *Assessing School Effectiveness: developing measures to put school performance in context*, London, Ofsted.

Schultz, T.W. (1961), 'Investment in human capital', *American Economic Review*, March 51, pp. 1-17.

Scott, C., Stone, B. and Dinham, S. (2001), '"I love teaching but ...": International patterns of teacher discontent', *Education Policy Analysis Archives*, 9, 28, http://epaa.asu.edu/epaa/v9n28.htm.

Shannon, P. (1996), 'Poverty, literacy and politics: living in the USA', *Journal of Literacy Research*, 28, 3, pp. 429-449.

Simon, B. and Chitty, C. (Eds) (1993), *Education Answers Back: Critical Answers to Government Policy*, London, Lawrence and Wishart.

Sinclair, J. and Coulthard, M. (1975), *Towards an Analysis of Discourse*, London, Oxford University Press.

Slee, R., Weiner, G. and Tomlinson, S. (Eds) (1998), *School Effectiveness for Whom? Challenges to the School Effectiveness and School Improvements Movements*, London, Falmer.

Smith, G. (2000), 'Research and inspection: HMI and Ofsted 1981-1996: a commentary', *Oxford Review of Education*, 26, 3+4, pp. 333-352.

Smithers, A. (2001), 'Labour creating a secondary maze', *The Guardian*, 24 April.

Smyth, J. (1999), 'Schooling and enterprise culture: pause for a critical policy analysis', *Journal of Education Policy*, 14, 4, pp. 435-444.

Smyth, J., Hattam, R., McInerney, P. and Lawson, M. (1997), 'Finding the "enunciative space" for teacher leadership and teacher learning in schools', paper presented at the Australian Association of Research in Education Conference, Brisbane.

Snow, C.E., Burns, S.M. and Griffin, P. (Eds) (1998), *Preventing Reading Difficulties in Young Children*, (National Research Council), Washington, DC, National Academy Press.

Spear, M., Gould, K. and Lee, B. (2000), *Who Would be a Teacher? A review of factors motivating and demotivating prospective and practising teachers*, Slough, England, National Foundation for Educational Research (NFER).

Strand, S. (1999), 'Ethnic group, Sex and Economic Disadvantage: associations with pupils' educational progress from Baseline to the end of Key Stage 1', *British Educational Research Journal* 25, 2, pp. 179-202.

Street, B. (1999), '"Hobbesian Fears" and Galilean Struggles: Response to Peter Freebody', Virtual Seminar 1, International Association of Applied Linguistics.

Stringfield, S., Millsap, M.A. and Herman, R. (1997), *Urban and suburban/rural special strategies for educating disadvantaged children: findings and policy implications of a longitudinal study*, Washington, DC, US Department of Education.

Taylor, B.M., Anderson, R.C., Au, K.H. and Raphael, T.E. (2000a), 'Discretion in the translation of research to policy: a case from beginning reading', *Educational Researcher*, 29, 6, pp. 16-26.

Taylor, B.M., Pearson, P.D., Clark, K.F. and Walpole, S. (2000b), 'Effective Schools and Accomplished Teachers: Lessons about Primary-Grade Reading Instruction in Low-Income Schools', *Elementary School Journal*, 101, 2, pp. 121-65.

Taylor, B.M., Pearson, P.D., Peterson, D., and Rodriguez, M.C. (2002), *The CIERA School Change project: Supporting schools as they implement home-grown reading reform*, (CIERA Report 2-016), Ann Arbor, MI: Center for the Improvement of Early Reading Achievement, University of Michigan. Also available from www.ciera.org/library/reports/inquiry-2/2-016/2-016.h.html.

Taylor, B.T., Pearson, P.D. and Clark, K.F. (2000), 'Effective schools and accomplished teachers: lessons about primary grade reading instruction in low-income schools', *Elementary School Journal*, 101, pp. 121-165.

Taylor, C.A. (1998), Surviving Ofsted, *Mape Newsletter*, Autumn, pp. 8-11.

Taylor, S., Rizvi, F., Lingard, B. and Henry, M. (1997), *Educational Policy and the Politics of Change*, London, Routledge.

Tharp, R. and Gallimore, R. (1998), *Rousing Minds to Life*, New York, Cambridge University Press.

Theakston, J., Robinson, K. and Bangs, J. (2001), 'Teachers talking: a teacher involvement in Education Action Zones', *School Leadership and Management*, 21, 2, pp. 183-197.

Thomas, H. and Martin, J. (1996), *Managing Resources for School Improvement*, London, Routledge.

Thrupp, M. (1998), 'Exploring the politics of blame: school inspection and its contestation in New Zealand and England', *Comparative Education*, 34, 2, pp. 195-208.

Times Educational Supplement (1987), reporting on the Conservative Party conference, 16 October.

Times Educational Supplement (1997), Estelle Morris and League Tables, 14 March, p. 8.

Tishman, S. and Andrade, A. (1995), *Critical Squares: games of critical thinking and understanding*, New York, IDES Press Books.

Tishman, S., Jay, E. and Perkins, D. (1992), *Teaching Thinking Dispositions: From Transmission to Enculturation*, Available from http://www.learnweb.harvard.edu/alps/thinking/docs/article2.html, Accessed 3 April 2003.

Toffler, A. (1970), *Future Shock*, New York, Random House.

Toulmin, S. (1990), *Cosmopolis: The hidden agenda of modernity*, New York, The Free Press.

Troman, G. (1997), 'Self-management and school inspections: complementary forms of surveillance and control in the primary school', *Oxford Review of Education*, 23, 3, pp. 345-384.

United Nations (1995), *Our Global Neighborhood: Report of the Commission on Global Governance*, Oxford University Press.

Universities Council for the Education of Teachers (1998), *UCET Evidence to the House of Common's Select Committee of Inquiry into Ofsted*, London, UCET.

Vincent, C. (2001), 'Researching home-school relations', In *Understanding Learning: Influences and Outcomes*, (Eds) J. Collins and D. Cook, London, Paul Chapman Publishing.

Vincent, C. and Martin, J. (1999), '"The committee people": school-based parents' groups – a politics of voice and representation?' Paper prepared for Parental Choice and Market Forces seminar, Kings College London, 2 March.

Vision 2020 Malaysia: 'The Way Forward', Malaysian Business Council available at http://www.wawasan2020.com/vision/.

Vygotsky, L.S. (1978) *Mind in society: the development of higher psychological processes.* Cambridge, MA, Harvard University Press.

Wade, S., Thompson, A. and Watkins, W. (1994), 'The role of belief systems in authors' and readers' constructions of texts', In *Belief about Text and Instruction with Text*, (Eds) R. Garner and P.A. Alexander, pp. 265-193, Hillsdale, NJ, Erlbaum.

Waggoner, M., Chinn, C., Yi, H. and Anderson, R.C. (1995), 'Collaborative reasoning about stories', *Language Arts*, 72, pp. 582-589.

Weir, S. and Beetham, D. (1999), 'Auditing British democracy', *Political Quarterly*, April-June, 7, 1, pp. 128-137.

Wells, G. (1999), *Dialogic Inquiry: Toward a Sociocultural Practice and Theory of Education*, Cambridge University Press.

Wharton McDonald, R., Pressley, M. and Hampton, J.M. (1998), 'Literacy Instruction in nine first-grade classrooms: Teacher characteristics and student achievement', *Elementary School Journal*, 99, 2, pp. 101-128.

Whetton, C. (1999), 'Attempting to find the true cost of assessment systems', paper presented at the International Association of Educational Assessment (IAEA) Bled, Slovenia, May.

Whitty, G. (1996), 'Creating quasi markets in education: a review of recent research on parental choice and school autonomy in three countries', *Review of Educational Research*, p. 22.

Whitty, G. (2002), *Making Sense of Education Policy*, London, Paul Chapman Press.

Wilkinson, R. (2000), *Mind the Gap: Hierarchies, Health and Human Evolution*, London, Weidenfeld and Nicolson.

William, J.D. and Randensbush, S.W. (1989), 'A longitudinal hierarchical model for estimating school effects and their stability', *Journal of Educational Measurement*, 26, 3, pp. 209-232.

Willis, A.I. and Harris, V.J. (2000), 'Political acts: Literacy, learning and teaching', *Reading Research Quarterly*, 35, 1, pp. 72-87.

Woodhead, C. (1995), *A question of standards: finding the balance*, London, Politiea.

Woods, P. (1989), 'Stress and the teacher role', In *Teaching and Stress*, (Eds) M. Cole and S. Walker, Buckingham, Open University Press.

Woods, P. and Jeffrey, B. (1998), 'Choosing positions: living with contradictions of Ofsted', *British Journal of Sociology of Education*, 19, 4, pp. 547-570.

Woods, P.A., Bagley, C. and Glatter, R. (1996), 'Dynamics of competition: the effects of local competitive arenas on schools', In *Reshaping Education in the 1990s: Perspectives on Secondary Schooling*, (Eds) C.J. Pole and R. Chawla-Duggan, pp. 11-25.

Index

ability groups 79
apprenticeship 36
    apprenticeship approaches 107
assessment 17, 19, 30, 40, 42, 102, 105,
    107, 109, 116

balance 77, 82
bench-marking 26

Campaign for Racial Equality (CRE) 39
Career Entry Profile (CEP) 38
Charter schools 21
child-centred education 35
citizenship 18, 113, 114
City Technology Colleges (CTCs) 20
classroom assistants 78
coaching 79, 80, 86
cognitive apprenticeship 7
computer literacy 116
constructivist 74, 106
convergence 6, 8, 81
Council for the Accreditation of Teacher
    Education (CATE) 36, 37
critical literacy 65–6, 86, 92
Cross Commission 36
culturally-sensitive pedagogies/culturally
    responsive practice 66–8, 87, 89

data extraction 75
deficit model 89
democracy 1, 7, 9, 13, 17, 23, 38, 46, 48,
    104, 123
democratic 5, 6, 9, 13, 22, 46, 47, 48, 49,
    50, 84
demographic change 53–4
descriptive map 73
dialogic 3, 81, 85, 89, 91, 99, 100, 119,
    120
differentiate 80-2
dispositions 106, 107, 109, 110, 111,
    113, 116
distributed cognition 112
diversity 2, 22, 104, 117, 120, 126

Education
    Act(s) 20, 25
    Action Zones (EAZs) 122
    Reform Act 16, 21
Equal Opportunities Commission 39
equity 104

funds of knowledge 87, 88, 89

General Teaching Council (GTC) 44–9,
    126
generalisability 75
globalisation 10–11
    economic 5–9
governing body 20, 22, 121
Grant Maintained Schools (GMSs) 20,
    22, 58

habits of mind 109
House of Commons Select Committee
    31, 43
household analogs 88
human
    capital 1, 11, 12, 15, 23, 116
    infrastructure 12

inclusion 63, 73, 74, 75, 76, 81, 102, 122
Information and Communications
    Technology (ICT) 115
Initiation Response Evaluation (IRE) 97,
    99, 100
instructional density 78
integration 77, 78, 82, 86
interaction(s)/interactive 81, 84, 89, 90,
    93, 99, 100, 107, 111
    classroom 101
    international patterns/modes/styles
    87, 89, 101

knowledge
    economy 5, 10–13, 60
    societies 12
knowledge-based infrastructure 52

language arts 76
league tables 2, 19, 60
letter-sound correspondence 76
level descriptions 68
lifeworld 85–6, 87
literacy
    achievement gap 53
    crisis 57–60, 63
    digital 115
    Hour 91, 92, 100, 101
    stance 91–2, 96, 97
Local Management of Schools (LMS) 21

Management Charter Initiative (MCI) 39
meta-analysis 74
meta-cognitive 71, 109, 110.
monologic 84, 85, 91, 100
multi-agency training 104
multi-media texts 64–5
multi-modal 56
multiple intelligences 107

narrative review 70, 72, 73, 84
National Curriculum 2, 16–18, 19, 26,
    35, 37, 60, 61, 68, 109, 110, 113
National Foundation for Educational
    Research (NFER) 33
National Literacy Strategy (NLS) 30,
    61–3, 64, 66, 67, 81, 84, 85, 90, 91,
    115
National Reading Panel (NRP) 14, 72
neo-liberalism 18
New Right 9

Office for Standards in Education
    (Ofsted) 1, 2, 18, 19, 25, 26, 27, 28,
    29, 30, 31–5, 36, 42, 43, 44, 57, 58,
    60, 81, 90, 125, 126
Office for Standards in Inspection
    (Ofstin) 27, 31–5, 43
open enrolment 21
Organisation for Economic Co-operation
    and Development (OECD) 7–8, 10,
    22, 116

parental choice 20–2
parents 1, 16, 19, 20, 21, 22, 26, 34, 40,
    41, 47, 48, 49, 50, 60, 67, 78, 79,
    105, 106, 119, 120, 121, 122, 123,
    124, 126

partnerships 8, 20, 38, 49, 50, 120, 123,
    124
performance tables 19
Plowden Report 49, 120
pluralism 104
popular culture 52, 67, 99
poverty 15, 28, 53–54, 68, 79, 80, 81,
    113, 117, 119, 122
professional
    autonomy 23, 24, 103, 124
    characteristics 73
    competencies 79
    control 124
    development 1, 3, 38, 45, 80, 83,
    118, 119
    independence 46
    knowledge 73, 79, 118
    lives 80
    practices 106
    reflection 104
    renewal 117
    self-interest 15
professionalism 2, 29, 30–5, 36, 37, 44,
    46, 47, 48, 49, 50, 57, 59, 106, 112,
    117, 118, 120, 124
    democratic 47–9, 50
    teacher 37, 44
Project Zero 110-12
protocol 73
punctuation 79

quasi-ethnographic 74
Qualified Teacher Status (QTS) 2, 35, 36
    38, 42
Quality Assurance Agency (QAA) 25

recitation script 102

scaffolding 79, 80, 86
school
    councils 123
    effectiveness 28
    governors 22
    improvement 15, 19, 28, 30, 31
scripted lesson 80
selection criteria 73
self-assessment 114
self-evaluation 31–5, 43, 44, 78, 79
situated cognition 118
situated practice 86, 87

situational literacies 87
small group teaching 80, 100
social justice 13, 23, 40, 104, 120, 122
socio-constructivist 112
socio-cultural 49, 80, 84, 85, 88, 89, 91
specialist schools 12, 20, 21
specialist teachers 78
spelling 79
staff development 118
Standard Assessment Tasks and Tests
    (SATs) 17, 19, 102
Standards 2, 14, 17, 19, 26, 28, 38, 39,
    40, 41, 42, 45, 104, 116
subject positions 97–100
synthesising (evidence) 74–5, 76
systematic review 70, 72, 73, 74, 84

talk story 88
target setting 19

teacher
    beliefs 79–80
    development 85
    modelling 111
Teacher Training Agency (TTA) 1, 2,
    25, 26, 35–43, 44, 45, 118, 119, 120
Testing 59, 60, 62, 66, 102, 111, 112,
    113
Third Way 9

University Council of Teacher Education
    (UCET) 37

weight of evidence 74, 75
whole class teaching 100
Woodhead, C. 28, 58–9, 62